Sanctuaries of Light in Nineteenth-Century European Literature

Studies on Themes and Motifs in Literature

Horst S. Daemmrich
General Editor

Vol. 102

PETER LANG
New York • Washington, D.C./Baltimore • Bern
Frankfurt • Berlin • Brussels • Vienna • Oxford

Hugo G. Walter

Sanctuaries of Light in Nineteenth-Century European Literature

PETER LANG
New York • Washington, D.C./Baltimore • Bern
Frankfurt • Berlin • Brussels • Vienna • Oxford

Library of Congress Cataloging-in-Publication Data
Walter, Hugo.
Sanctuaries of light in nineteenth-century European literature / Hugo G. Walter.
p. cm. — (Studies on themes and motifs in literature; v. 102)
Includes bibliographical references and index.
1. European literature—19th century—History and criticism. 2. Wordsworth, William,
1770-1850—Criticism and interpretation. 3. Hoffmann, E. T. A. (Ernst Theodor Amadeus),
1776-1822—Criticism and interpretation. 4. Eichendorff, Joseph, Freiherr von, 1788-1857—
Criticism and interpretation. 5. Brontë, Charlotte, 1816-1855—Criticism and
interpretation. 6. Refuge in literature. I. Title.
PN761.W348   809'.034—dc22   2009052365
ISBN 978-1-4331-0913-3
ISSN 1056-3970

Bibliographic information published by **Die Deutsche Nationalbibliothek**.
Die Deutsche Nationalbibliothek lists this publication in the "Deutsche
Nationalbibliografie"; detailed bibliographic data is available
on the Internet at http://dnb.d-nb.de/.

This work is dedicated to my mother, Elli R. Walter.

✳ *Table of Contents*

❋ Acknowledgments

I would like to thank the following professors for their guidance, encouragement, and supportiveness during and after my years of graduate study at Yale University and at Drew University: Jeffrey Sammons, Peter Demetz, Robert Ready, and John Warner.

I would also like to thank the many professors, administrators, students, and staff members at Berkeley College who have been so supportive and thoughtful to me during the past several years. In particular, I would like to thank the following members of the Berkeley college community: Kevin Luing, Randy Luing, Brian Luing, Glen Zeitzer, Marianne Vakalis, Dario Cortes, Marisol Abuin, Mary Jane Clerkin, Luisa Ferreira, Michael Frew, Lisa Karakas, Rich Schultz, Marilyn Kulik, Mary Slavin, Bill Cipolla, Cathy St. John, Mike Jacobs, Georgette Coffey, Leslin Charles, Marlene Doty, Corazon Estavillo, Jim Leftwich, Todd Eglow, Ellen Thomas, Gail Miller, Arthur Blumenthal, Mary McDonough, Thayer Draper, Martin Shapiro, Guy Adamo, John Rapanos, Rose Mary Healy, Kristin Rowe, Don Singer, Mitch Serels, Sam Lloyd, Mike Samman, Steve Streeter, Christopher Vinger, Beth Coyle, Roseann Torsiello, James Pacello, the Online Dean, and the Online Programs administration.

I would also like to thank Professor Horst Daemmrich of the University of Pennsylvania and Dr. Heidi Burns of Peter Lang Publishing for their insightful and thoughtful comments regarding my manuscript.

Finally, I would like to thank Nicole Grazioso and the Production Department of Peter Lang for their helpful assistance and patience in the production of the manuscript.

I would like to acknowledge the following institutions for permission to reprint from the following works:

The Apostrophic Moment in Nineteenth and Twentieth Century German Lyric Poetry, by Hugo Walter, Copyright © 1988, Peter Lang Publishing, reprinted with the permission of the publisher.

Sanctuaries of Light

Space and Time on the Magic Mountain: Studies in Nineteenth- and Early-Twentieth-Century European Literature, by Hugo Walter, Copyright © 1999, Peter Lang Publishing, reprinted with the permission of the publisher.

THE PRELUDE 1799, 1805, 1850 by William Wordsworth: A Norton Critical Edition by William Wordsworth, edited by Jonathan Wordsworth, M. H. Abrams. Copyright © 1979 by W. W. Norton & Company, Inc. Used by permission of W. W. Norton & Company, Inc.

"The Golden Pot" and "The Nutcracker," by E. T. A. Hoffmann, Copyright © 1993, Dover Publications, reprinted with the permission of the publisher.

Jane Eyre, by Charlotte Brontë, Copyright © 1982, Penguin Books (A Signet Classic), reprinted with the permission of the publisher.

✳ *Introduction*

In Act II, Scene V of Percy Shelley's *Prometheus Unbound,* Asia describes the "enchanted boat" (II.V. 72) of her soul wandering with the angelic guidance of her companion spirit through "a paradise of wildernesses" (II.V. 81) and subsequently through "Elysian garden islets" (II.V. 91) where the spirit of love creates a dynamic aura of harmony in the earth and the heavens. As Act II, Scene V concludes Asia declares:

> We have passed Age's icy caves
>
> And Manhood's dark and tossing waves,
>
> And Youth's smooth ocean, smiling to betray: . . .
>
> Through Death and Birth, to a diviner day;
>
> A paradise of vaulted bowers,
>
> Lit by downward-gazing flowers,
>
> And watery paths that wind between
>
> Wildernesses calm and green,
>
> Peopled by shapes too bright to see . . . . (II.V. 98-100, 103-108).

Such a "paradise of vaulted bowers" (II.V. 105) signifies a sanctuary of light, harmony, beauty, and tranquility. This is a sanctuary beyond the vicissitudes of death and mortality which can comfort, heal, inspire, and soothe the heart and the soul of the sensitive individual, the lyrical wanderer.

In Act III, Scene iii, Prometheus, after being unbound by Hercules, addresses Asia and asks her to dwell with him in a cave which contains various plants, is "paved with veined emerald" (III.iii.13) and secluded, contains a vital fountain, and represents a place where they can "talk of time and change, / As the world ebbs and flows, ourselves unchanged" (III.iii. 23-24). This is a sanctuary of profound peace and subtle radiance beyond the ravages and tribulations of mortality.

In a subsequent passage the Earth describes her cave as an extraordinary space:

> There is a cavern where my spirit
>
> Was panted forth in anguish whilst thy pain
>
> Made my heart mad, and those who did inhale it

Became mad too, and built a temple there, . . .

Which breath now rises, as amongst tall weeds

A violet's exhalation, and it fills

With a serener light and crimson air

Intense, yet soft, the rocks and woods around. (III.iii.124–27, 131–34)

The atmosphere of a special refuge which such a space instinctively possesses is further reinforced when the Earth calls forth a spirit who is portrayed as her torch-bearer to guide the present company to a beautiful natural place where there is a temple which is "populous with most living imagery, / Praxitelean shapes, whose marble smiles / Fill the hushed air with everlasting love" (III.iii. 164–66). The temple is further defined as having once celebrated Prometheus. At the end of Act III, Scene iii the Earth proclaims that "the destined cave" (III.iii. 175) is beside the temple.

Edward Hungerford in *Shores of Darkness* argues insightfully that the temple "must be near Athens, for there the Attic cult of Prometheus celebrated the worship of the Titan" (197) and that the temple "must have reference to the Academy, the famous grove outside the walls of Athens" (197). Hungerford makes the following interesting observation about this site:

> There were two places in ancient times connected with the Attic cult of Prometheus: one was his sanctuary in the Academy; the other was the sacred grove at Colonus, a deme outside the walls of Athens, about a mile and quarter to the northwest, and contiguous with the grove of the Academy. It is the spot where Plato once taught and where the action of Sophocles' tragedy *Oedipus at Colonus* takes place.

Hungerford proceeds to argue that the life of Prometheus and Asia in this refuge will represent not only "the enjoyment of the Promethean gift of love no longer enslaved to mutability" (201) but also "the cultivation of the capacities of the mind" (201) in a spirit of enlightenment. For Prometheus asserts in Act III, Scene iii to Asia, as he addresses her as "thou light of life" (III.iii.6), that they will create a healing space of exceptional natural beauty, divine harmony, and extraordinary effulgence where the arts of painting, sculpture, and poetry will be nurtured.

In this series of essays I will examine several sanctuaries of light (whether motivated by an inner effulgence or generated by an external radiance), natural beauty, creativity, harmony, and serenity in nineteenth-century European literature which celebrate and exemplify the spirit of and some of the characteristics and qualities so vitally apparent in the places of luminescent refuge in Shelley's *Prometheus Unbound*. I will focus on various descriptions, depictions, and portrayals of sanctuaries of light in the works of William Wordsworth, E. T. A. Hoffmann, Joseph von Eichendorff, and Charlotte Brontë.

In Chapter 1, I will discuss various extraordinary sanctuaries of light, natural beauty, harmony, and tranquility in the poetry of William Wordsworth from "Tintern Abbey" to *The Prelude*. In "Tintern Abbey" the persona experiences a sense of aesthetic and spiritual inspiration and comfort in the presence of a beautiful natural environment. In the "Ode: Intimations of Immortality from Recollections of Early Childhood" the persona emphasizes the importance of significant moments of experience in childhood and youth which guide and motivate the future development of his life. Even though the past glory of beauty and vitality cannot be directly revived, the poet will find comfort and strength in the creative process and in his lyrical achievements, in a holistic sense of connectedness to the world around him, and in a faith which envisions a future beyond mortality. In "Nuns Fret Not at Their Convent's Narrow Room" the poet emphasizes the capacity of a hermetic space to provide sufficient aesthetic and spiritual inspiration and serenity. In "I Wandered Lonely as a Cloud" Wordsworth celebrates the vitality of a beautiful and luminescent natural space to heal and soothe his mind and soul forever. In *The Prelude* Wordsworth stresses the importance of various lovely natural spaces, beautiful sanctuaries of light, which comfort his heart and soul and inspire and generate his creativity. As in the "Ode: Intimations of Immortality from Recollections of Early Childhood," Wordsworth also affirms in *The Prelude* the importance of an emotional sensitivity and of a generous heart and spirit which would include in its perception and vision all aspects of the natural world, whether prominent, dynamic, and spacious or more fragile, subtle, and gentle.

In Chapter 2 I will explore sanctuaries of exceptional effulgence in several stories by E. T. A. Hoffmann. Whereas in the poetry of Wordsworth the sanctuaries of light and serenity typically exist and thrive in the world of nature, in the stories of Hoffmann sanctuaries of light and tranquility are present in interior environments and domestic interiors. For example, in "Ritter Gluck" the most vital sanctuary in the story is a sanctuary of radiance and musical harmony and vitality which exists in the private room of the composer Gluck. In "The Golden Pot" the most important sanctuaries throughout most of the narrative are present in the magnificent house of the Archivist Lindhorst. When Lindhorst takes Anselmus through his remarkable house there are several rooms, especially the library and the room which contains the golden pot, which exhibit not only an extraordinary radiance but also a rich array of colors, fragrances, and melodies. One might even claim that the house of Lindhorst itself signifies a refuge from the exigencies and idiosyncratic encroachments of the world of everyday mortality. The ultimate sanctuary of luminescence which Serpentina and Anselmus enjoy in Atlantis could be interpreted as a beautiful refuge in the natural environment or even as a lovely and spatially expansive "interior" which has the aura of an exceptional space in the external environment.

In "The Sandman" and "Mademoiselle de Scudery" the sense of sanctuary, although not as vibrantly abundant and dynamically effulgent as in "Ritter Gluck" and "The Golden Pot," is also depicted in interior environments. In "The Mines at Falun" the sense of refuge is prominently displayed in an underground ambience. The world of the mine possesses an aura of crystalline exuberance and shimmering radiances which allures the protagonist. In this story the protagonist is thoroughly entranced by the sparkling jewels and rich stones which seem to be embedded in the profundity of the mine.

In Chapter 3 I will analyze numerous sanctuaries and "transitory enchanted" moments of sanctuary in the poetry and stories of Joseph von Eichendorff. The sense of sanctuary in the work of Eichendorff is present not only in various beautiful dimensions of the natural world, as in Wordsworth, but also within the depths of the creative, lyrical self. In "Der frohe Wandersmann," for example, the persona claims that the life of the wanderer is blessed and sanctified by god, by a divine presence. As he travels throughout the world he feels the presence of god in him and near him as an emotional guide and a spiritual support. In "Abschied" the poet states that even though he must leave the beautiful natural space which has been his greatest joy and source of delight to travel into and through the world of everyday mortality, he will always reflect on the beauty, harmony, and luminescence of this gorgeous place. Such reflections, as those of W. B. Yeats in a similar situation in "The Lake Isle of Innisfree," will perpetually comfort and sustain him.

Light and radiance are important thematic concerns for Eichendorff in numerous poems focusing on different times of day. Perhaps the most inspirational temporal moments for Eichendorff are the morning and the evening, threshold moments between day and night and more symbolically between life and death which reveal or generate epiphanies of light and shadow. In "Sehnsucht" the persona describes a nocturnal ambience which is permeated by the golden light of the stars. As he listens to the song of distant travelers the persona expresses an explicitly vital longing to wander with carefree ease and lyrical expectation through the lovely natural environment. In "Sehnsucht" the persona imagines that he hears the travelers singing of sublime natural landscapes and of gorgeous palaces and gardens which appear to come alive in the moonlight. One might argue that such palaces and gardens thrive in the twilight arbors of the poet's creative imagination. In "Der Einsiedler" the persona, wearied by the cares and tribulations of mortality, longs for the tender comfort of the night and anticipates the coming of eternity, of an eternity of rest and serenity for his soul.

In Chapter 4 I will discuss the theme of sanctuary in the work of Charlotte Brontë and especially in *Jane Eyre*. There are sanctuaries which exist for Jane Eyre in domestic interiors such as at Gateshead and at Lowood. For example, the special meal which Jane shares with Miss Temple and Helen at Lowood represents a sanctuary of intellectual illumination and aesthetic inspiration for her. Jane also feels a sense of sanctuary in some of the aesthetically interesting and elegant rooms at Thornfield before her emotionally strained departure in chapter 27 and the eventual conflagration. Brontë also depicts the relationship of Rochester and Jane as signifying a sanctuary. For example, in chapter 22 of the novel Jane says to Rochester that her only home is wherever he is—the material aspects of such a refuge are secondary compared with the presence of her beloved. For Jane the sense of sanctuary at this point in the novel before the cataclysmic day of the intended wedding and again at the end of the novel at Ferndean derives from the emotional, intellectual, and spiritual closeness and presence of Rochester.

The utter despair which Jane feels in the environs of Whitcross in chapter 28 of *Jane Eyre* as she tries to establish a new life for herself is somewhat mitigated by her conviction in the power of nature and God to help and guide her. Jane's battered soul and wretched spirit find some solace in the sanctuary of a comforting and accepting natural environment which does not disdain and shun her as the human world had done and would do in the very near future. Jane does find emotional and spiritual solace in being close to nature, a solace which is abruptly diminished by the mistreatment she receives when she goes into the village to look for work and for something to eat. Despite this painful experience for Jane, she is drawn to the light in the wilderness which leads her to another sanctuary of effulgence and happiness, the house and life of the Rivers family. The ultimate sanctuary in the novel, Jane's return to Rochester at Ferndean and their shared love, life, and bliss, encompasses both a domestic interior, the manor-house, and the natural environment surrounding and enclosing it. In this last phase of the novel, as in chapters 21, 22, 23, and 24, Jane represents a source of light and radiance for Rochester. Especially at Ferndean Jane is Rochester's sight and describes and envisions the world for him as he struggles with his blindness. That Rochester regains his vision in one eye is a consequence of and a tribute to the profound love which Jane shows him as well as a manifestation of the luminescent power of this sanctuary to heal and soothe such a chastened and suffering individual.

Maria Tatar states in *The Classic Fairy Tales* that the "life story of the heroine of *Jane Eyre* can be read as a one-woman crusade and act of resistance to the roles modeled for girls and women in fairy tales" (xvii). Tatar proceeds to argue that Jane Eyre writes and develops her own story to a considerable extent and does not passively accept a role in the fantasies of others:

> Jane Eyre rejects the cult of suffering and self-effacement endorsed in fairy tales like "Cinderella" and "Beauty and the Beast" to construct her own story, renouncing prefabricated roles and creating her own identity. She reinvents herself and produces a radically new cultural script, the one embodied in the written record that constitutes her own autobiography. (xvii–xviii).

In constructing her own story Jane Eyre depends on several important occasions on sanctuaries of light, serenity, and natural beauty to enable her to confront effectively and even to transcend the vicissitudes of everyday mortality as she shapes a new and a more congenial life for herself.

The idea of a sanctuary and the desire to create or participate in a sanctuary are motivated to some extent, if not to a considerable extent, by a profound concern about and by an acutely sensitive response to time and the inevitability of mortality. From Shakespeare's sonnet "When I Have Seen By Time's Fell Hand," Thomas Gray's "Ode on a Distant Prospect of Eton College," William Wordsworth's *The Prelude*, Percy Shelley's "Ozymandias," E. T. A. Hoffmann's "The Golden Pot," and Emily Dickinson's "Because I Could Not Stop for Death," to Joseph von Eichendorff's "Der Einsiedler," Walt Whitman's "Song of Myself," Charlotte Brontë's *Jane Eyre*, Thomas Hardy's "Hap," Tennyson's "The Poet," and Thomas Mann's "Death in Venice," just to name several works which are attentively, intimately, and sensitively aware of the flux of mortality, the protagonist in literary works dealing with mortality and transience may try to conquer time, to challenge it, to reshape it, to measure it, to eliminate it, to mask it, to transform it, or even to coexist in a complementary relation with it. The protagonist may even try to reaffirm or redefine his own existence through his relation to time and mortality.

There are multiple strategies of approaching and confronting the issue of time and mortality in a thoughtful and viable manner. One strategy is to believe in the eternity of the creative individual or the creative work as having the capacity to vanquish time and mortality. This philosophy of time is exemplified by Shakespeare's "Devouring Time." In this poem Shakespeare addresses time as a destructive force which can "blunt the lion's paws" (1) or "Pluck the keen teeth from the fierce tiger's jaws" (3). As negative and hostile as the presence of such a force is in the universe, the poet does not fear it because he believes in his immortality as a writer and in the creative eternity of his literary achievements.

In the first quatrain of "Devouring Time" the persona describes some of the most destructive aspects of time. In the second quatrain of this sonnet the persona proclaims that time can do whatever it wants to the world, but he forbids it "one most heinous crime" (8). The crime which the poet forbids time, concisely described in the next four lines, is that time should not effect or age his love. The assertive plea of the third quatrain becomes the aggressive proclamation of the final couplet: "Yet, do thy worst, old Time: despite thy wrong, / My love shall in my verse ever live young" (13-14). The persona is so thoroughly confident of his creative vitality that he can challenge time to be as destructive as it chooses or wishes to be. Despite the evil which time (the persona addresses time here as "old Time," implying that time itself is subject to mortality) may and does inflict upon the world of humanity, the poet is instinctively certain that the immortality of his love will be achieved and affirmed through the eternity of his poetry.

In "Not Marble, nor the Gilded Monuments" Shakespeare also discusses the theme of the challenge which mortality offers to his creative endeavors. This poem adds two corollary thematic emphases to the discussion of the theme of time which was offered by "Devouring Time." In the first two quatrains of "Not Marble, nor the Gilded Monuments" the persona argues that his creativity, his poetry (and, by implication, any such vital poetic expression) is more powerful and more everlasting than any material object, even more than the marble and "gilded monuments / Of princes" (1-2). In the third quatrain the persona declares that the aesthetic and intellectual power of the poem and of its thematic object (the "you") will be perpetuated in future generations of readers. The final couplet argues for the eternity of the poet's love through the existence of the poem and through generations of lovers' eyes who read and appreciate the poem. The final couplet also implies the capacity and the vitality of the effective and thoughtful literary work to transcend mortality. Shakespeare creates a sense of sanctuary in the poem itself. Or one might say that the poem represents an atmosphere of sanctuary against mortality which is perpetuated in the interpretive awareness and thoughtfulness of future generations of readers.

Alfred, Lord Tennyson's "The Poet" depicts the poet as a visionary, a sage, and a supreme creator secure from the ravages of mortality and portrays the vital ambience of a radiant sanctuary. In the first stanzas of "The Poet" Tennyson describes the essential features of the poet—the golden, life-affirmative heritage, the capacity to experience a spectrum of human emotion, and the ability to develop and nurture a visionary imagination. These qualities are elaborated upon in stanza four which stresses the energy of his thought, in stanza seven which proclaims his capability to disseminate truth and to revitalize the world, and in stanza nine which implies the poet's potential to create, or even recreate, a Garden of Eden-like existence.

The first lines of the poem suggest that the poet belongs to a favored world in the spirit of Friedrich Hölderlin's statement in "Youth" that the poetic persona grew up in an aesthetically and emotionally privileged and refined environment:

> In my days of boyhood
>
> A god saved me often
>
> From the shouts and the rod of mankind.
>
> Then, safe and virtuous, I played
>
> With flowers of the forest,
>
> And the breezes of Heaven
>
> Played with me.

In Tennyson's "The Poet" the persona not only experiences a similar upbringing but also reveals a capacity to participate in, and, by implication, to shape a world of light. The timeless quality of this aura is seen in the fact that the golden light pervades not only the day but the night as well, exemplified in the image "golden Stars" (2). Lines three and four of the first stanza of "The Poet" proclaim the capacity of the poet to appreciate and participate in a range of emotion while striving beyond hate and disdain to resolve such emotional tensions in "the love of love" (4). Tennyson's persona is endowed with the conviction, expressed so eloquently by Demogorgon in Shelley's *Prometheus Unbound*, that love folds over the world its healing and comforting powers.

Stanza two of Tennyson's "The Poet" presents the poet as a visionary who can see through life and death, through good and evil, and even into the depths of his own soul. This persona's vision is as powerful as the faith of Wordsworth's persona in the "Ode: Intimations of Immortality" who looks through death in shaping the philosophic and reflective mind. The capacity to appreciate the depths and intricacies of human emotion and thought enables the poet to understand the everlasting will of the universe and perhaps even help in forming and expressing it.

The visionary mind is so vital that its thoughts, "winged with flame" (12), fill with light and melodies the winds of the world. If we interpret the winds as manifestations of the Aeolian lyre, then Tennyson seems to be suggesting here the capability of the poet to inspire and to shape the creative energy and the healing power of the world. The emphasis on light is intimately linked to and reinforces the golden aura of the first stanza. The hermetic uniqueness of the visionary mind and its affinity for a sense of sanctuary is suggested in the image of the echoing feet threading the most secret walks of fame. That the poet is able to explore these hallowed corridors reaffirms his appreciation of the importance of a sanctuary and his differentiation from the world of everyday mortality.

Stanzas three through seven are permeated by a dynamics of development and growth. Not only does the verse of the poet have a melodic mellifluousness but his thoughts flow through the world by their own innate incantatory power. As Keats' poetic voice is heard in the music of nature in Shelley's "Adonais," so the voice of Tennyson's poet infuses nature with its luminescent, melodic energy. The imaginative thoughts, after moving earthward from their lofty, majestic source, will continue to participate in a dynamic process of eternal cyclicality, growth, and renewal. As "arrow-seeds of the field flower" (19) they will take root and spring forth anew, culminating in a golden flower, in a bloom of effusively luminescent radiance. Such a flower, the symbolic representation of the poet, disperses the "winged shafts of truth" (26) and perpetually revitalizes a spirit of hope and youth. Stanzas three through seven, culminating in an image of expansive effulgence, emphasize not only the capacity of the poet to illuminate the world of everyday mortality with a powerful and an enduring aesthetic vision and to establish an intimate and sensitive association with nature but also to develop a vision of truth and to revitalize the emotional and the spiritual soul of humankind.

One might claim that Tennyson's poet fuses Wordsworth's and Shelley's conceptions of the poet. He desires to be, in the spirit of Wordsworth's assertions in the Preface to the Second Edition of the *Lyrical Ballads*, "a man speaking to men," aspiring to fulfill the challenge of the open scroll, while sustaining and strengthening a unique emotional, aesthetic, and spiritual sensibility. Not only does this poet sing a song in which all beings can join, but he rejoices in the presence of truth and portrays poetry as "the breath and finer spirit of all knowledge" (Perkins 324–326). Moreover, in his illuminating power Tennyson's poet, in the spirit of Shelley's "A Defence of Poetry," lifts the veil from the hidden beauty of the world (as in stanza nine); turns all things to loveliness (Perkins 1076, 1085), as in stanza one, transforming hate and scorn to love; and enlarges the range of the imagination by infusing it with innovative images, with provocative ideas, and with radiant reflections.

The image of the poet as sage, as a harbinger of and a guide to truth, implied in stanza two (an individual who has the wisdom to see through the intrigues and the machinations of the world of everyday reality) and strengthened in stanza seven (in the facility of dispersing "the winged shafts of truth"), culminates in stanza nine where the vitality of truth is reaffirmed in the resplendent aura of a great garden. The dreams of desire of stanza eight are fulfilled in stanza nine in the creation of the Garden of Eden by expanding the range and intensity of the aesthetic-intellectual vision.

Tennyson's Garden of Eden in "The Poet" is a garden of light, reinforcing the aura of the golden clime in which he was born and affirming a profound devotion to truth as an integral aspect of the holistically motivated luminescence. The sense of time in "The Poet" believes in and celebrates the potential harmony of past, present, and future through the creative, aesthetic vitality of the poet. While images of a natural refuge from the world as a space of reflection on the past, self-revitalization, or poetic inspiration are present in various poems of Tennyson, the Garden of Eden image in "The Poet" is especially interesting because of the golden luminescence which creates and pervades it. The lovely sunrise is the "fountain-light" of the aesthetic vision which will perpetually reenergize itself by preserving and strengthening the power of its inner radiance.

As the golden light in Joseph Turner's painting *Angel Standing in the Sun* congeals into the supernatural form of an angel, so "Freedom" (37) in Tennyson's "The Poet" emanates from the golden light of the Eden-shaping sunrise. One might even suggest that "Freedom" (37) is the crystallization of the essence of the orphic, outward-directed dimension of the poetic scroll. "Freedom" (37) also represents the mirroring of the soul of the poet—his eyes are burning perhaps because in the sense of a creator who has shaped a work of an intensity and power that he was not fully aware of, the figure of Freedom is the activated, the publicly engaged poetic soul, the creative spirit who is and will remain "an unacknowledged legislator" of the world through devotion to "the progeny Immortal / of Painting, Sculpture, and rapt Poesy" (*Prometheus Unbound*, III, iii, 54–55).

The final stanza of "The Poet" asserts the power of the pen over that of the sword. The open scroll of the poet is so vital that it has the capacity not only to illuminate and revitalize the world through its emanation, or manifestation of the figure of Freedom, but also to renew itself perpetually in epiphanic moments of orphic luminescence. The creation of the Garden of Eden ambience in stanza nine is such a dynamic moment which evolves the golden light which will influence and shape the world in an epiphany of self-generating radiance.

The ending of "The Poet" revitalizes and redefines the affirmative, dynamic power of the beginning of the poem. Although it is not the poet directly but a manifestation and symbol of the poet, "Freedom," that emerges, at the end the powerful creative presence of the poet who "saw thro' life and death" (5) is proclaimed. The creative vitality of the persona in "The Poet" fulfills the challenge of Walter Pater in *The Renaissance* that art and life should be infused with a dynamic energy and a passionate creative vitality. As Tennyson's "The Poet," so Pater's conclusion to *The Renaissance* draws on imagery of fire and flame to signify its artistic power. Whereas Tennyson's "The Lady of Shalott" ends with the night of the poet and the ending of "The Palace of Art" is pervaded by the aura of a metaphysical twilight, "The Poet" represents a paean to light, to the luminescent vitality and self-regenerative effulgent cyclicality of the poetic power.

In Tennyson's "The Poet" the persona creates not only for himself but also for the world; in contrast, in Tennyson's "The Palace of Art" the persona creates only for herself. In "The Palace of Art" the poetic persona creates a hermetic, self-contained world of beauty which would accommodate every mood of her tranquil soul. The images which soothe and inspire her—images which seem to have an external existence in the halls of the palace—may also be construed as landscapes of the mind. The construction of the palace demonstrates the supreme creative vitality of the persona. Whereas the persona of "The Poet" creates an inner expansiveness of mind which has the world of mortality as its domain, the persona of "The Palace of Art" shapes an outer expansiveness of spirit which has as its realm the spaciousness of its own creation. The persona of "The Palace of Art" revels in her own courts, lawns, cloisters, fountains, and gallery. While the personae of the two poems have different aesthetic conceptions and philosophies of art they do share an interest in and an emphasis on dazzling brilliance of light and flame in their visions. The "viewless arrows" (11) of the persona's thoughts in "The Poet" are "wing'd with flame" (12), whereas in "The Palace of Art" "The light aerial gallery, golden-rail'd, / Burnt like a fringe of fire" (47–48). Moreover, the deep-set windows of the palace "Would seem slow-flaming crimson fires / From shadow'd grots of arches interlaced, / And tipt with frost-like spires" (50–52).

Like Shelley's "Witch of Atlas" the persona of "The Palace of Art" develops and nurtures a hermetic existence beyond good and evil, indifferent to the events and the activities, to the happiness and the suffering of the world of everyday mortality. The absolute contentment and complacency of the persona in "The Palace of Art" with her exclusively hermetic situation is the tragic flaw which will ultimately lead to her downfall. Perhaps the flaw of the persona in this poem is not only her complacency but also her attempt to "possess" the world of her creation. When she possesses it, as she asserts in line 181, she undermines its potential for further refinement and growth, undermining its capacity to renew and regenerate its own aesthetic vitality. The persona's indifference to mortal concerns and suffering and her hubris of functioning as "God holding no form of creed" (211) also precipitate her demise as the creative demiurge of the palace of art.

In the fourth year of her sojourn in the palace of art the persona is plagued by God with despair so that she disdains her solitude. The once self-assured dynamic persona is no longer in control of her spacious mansion which now reveals uncertain shapes standing in dark corners. Now oppressed by her incapacity to govern her own mind, for which the mansion serves as a metaphor, and the stillness of her world through which no voice penetrates, the persona experiences absolute despair. Unable to find solace in life or in death, in time or in eternity, the persona feels that she is decaying in her own "crumbling tomb" (273). As the persona of "The Poet," the persona of "The Palace of Art" experiences the heights and depths of emotional vitality. Yet, this is ultimately a very different emotional intensity which the persona of "The Palace of Art" experiences, for when she cries out in her despair that she is on fire within (not the same flame as in "The Poet" but instead more in the sense of the dying embers of inspiration mingled with the flames of existential despair) there is no reply, no appeasement of her suffering.

At the end of four years the persona throws her royal robes away and intends to find a modest cottage, a more emotionally and spiritually congenial place, where she may "mourn and pray" (292). Ultimately, the persona does not wish the palace of art to be destroyed, not only because she still may view it as a semblance of the beautiful but also because it may serve as a reminder or admonition to her of her earlier folly. Moreover, the persona wishes to return with other people to this lovely palace someday to stress the moral of her experience there and perhaps even to reshape it or to revitalize it according to the aesthetic values of her new artistic conception when she has liberated herself from the spirit of absolute solitude.

In Friedrich Schiller's "Die Teilung der Erde" the poet, the creative figure, although undervalued and devalued by the world of everyday reality, is privileged above everyone else by the divine figure. This poem stresses not only the vitality of the lyrical creator but also the eternal connectedness of the poet and heaven, the divine realm. By virtue of his creativity, his creative vitality, and his character the poet will always be welcome in the divine realm. In the first stanza of "Die Teilung der Erde" Zeus calls from the Olympian heights and exhorts humankind to take possession of the world. In stanzas two and three various individuals annex material objects and property for their own benefit.

In stanza four the poet arrives too late to participate in the distribution of material wealth and property. Stanza five describes the melancholy lament of the poet, who feels that as "dein getreuester Sohn" (as the most loyal son or follower of the divine) he should not be forgotten and excluded from such gifts. The response of the divine figure is to suggest that if the poet was spending his time in the land of dreams and reveries, then he should not expect anything. This relatively harsh reaction continues as the divine figure proceeds to ask the poet where he was when the distribution of material wealth was taking place. The poet responds eloquently and thoughtfully that he was devoting himself to reflections and visions of the divine and of heaven. Moreover, he was so enraptured by the light of the divine that he temporarily forgot about the world of everyday mortality.

Zeus, the supreme god, is certainly impressed with the sensitive and tactful answer of the poet. After admitting that he has given away the material aspects and dimensions of the world of everyday mortality, Zeus says: "Willst du in meinem Himmel mit mir leben~ / So oft du kommst, er soll dir offen sein." In making this offer of a perpetual welcome to the poet to come to and to be a part of heaven, in assuring the poet that the divine realm will always be open to him, Zeus comforts and soothes the poet considerably.

This poem by Schiller affirms the differentiation of the poet, the creative artist, from the acquisitive, self-aggrandizing world of everyday mortality and its expectations and ambitions. While every other member of society shows his ambition and his desire to acquire various material objects and to enrich his personal socioeconomic position, the poet, the creative artist, alone is committed to the world of the soul and the spirit. Moreover, the poet, the creative artist, is emotionally and intellectually closer to and more intimately connected to the divine and the world of eternity than are the other individuals in society.

Another approach to the theme or issue of mortality is a belief in spiritual eternity, in the capacity of the soul to exist beyond the destructive reach of mortal time. Various works of John Donne and John Milton exemplify this belief in and strategy of spiritual eternity. Both of these poets reveal a strong belief in the eternity of the individual soul and share the conviction that the individual soul (especially the aesthetically, intellectually, and spiritually sensitive soul) will ultimately ascend to the ambience of eternity beyond the ravages and vicissitudes of mortality.

Donne's "Death, Be Not Proud" offers a scathing criticism of Death personified. Donne's premise, like that of Milton, is that the eternal soul has the capacity to vanquish death and to overcome mortality. The apostrophic vitality of Donne's poem not only asserts that "poor Death" (4) has no power over the persona, but also proclaims that death is actually weak and not as powerful as it believes that it is. In the third quatrain the persona criticizes death as being a "slave to fate, chance, kings, and desperate men" (9). Not only is death dependent on other aspects of life for the sources of its power and to enhance its destructive prowess, but it is prominently associated with negative features or qualities of existence such as "poison, war, and sickness" (10).

The persona's attempt to diminish the potency of death culminates in two declarations. The first point which the persona confidently makes is that the use of "poppy or charms" (11) can produce the same kind of effect as that of death. Moreover, such an effect is certainly more pleasurable than death. The persona's concluding argument is that death is mortal in contrast to the individual with the eternal soul who has an everlasting presence in the universe. Although Donne's persona does not describe eternity or the aura of eternity as elaborately or in as much detail as Milton does in "On Time," his belief in eternity and in the capacity of the eternal soul to vanquish death is as vital and resilient as that of Milton.

John Milton, like John Donne, views time (and mortality) as an antagonist which can be vanquished and eradicated by the immortality of the soul. In the first several lines of "On Time" Milton criticizes time (in the sense of mortality) as being short-lived and transient. Milton asserts that time is not only a limited phenomenon, but it is also vain and characterized by "mortal dross" (6). The temporal limitation of time and the capacity of the eternal soul to overcome mortality are stressed in the following lines: "For when as each thing bad thou hast entomb'd, / And last of all, thy greedy self consum'd, / Then long Eternity shall greet our bliss / With an individual kiss" (9–12).

Such a passage is especially noteworthy not only because it suggests an absolute end to mortality but also because it implies through the use of the comma after "consum'd" a sense of continuity between mortality and eternity for the individual soul. There is no fear of death here, for the individual who receives the "kiss" of eternity already experiences a sense of bliss (perhaps in anticipation of the vital experience of eternity or from a feeling of confidence that death will be overcome).

As the ambience which time governs in its transient condition is characterized by negative qualities, by what is false and vain, so the world of eternity represents for Milton everything that is "good and perfectly divine" (14–15). The focal point and source of vitality of eternity for Milton is the figure and throne of Jesus. The exemplary qualities of "Truth" (16), "Peace" (16), and "Love" (16) represent not only the essence of eternity; they are so powerful and gloriously radiant that they illuminate the environment of eternity. The stark contrast between mortality and eternity is affirmed in the last several lines of the poem where the persona distinguishes emphatically between the "Earthy grossness" (20) which the eternal soul shall leave behind and the exuberant, stellar experience of eternity which represents the eternal resting-place of such a soul.

The final line of "On Time" brings the poem full circle. As in line one, so at the end of the poem the persona addresses time (and its corollary phenomena "Death" and "Chance") as secondary to and as easily overcome by the eternal soul. The image of light at the end of "On Time" is comparable in intensity and vitality to images of light in other poems by Milton. For example, in "Ode on the Morning of Christ's Nativity" the poet speaks of an extraordinary radiance in heaven which Jesus left to be a part of the world of everyday mortality. The radiance of eternity which Jesus reveals in heaven is described as a "glorious Form" (8) and a "far-beaming blaze of Majesty" (9). Such a light is comparable to the radiance which pervades the eternal soul "Attir'd with Stars" (21) in the heavenly domain.

William C. Bryant's "Thanatopsis" offers several interesting insights about mortality in the process of articulating a belief in spiritual eternity. In the opening section of the poem Bryant suggests that one viable strategy of confronting and diminishing the anguish of mortality is to venture into the expansiveness of the world of nature and listen to its wisdom, to the profundity of the silence and of the murmurings of the natural world. Yet, when death comes, it represents a return to nature, to natural elements which will then revitalize themselves in new forms of existence. This is reminiscent of Whitman's assertion in "Song of Myself" that the mortal individual achieves a sense of immortality by participating in the eternal cyclicality of nature.

In the second stanza of "Thanatopsis" Bryant states that in death the individual becomes an integral part of the vast realm of the dead. Bryant proceeds to suggest that in death the sensitive individual will be associated with the great and prominent individuals of the past: "....Thou shalt lie down / With patriarchs of the infant world—with kings, / The powerful of the earth—the wise, the good, / Fair forms...." (33–36) Bryant also suggests that even if no one acknowledges or mourns the death of a particular individual, such an individual is not alone—for in the future everyone will share this individual's destiny and follow him to the grave.

In stanza three of this poem Bryant encourages the reader to live now and not to be in fear of death. The realm of death is described as a pleasant, congenial place. Bryant's poem seems to stress the eternity of the spirit rather than the immortality of the soul in a religious sense. That Bryant's eternal resting-place is not religious in the sense of Donne or Milton appears to be affirmed not only by the absence of an emphasis on God or a divine figure as the guiding force in the realm of the dead but also by Bryant's vision or anticipation of this "resting-place" as a space which does not discriminate or distinguish according to religious persuasion. Kings and powerful figures from the distant past (from the pre-Christian past, one might say) are just as welcome in the realm of the dead as uncommon or common individuals from contemporary society. The connectedness of individual lives which Bryant envisions in the realm of the dead is similar in spirit and intensity to the assertion of R.W. Emerson in "Each and All" of the connectedness of individuals and of multiple aspects and dimensions of life.

Although Bryant believes in an afterlife as do Milton and Donne, there are two crucial differences in their approaches to this issue. First, Milton and Donne view death and mortality as antagonistic and hostile forces, whereas for Bryant death represents a congenial ambience. Second, while Milton and Donne believe in the immortality of the soul in a religious sense, Bryant believes in an afterlife, in an eternity of the spirit without strictly religious implications or overtones. Moreover, Milton seems to suggest that eternity exists beyond mortality and beyond the physical parameters of the earth. Bryant, on the other hand, locates the afterlife on the earth, implying that the world of the dead is omnipresent, that it is all around us, merely in another dimension of temporal existence.

The theme of spiritual eternity is of paramount importance in a number of poems by Emily Dickinson. In "I Never Saw a Moor" the persona expresses an instinctive faith or confidence in the existence of God and heaven. In "Because I Could Not Stop for Death" the persona sees Death not as an antagonist but as a friend, as a congenial companion: "Because I could not stop for Death, / He kindly stopped for me; / The carriage held but just ourselves / And immortality" (1-4). The persona implies the existence of an aura of friendly congeniality between herself and death. In the next several stanzas the persona says that she did not fight against death when he made his appearance. She acknowledged his civility and let him lead onward to another realm.

On the way to the cemetery the persona experiences, or perhaps one should say reexperiences, her personal past ("We passed the school where children played" (9)). The house that appears to be a "swelling of the ground" (14) is her final resting-place in the world of mortality. Even though the persona implies a friendly connectedness between herself and death, the final stanza of the poem does suggest that her last day on earth was not completely tranquil or pleasing, and perhaps even somewhat painful: "Since then 'tis centuries; but each / Feels shorter than the day, / I first surmised the horses' heads / Were toward eternity" (17-20).

The persona is writing the poem from the perspective or vantage-point of eternity. She has been dead for a very long time, for centuries. Yet, even though the persona has been gone from the world of mortality for such a long time, this interval seems as nothing compared to the duration of her final day on earth. That is, the interval of time which she has spent in eternity does not seem as long and protracted as her final day in the world of mortality when she sensed that death had come for her. Such a statement does insinuate a somewhat negative undertone about her experience of her last day of mortal life. Although Dickinson does not elaborate on eternity as does Milton in "On Time," that her persona in the poem would speak of having experienced eternity for centuries affirms her conviction and faith in a vital, dynamic eternity.

Another strategy of approaching and confronting mortality is represented by an attempt to focus exclusively or primarily on the present time or the present tense. This strategy is exemplified effectively in poems by Robert Herrick and Andrew Marvell. Herrick's "To the Virgins, to Make Much of Time" articulates the "carpe diem" life-philosophy. Only the present, the life on this earth, is available to the individual, and he or she should therefore live life to the fullest and take advantage of every opportunity to explore and exploit life's possibilities. Herrick begins his argument by emphasizing the inevitability of transience illustrated by the image of the flower which has a fleeting existence. Herrick also uses the rising and setting of the sun, the progression of the daily cycle of time, to exemplify the necessity and the inevitability of change.

The persona privileges the earlier, more youthful stages of life, suggesting that the aging process will always produce increasing difficulties and problems which are not easily addressed or confronted. The culminating stanza deals on one level with the issue of matrimony—the individual is encouraged to marry before it is too late, that is, before the passage of time might make it increasingly challenging to find an appreciative partner. One could argue that the final stanza represents also a symbolic reminder to try to achieve a significant goal or mission in one's life while one has the energy, the creativity, and the vitality to do so.

Andrew Marvell's "To His Coy Mistress" represents an intensification of the carpe diem theme. Like Herrick, Marvell believes not in the option of eternity, but rather only in the possibility of a dynamic and vital present existence on the earth. In the first two stanzas of "To His Coy Mistress" Marvell raises the subjunctive possibility of having an abundance of time and space. If he and his lover had "world enough, and time" (1), they could enjoy a profoundly energized love as well as a strong sense of spatial and temporal expansiveness. In the first twenty lines of the poem the persona envisions a love of timeless quality which would not only affirm his vitality as a lover, but also acknowledge and proclaim the worthiness of his love.

Line 21 introduces a change in spirit and tone in the poem. The possibilities and opportunities raised by the subjunctive aura of the first twenty lines of the poem abruptly cease in line 21 with its awareness of the inevitability and of the presence of mortality. Lines 21–32 offer no paean to the eternity of love as in numerous Shakespearean sonnets; instead, Marvell argues for an inevitable ending to love, culminating in the effectively crafted lines: "The grave's a fine and private place, / But none, I think, do there embrace" (31–32). Mortality signifies an absolute ending to love and cessation of love—death will vanquish not only his song, his melodious love-lyric, but also the beauty of the lover.

In lines 33–46 of "To His Coy Mistress" the persona, painfully aware of the inevitability of mortality, asserts that the only viable strategy to confront and to respond to this awareness is to live as vitally as possible in the present. The verbs of this final stanza ("sport," "devour," "tear," "run") consistently have an active, assertive tone. The persona and his love will challenge time through the intensity and vitality of their love and life. Although the persona is clearly and poignantly aware of and sensitive to the destructive power of time, he even suggests a desire and a capacity to overcome time, though only temporarily, by the intensity of his activities and experiences in the present. However, ultimately, the intensity can only prolong or postpone the inevitable: "Thus, though we cannot make our sun / Stand still, yet we will make him run" (45-46). There is an undertone of melancholy here for even with all of the strength and power which an individual can develop, nurture, and produce and even with all of the love and passion which can be congenially and vitally shared, death will inevitably and objectively intervene to conquer all.

Alexander Pope's "Solitude" offers another perspective on the strategy of focusing on the present or thoroughly savoring the present existential condition. In this poem Pope describes a life of quiet contentment away from society and its demands and expectations. The persona lives in splendid isolation in a self-contained environment of his own creation, nurturing, and development. The individual who has achieved the physical well-being and intellectual serenity depicted in "Solitude" experiences a sense of harmony or unity with time. Unlike the awareness of time or approach to time in the poems by Herrick or Marvell, for Pope, mortality is not an antagonist or a hostile force. Time or mortality is merely an aspect of the human condition to be accepted and not feared.

The persona in "Solitude" is unconcerned not only about mortality, but also about eternity: "Thus let me live, unseen, unknown; / Thus unlamented let me die, / Steal from the world, and not a stone / Tell where I lie" (17-20). This final stanza of the poem shows how instinctively and profoundly serene and dispassionate the persona is about life and death. He aspires to achieve neither the creative eternity of Shakespeare nor the spiritual eternity of Milton. Nor is such an independent-minded persona concerned about fame, recognition, or public acknowledgement of his presence. This persona's indifference to or lack of abiding concern about mortality and mortal fame affirms his belief in the importance of solitude. Not only does the persona in "Solitude" wish to be unlamented at death, but he also wants to leave this mortal, earthly existence with not even a gravestone to memorialize his presence in the world. The individual who would achieve such an existence of profound connectedness to nature is similar to some extent to those personae such as Whitman's in "Song of Myself" who aspire to participate ultimately in the cyclicality of nature. The essential difference between the approaches of Pope and Whitman is in the awareness of the duration of this connectedness. The persona in Pope's poem enjoys being a part of the annual cyclicality of nature, a participation which will end at his death. The persona in Whitman's "Song of Myself" believes in his eternal presence in the world of nature.

Whitman's persona, although aware of mortality, believes that he transcends it by virtue of his becoming ultimately a part of the eternal cyclicality of the natural environment.

Another approach to time and mortality is the belief that death and mortality are inevitable with little, if any, redeeming features or qualities at the end of the cycle or process of mortality. Edgar Allan Poe's "The Conqueror Worm" suggests that the life and development of humankind is a tragedy which leaves even the angels "pallid and wan" (37). The hero of this tragedy is the conqueror worm, implying that mortality conquers all and is relentless in its destructive force.

Poe's "Annabel Lee" not only asserts the inspirational importance of beauty, even in death, but also proclaims the inevitability of mortality. Despite the tragic aura of this poem and Poe's emphasis on this world as the only one of experiential validity, there is an implication of the eternity of the spirit in the last stanza of "Annabel Lee." Here the persona states that neither the angels in heaven nor the demons in hell can ever separate his soul from the soul of his beloved Annabel Lee. Poe's sense of eternity in this instance appears to be more similar to that of Bryant in "Thanatopsis" than to that of Milton or Donne. For Bryant, as for Poe, the individual spirit may or will exist through eternity. However, this is not a religiously motivated eternity—this is not a sense of eternity with any religious implications or overtones. In "Annabel Lee" Poe suggests a perpetual coexistence and consanguinity of two kindred souls, the soul of the persona and the soul of Annabel Lee.

Thomas Gray's "Ode on a Distant Prospect of Eton College" also suggests the inevitability of mortality. The first five stanzas of the poem elaborate on happy, congenial aspects of life. Stanza two is especially indicative of the pleasant tone of the first half of the poem. In this stanza the persona describes his childhood as characterized by a carefree atmosphere and a spatial expansiveness. The sixth stanza introduces a new tone into the process of the poem. The poet speaks in this stanza of how unaware people appear to be of the dangerous situations that await them in the world of everyday mortality. From stanza six through the end of the poem various dark and destructive aspects of time and mortality are personified and described from "black Misfortune's baleful train" (57) to the "painful family of Death (83). This detailed and graphically presented litany of destructive and hostile emotions and forces represents a frightening array of mortal danger.

As one proceeds through this series of negative and even terrifying circumstances and qualities one might reflect upon stanza four and appreciate more thoughtfully the significance of the "fearful joy" (40) which is mentioned. Even the audacious and intrepid individuals who adventurously dare to challenge the limits of human endeavor realize consciously, if not intuitively, that they must be aware of what lies behind them and of what might suddenly emerge to make their situations perilous. The "voice in every wind" (39) which the adventurers, pioneers, and explorers of new intellectual, emotional, and physical terrain hear could be interpreted in different ways. This voice could be interpreted as having a threatening tone which reminds the traveler or adventurer that mortality is always present and near. Or the voice could be construed in a more positive light, suggesting the presence of a beautiful image, melody, or memory which should be appreciated while it lasts. The next line does reinforce the message that a mortal bliss, joy, or sense of exuberance must be valued as much as possible in its present context, for such bliss, joy, or sense of exuberance can only be fleeting and transient in the world of everyday mortality.

The final stanza of the poem stresses initially the inevitability of mortality and suffering. In the last six lines the poet shifts his focus from the description of the anguish of mortality to a consideration of possible strategies to counter mortality and suffering. On the one hand, the persona seems to be suggesting that it is better not to think about the ills and misfortunes of mortal existence, and instead to try to find enjoyment and pleasure in life. The last two lines— "...where ignorance is bliss / 'Tis folly to be wise" could be interpreted as suggesting that it is better to develop a sense of carefree indifference to the trials and tribulations of mortality than to be fully aware of its range of anguish and danger. On the other hand, the persona might perhaps be criticizing this approach and arguing that a mature awareness of and wisdom about the world, its complexity, and its diversity of good and evil is most important. While leaving open different interpretive possibilities at the end, the poem offers no return to the careless and carefree childhood of the first part of the poem, thus affirming the notion that mortality vanquishes all animate beings.

Henry Wadsworth Longfellow's "The Tide Rises, the Tide Falls" discusses mortality in the context of the cycles of nature. In stanza one of the poem the traveler, walking along the shore in the twilight, participates in the cyclicality of the natural world and of the universe. In stanza two, however, darkness covers everything and "the little waves" (8) wash away the footprints of the traveler. The use of the descriptive adjective "little" here suggests that the sea is so powerful that even the smallest examples of its power can vanquish and eliminate the human presence. Stanza three depicts the return of the day— however, the traveler has vanished forever from the scene. In contrasting the eternal cyclicality of nature to the mortality of humankind, Longfellow affirms the perpetual dynamism of the sea and the inescapability and inevitability of mortality. As the tide of the sea will continue to rise and fall, so time will continue to move onward—the sphere of human endeavor seems almost incidental in the context of these dynamic cyclical and universal forces.

Percy B. Shelley's "Ozymandias," as several of the poems discussed above, argues effectively for the inevitability of mortality and transience, although in a different geographical context. The persona of "Ozymandias" meets a traveler "from an antique land" (1) who tells him of his experience of the limited longevity or transience of mortal fame. The traveler says that he encountered a broken image or sculpture of Ozymandias, a powerful and prominent king of the ancient world, in the desert. Only "two vast and trunkless legs of stone" (2) and a "shattered visage" (4) remain of the once seemingly colossal and imposing structure. These broken, isolated objects sundered from the whole are all that remains, literally and symbolically, of the once great realm of Ozymandias.

The pedestal of the sculpture, which contains the moral of the poem, is interestingly enough, still intact. The message connected to these sculptured fragments is: "My name is Ozymandias, king of kings: / Look on my works, ye Mighty, and despair!" (10-11). One interpretation of this passage is that these lines are added by the sculptor to complement his work. The sculptor, and by implication, the artist in a universal sense, asserts that even the illustrious accomplishments of such a famous and powerful king as Ozymandias, are fleeting and impermanent in the world of mortality. It is noteworthy that the sculptor says that this is a direct quote from Ozymandias, suggesting that the message is not merely the artist's interpretation. Ozymandias uses the word "despair" to proclaim to posterity the inevitability of mortality and the painful awareness that mortality conquers and vanquishes everything. Even the great monuments of such an important and prominent individual as the king, or any regal ruler, will not last. It is also interesting that Ozymandias is not even addressing the general public in this statement—he is only making his pronouncement to "ye Mighty," who are presumably other prominent, famous, and powerful rulers such as he is.

Another plausible interpretation of this passage is that Ozymandias was alive when the sculpture was created and commanded the sculptor to add these specific words to the pedestal. Whether or not this is a historically accurate comment from such a king as Ozymandias, that the statement derives from such a royal personage affirms its validity and makes the implications of the remark all the more poignant.

The destructive power of mortality is further made manifest by the fact that these sculptured fragments are alone and isolated in the middle of the desert—there is only an endless expanse of sand stretching around and beyond the decayed wreck. If there is anything positive about the persona's awareness of mortality here it is to be found in lines 4-8. Perhaps the poem is suggesting that although mortality conquers and diminishes all material things, the spirit of the creative enterprise will always endure. Although Ozymandias is dead and although his realm no longer exists, and although only a broken piece of sculpture remains as a testament to his former greatness, the artist's genius in capturing the spirit of his character and empire is perpetuated by the appearance of his countenance.

There is also the strategy of confronting mortality and the flux of time by attempting to return to the aura of the past and by an attempt to revitalize the spirit of the past. For example, Henry Vaughan in "The Retreat" describes the longing of the persona for the past, for an existential condition that was much more enjoyable and beautiful than the present. Vaughan's persona contrasts the burden and oppression of the present with the celestial vitality of his "Angel-infancy," when he achieved an emotional and a spiritual closeness to the divine and to eternity.

Friedrich Hölderlin's "Da ich ein Knabe war" privileges the earlier stages of life and emphasizes that the persona was reared in an especially nurturing environment beyond the limitations and clamor of everyday mortality. The persona implicitly longs for this extraordinary environment of the past which has given his life meaning and a sense of vitality. In his youth the persona developed in the atmosphere of the gods and of a beautiful natural environment. Although there is now a temporal distance between him and his golden past, he remembers the friendly gods very fondly as well as his love for them.

The persona in Hölderlin's "Da ich ein Knabe war" proceeds to assert that he knew the gods and the divine realm better, more instinctively, and more vitally than he ever knew the world of humankind. This persona even proclaims that he understood the serenity, the existential stillness of the divine realm, whereas he never really understood the language and the discourses of humankind. Perhaps the persona is suggesting that because he was reared in the pristine beauty of nature and in a realm with a divine aura he will never truly be able to feel that he is a part of the world of everyday mortality. The spirit of the persona was influenced and shaped in such a way by his contact with the divine world that he is too refined and too sensitive to become an active and an ordinary participant in the complications and machinations of everyday mortality.

Lyubov in Anton Chekhov's *The Cherry Orchard* tries to revitalize her life by returning to the place of her beautiful childhood and youth. However, the anguish of the intervening years of her life and the family's financial situation make it difficult for her to sustain the vitality of the image of the past. Mrs. Lyubov Ranevsky attempts to revitalize the past because she believes that the past, her past in the ambience of the lovely cherry orchard, represents a conspicuously more glorious time than the present. Lyubov thinks of her experience of the cherry orchard and its enchanting environment as a period of innocence and beauty.

In F. Scott Fitzgerald's *The Great Gatsby* the protagonist, Gatsby, believes strongly that he can revitalize the past. Gatsby aims to challenge mortality by creating an enchanted moment of timelessness, of timeless continuity with the past. The space of his splendid mansion is the space which will initiate and motivate his revitalization of the past. Gatsby tries to revive the past so he can displace the unpleasant present and bring Daisy back into his life. To some extent Gatsby is attempting to recreate the past enchanted time which he and Daisy shared together. Unfortunately, the vicissitudes of mortality and the human capacity for destructiveness undermine his valiant attempt to revitalize the past.

One key difference between these two encounters with the past or approaches to the past is that Gatsby's experience with the past was not completely positive because Daisy's family was against Daisy's connection with Gatsby. For Lyubov the distant past, especially her childhood and youth on the estate, symbolized by the cherry orchard, was a time of happiness and joy unadulterated by contact with the tribulations of everyday reality. It is also noteworthy that Lyubov feels a strong personal, temporal connectedness with the distant past in her home environment. While Gatsby has no roots in the world of Daisy's youth (in the world where Gatsby initially met Daisy), Lyubov has the deepest roots and connections possible in the world symbolized by the beautiful cherry orchard. For Lyubov was born in the house surrounded by the cherry orchard. Moreover, her mother, father, and grandfather lived in the house. Lyubov's profound attachment to and devotion to the cherry orchard are affirmed in her statement in Act 3 that without the cherry orchard life has no meaning for her.

Gatsby tries to revive the past more literally than symbolically. He believes that if he can "return" to the past moment of his relation with Daisy, then he can revitalize his life and make a new beginning. In contrast, Lyubov aspires to revive the past more symbolically than literally. It is as if Lyubov has returned home to Russia to recapture the spirit of the past so when she leaves again she will take the reawakened "spirit of the past" with her to inspire and regenerate her present life. Of course, Lyubov has returned ostensibly to liberate herself from the misery and suffering of her recent past in Paris where her partner robbed and deserted her, after which she tried to poison herself. In Act 2 Lyubov says that she wished to return to Russia with her little girl; certainly another reason for the return is Lyubov's desire to cleanse herself of the recent anguish and to reenergize her life.

Although Lyubov disagrees instinctively and strongly with Lopahin's decision to cut down the cherry orchard, which would vanquish an important symbol of her past, there is a sense that she had an intuition about this or perhaps even expected this subconsciously to happen. That is, one could argue that Lyubov seems to anticipate only a brief return to her home, sensing that she can merely re-engage with a beautiful and transient symbol of her glorious past. In longing for the innocence and happiness of her childhood Lyubov is also thinking not only about the beauty and loveliness of the cherry orchard but also about its pristine and extensive spaciousness. At one point in the drama Lyubov even believes, although only temporarily, that she sees her mother, who is dead, walking in the orchard. It is as if the spaciousness of the cherry orchard has removed or sublimated all sense of temporality and temporal flux.

Gatsby, by contrast, does not inherit an estate—he purchases and creates a house of cosmopolitan, eclectic ambience. The incorporation in the house of various architectural and aesthetic styles affirms implicitly this interest in transcending the parameters and limits of the present tense. But the house, as the character and owner, also lives in and is contiguous with and connected with the past. One might claim that Gatsby, although creating an aesthetically interesting house, is more interested in the spirit and the aura of the house than in its material substance and features. For Gatsby wealth is a means to an end, to the revitalization of his past with Daisy. Gatsby's house seems to represent a continuation of and an extension of the past—the sense of continuity established here will enhance the process of his revitalization with Daisy, or so he believes.

As vitally material and aesthetically dynamic as Gatsby's house is or seems to be, there is something inherently and profoundly ethereal about it as well, epitomized in the scenario in which Daisy makes the very romantic statement that she would like to push Gatsby gently around in a cloud. Perhaps such a textual moment even possesses the aura of an Ibsenesque "castle in the air."

As for Solness in Henrik Ibsen's *The Master Builder*, so for Gatsby there is a beautiful dimension which such a creation possesses which a regular house grounded completely or thoroughly in the world of everyday mortality can never have. The "castle in the air" represents for Solness and for Ibsen the triumph of the ideal over the real—it is a potent tribute to the perpetual vitality of the creative imagination. Gatsby's mansion has the aura of a "castle in the air" about it. Certainly such a mansion has a solidly material and strongly materialistic dimension. But this is merely the façade. What is most important is the creative spirit behind the façade, behind the public, outward appearance. Daisy shows her intuitive knowledge of Gatsby and of his house when she evokes or creates the image of the pink cloud which represents the spirit of the place and its capacity for transcendence.

Such are the primary strategies for confronting, challenging, and even trying to overcome the tribulations and vicissitudes of everyday mortality: a belief in the creative eternity of the writer or artist, in the creative eternity of his or her work, and in the eternity of the love, the emotional vitality which is sensitively and vitally expressed in such artistic or literary works; a belief in the eternity of the soul and the eternity of the spirit, motivated and informed by religious concerns and inclinations or primarily secular; a focus on the present motivated by an attempt to enjoy the present life fully and dynamically as the only effective antidote to the flux of mortality; a focus on the present motivated by a desire to exist in splendid isolation away from the energy and experiential abundance of the world of everyday mortality; an emphasis on the present which reveals an awareness of and a sensitivity to the past and the future; a present-focussed existence which believes that mortality is inevitable and omnipotent and that the flux of time cannot be vanquished or transformed; a belief in the power of the past to heal and to redeem the present; a devotion to the past, to a vision of the past, which can make the present more meaningful and which can make the exigencies and sufferings of the present more endurable; a belief in the capacity of special spaces, of sanctuaries of light, harmony, and serenity, to mitigate, diminish, eradicate, or transform the flux of mortality; a belief in and a devotion to sanctuaries of light, harmony, and serenity as possessing an inherent capacity to heal and soothe the mind, the heart, and the soul.

The sanctuaries of light and effulgence which are described in this book may have an aura of absolute permanence and stability generated by their own vitality or by a sense of participating in a cycle of eternal renewal, an atmosphere of relative security and peacefulness, or even an ambience of delicate radiance and transitory enchantment as fragile as the vision in S. T.

Coleridge's "Kubla Khan" and as ethereal as Henrik Ibsen's "castle in the air." Yet, what all of these sanctuaries share is an innately strong belief in the power and the profundity of the light which creates, infuses, motivates, and nurtures them. This is a light as radiant and as sublime as the Apollonian luminescence in Shelley's "Hymn to Intellectual Beauty" which may comfort, revitalize, and regenerate the heart and the soul and which may inspire the creative spirit to develop, to sustain, and to strengthen his own artistic vision:

> Thy light alone—like mist o'er the mountains driven,
>
>   Or music by the night-wind sent
>
>   Through strings of some still instrument,
>
>   Or moonlight on a midnight stream,
>
> Gives grace and truth to life's unquiet dream. (32–36)

✳ *William Wordsworth*

In *William Wordsworth: A Life* Stephen Gill writes that "Tintern Abbey" (written in 1798) is Wordsworth's "hymn of thanksgiving" (120) for the "energies in the natural order that make for unity, which enable man to know himself part of the great whole of the active universe" (129–130). Wordsworth's persona (the "I" in the poem) overcomes the fragmentation of the self that occurs in "Yew-tree Lines" by appreciating profoundly the "sense sublime / Of something far more deeply interfused" (95–96) which inspires him to see in nature the emotional, spiritual source of his experience of a diastolic, expansive sense of space and time. In "Tintern Abbey" Wordsworth reveals a diastolic sense of space and a sense of time that is both hermetic and orphic, hermetic in the sense that the persona is more aware of mortality, orphic in the sense that the persona believes intuitively that any expansiveness of space may lead to a feeling of expanding time.

The importance of a sense of space is stressed from the beginning of "Tintern Abbey." In the first ten to fifteen lines Wordsworth speaks of the significance of the "steep and lofty cliffs" (5) which not only inspire profound thoughts, but also represent the link between the earth and "the quiet of the sky" (8). The aura of heavenly tranquility is subsequently applied to the repose which the persona experiences under the dark sycamore. Wordsworth views with admiration various features of his immediate natural environment, including the "orchard-tufts" (11) and the "hedge-rows" (15). He asserts that although he has not seen "these beauteous forms" (22) directly for several years, these lovely images of nature have influenced his mind and heart powerfully from a distance. These images have not only given him "sensations sweet" (27), but they have also infused his soul with a semblance of the tranquillity which characterizes "the quiet of the sky" (8).

The sensitive contemplation of the beautiful forms of nature creates a mood of profound serenity in which the individual experiences a psychic suspension of corporeal existence and becomes a living soul. In attaining this existential condition the persona prepares himself (as lines 46–48 suggest) to achieve a diastolic sense of space and time. At this epiphanic moment of harmony and joy the persona sees "into the life of things" (49). This vision or visionary capacity seems to be a precursor of and perhaps even comparable to the "faith that looks through death" (185) of the Immortality Ode. Such a visionary capability coupled with an exceptional sensitivity for nature is also seen in Samuel Palmer's *The Magic Apple Tree*. The persona in Wordsworth's poem and the primary individual in Palmer's painting achieve a similarly vital epiphanic moment of harmony and a sense of a serene sanctuary.

In the next section of the poem starting with line 49 the persona claims that he has often turned to the sense and spirit of the "sylvan Wye" (56) and its surroundings to help and guide him through his present existence. The persona declares that reflecting on this beautiful natural environment often illuminated his mind and spirit and gave him a sense of hope when he was experiencing spiritual or physical darkness. The sense of spatial fluidity which was established in the first fifteen lines of the poem is reinforced by the image of the "sylvan Wye" (56) wandering through the forest. Although the Wye represents an image of water and not of earth (in contrast to the previously foregrounded images of nature) all of the dominant features of nature described so far in the poem possess an inner energy. The "orchard-tufts" (11) and "hedge-rows" (15), like the "sylvan Wye" (56), are infused with a dynamic motion which affirms the vitality of nature and perhaps even enhances the capacity of the living soul to see into the life of things. This vital energy in nature encourages the persona to feel that his present observations of this lovely environment will generate a host of congenial images and reflections for many years to come and will provide an inner illumination of the soul in the future.

The return to this inspirational place is important not only for the present revitalization of the individual, but also for his future development. Although the persona is able to revive some of the past spirit of this space and of his feeling for nature, he realizes the noticeable difference between his earlier and his current experience of nature. The emotional passion which the persona felt as a youth in the presence of nature has been toned down to a more serene awareness of and feeling for nature. Yet, there is still a unity of past and present through the power of memory which sustains and will continue to preserve the poet's faith in the vitality of the present. Moreover, change is not seen necessarily as a negative dimension of life; rather, it produces "abundant recompense" (88), perhaps most of all in the increasing development of a more mature and insightful creative vision.

The persona, in becoming a more mature and profound observer of and participant in nature, feels a presence that disturbs him "with the joy / Of elevated thoughts" (94–95). This "sense sublime" (95) is characterized above all by a spatial expansiveness—the motion and the spirit which the persona senses as the source of nature's creative energy and sublimity is a diastolic spatiality that encompasses not only sky, earth, and water, but also the mind of man. Wordsworth's persona asserts that because he feels vitally this spatially generated energy, light, and vitality which "impels / All thinking things" (100–1) and "rolls through all things" (102) he is a nature-lover, a lover of the spatial expansiveness of nature. This awareness of the diastolic power of nature inspires the persona to proclaim that nature (and the language of the sense) represents the guide and the guardian of his heart, soul, and moral being.

Line 97 offers one example of the power of the diastolic spatiality of nature to influence significant dimensions of the surrounding world. In line 97 the persona perceives, or perhaps conceives of, time in terms of space. In suggesting that the dwelling of this presence in nature is "the light of setting suns" (97), the persona implies the transcendence of time through space. The phrase "setting suns" (97) suggests a series or a succession of evenings which are unified in the spatially motivated aura of their light. This emphasis on space as the defining quality of this experience of the presence of nature, exemplified by the use of the image "dwelling" (97), is reinforced by the following phrases, "round ocean" (98), "living air" (98), and "blue sky" (99), all of which are spatially vital and spatially motivated images.

The "sense sublime / Of something far more deeply interfused" (95–96), which is fulfilled in the conception of a motion or a spirit pervading nature, has already been presented in the poem prior to line 95. For the description of the "orchard-tufts" (11) losing themselves "Mid groves and copses" (14), the "hedge-rows" (15) running wild, and the sylvan Wye wandering through the woods are all examples of the "motion" (100) and the "spirit" (100) which rolls through all things. The potential for diastolic spatiality is perhaps even implied in the first few lines of the poem where the persona speaks of hearing the waters "rolling from their mountain-springs" (3), implying his capacity to envision an existential vitality beyond the immediate natural space. The persona's capacity for experiencing and participating in, as well as creating, a spatial expansiveness is affirmed in the ensuing lines in his perception of the cliffs connecting the landscape with the quiet of the sky.

The spatial metaphor is reaffirmed in the last section of the poem, lines 111–59, where the persona speaks, for example, of the importance of the mind, which through the benevolent and pervasive influence of nature "shall be a mansion for all lovely forms" (140) and of the significance of the memory which shall "be as a dwelling-place / For all sweet sounds and harmonies" (141–42). The structural framework of this spatial metaphor reinforces the sense of space established by the initial experience of the sycamore. The poet grounds or establishes himself in a particular space from where he envisions the beauteous forms of nature and the motion and spirit that vitalizes those forms. From this secure, or seemingly secure, space the persona perceives and conceives the diastolic spatiality of his natural environment.

Helen Vendler in "'Tintern Abbey': Two Assaults" asserts the importance of the "continuing force of various paradigmatic identity roles preferred by lyric to centuries of readers" (185). The continuity of the Wordsworthian "I" can be maintained without seeing it as "factually mimetic of its own historical moment of social experience" (185). Vendler is responding to Levinson's argument that Wordsworth has suppressed facts about the description of Tintern Abbey and its environment in a strategy of historical denial as well as to "Barrell's insistence that Wordsworth must have endorsed a connection between gender and language because some of his contemporaries did" (183) by saying that both are "examples of a misplaced historicizing of lyric" (183).

Vendler proceeds to say: "If Wordsworth's aim in 'Tintern Abbey' is, as I believe, to write in longer form 'My heart leaps up,' then he is constructing a geometrical figure for the ego over time, connected by lines between four points" (184). Vendler continues to assert that if "these are the four different immersions in the landscape that generate the poem, nothing could be more irrelevant to them than the industrialism and the vagrant-haunted Abbey" (184–85). The Wordsworthian "I" can attain a sense of continuity in his own landscape vision, in his own context of emotional, intellectual, and spiritual vitality, which may include, but is not necessarily determined by, the historical experiences which occur simultaneously.

Vendler suggests that the change in the way the word "nature" is used in the poem, especially in the shift from the unpersonified presence of nature meaning "the natural world" in the second part to the personification of nature as female in the third part "was enabled by the entrance of the thought of the speaker's sister, who becomes the genius loci" (187).

Whether or not one argues that the maturation of "wild ecstasies" (138) into "a sober pleasure" parallels or represents a transformation of time and space, it is the aura of spatial expansiveness which possesses and reveals dynamic healing qualities. Only the individual who is aware of and sensitive to the beauteous forms of nature and who develops a profound feeling for nature may achieve this sense of a spatial expansiveness of the soul.

Percy Shelley's "Lines Written among the Euganean Hills" and "Hymn to Intellectual Beauty" offer approaches to space, time, and mortality which are similar to Wordsworth's sense of space and time in "Tintern Abbey." The "sense sublime" (95) which Wordsworth's persona feels is comparable to the power of the light of intellectual beauty which Shelley's persona experiences as giving "grace and truth to life's unquiet dream" (36). In "Lines Written among the Euganean Hills" the persona, wandering across the sea of mortality, finds flowering isles, temporary epiphanies of light and happiness, which not only revitalize him emotionally and spiritually but also regenerate the potential of the earth to renew itself. The flowering isle is comparable to Wordsworth's locus amoenus at Grasmere, though Wordsworth's spatial paradise seems to offer more permanent security and stability than Shelley's. Wordsworth's "I" describes a seemingly hermetic and self-sustained paradise, an aesthetic unity which will perpetually inspire him. However, Shelley's "I" in "Lines Written among the Euganean Hills" must keep moving from flowering isle to flowering isle, from epiphany to epiphany, to sustain and develop his creative vitality and his sense of transcending mortality.

Moreover, only such an individual who loves, admires, and reveres nature may experience a continuity of self by participating in a series of epiphanic moments in which nature so influences the mind and impresses the soul with quietness and beauty that it cannot be adversely affected by the harsh, unsympathetic experiences which may occur in the world of everyday mortality. The highest and most vital condition of mortal existence is signified by a continuity of self in the spirit of the epigraph of the Immortality Ode: "And I could wish my days to be / Bound each to each by natural piety."

The sense of continuity is enhanced by Wordsworth's belief in the presences or Presence of nature. Perkins in English Romantic Writers says that for Wordsworth (especially for the Wordsworth of The Prelude but manifest throughout his work) "in the natural world there is not simply a congeries of objects but a Consciousness, a pervading Being, or. . . a Presence" (172). Wordsworth's awareness of continuity—his assertion of the importance of achieving a continuity of self—is connected to and reinforced by his philosophy of organicism. As the universe is a living, dynamically growing and maturing whole, so the self aims to develop organically by encompassing a series of "selves," or moments of existence of the self, in a perpetually self-generating unified vision. However, sometimes the unified vision falls apart and fragments into countermoments of "sightings," not vision.

It is noteworthy that Wordsworth uses the "light of setting suns" to motivate his awareness of a vital presence, a divinely powerful presence, in nature. One might ask why he does not speak of rising suns, suggesting directly an aura of beginnings and renewal. Perhaps one might argue that it is at this threshold moment of evening, of the interface of day and night, and symbolically of life and death, that the persona feels he may most vitally or even exclusively experience the spatial expansiveness of nature. Through his awareness of the spatial expansiveness of nature the persona experiences an expansiveness, spatial and ultimately temporal, of the creative self as powerful as the holistic vitality of the self in Samuel Palmer's painting *Cornfield by Moonlight with the Evening Star* (1827) and in John Constable's *The Hay Wain* (1821).

Wordsworth's "I Wandered Lonely as a Cloud" exemplifies with similar intensity the spirit of devotion to nature which is represented in "Tintern Abbey." "I Wandered Lonely as a Cloud" signifies the illumination of the mind and the soul inspired by the beauty and the magnificence of nature. This poem reveals an epiphanic moment of Turneresque luminescence. In stanza one the persona describes himself as wandering through a beautiful natural environment whose most prominent features are the daffodils, the lake, the trees, and the breeze which creates the dancing motions of the flowers. That the persona feels an intimate kinship with nature is suggested by the first line of the poem. The persona feels not only that his lonely wandering is comparable to that of a cloud floating across the sky but also that he is as a cloud moving through this distinctively lovely landscape.

The light of the golden daffodils becomes especially vital and potent in the second stanza. The great abundance of daffodils creates an aura of golden radiance. The continuity and the power of this radiance is even compared to "the stars that shine / And twinkle on the milky way" (7-8). The daffodils represent luminescent "spots of time" which inspire the persona to feel a sense of awe and admiration for the natural environment. In the last two lines of stanza two—"Ten thousand saw I at a glance, / Tossing their heads in sprightly dance" (11-12)—the persona implies an almost impressionistic infinity of color and light.

The vitality of this lovely natural scene is emphasized in stanzas two and three, especially in the image of the dancing daffodils, fluttering in the breeze. Even though the waves of the lake are dynamic, the daffodils are even more vital in their energetic and dazzling display of color and light. In stanza three the persona also asserts that such a beautiful natural place inevitably encourages the poet to feel happy and connected to the aesthetic delight of the moment. The persona also admits that as beautiful as this scene is, he could not envision all of the future happiness and pleasure which such an experience would offer him.

In stanza four the persona declares that even when he is distant from such a picturesque natural space, he only needs to reflect upon the beautiful daffodils and other lovely aspects of nature and his mind and spirit are comforted and soothed: "And then my heart with pleasure fills, / And dances with the daffodils" (23-24). The fourth and final stanza describes a sanctuary of light and tranquility which soothes and enlivens the mind, heart, and soul of the persona.

It is not only that the persona is inspired by his reflection on and vision of the beauty of the daffodils and the surrounding nature. The spirit of the persona also actively participates in this visionary moment by dancing emotionally and spiritually with the daffodils. The radiance and the vitality of the daffodils and the natural scene which embraces them illuminates the heart and the soul of the poet and has the "power to make / Our noisy years seem moments in the being / Of the Eternal Silence" (The Immortality Ode, 153-55).

The power of such a moment of inner illumination is reminiscent of the radiance which the light of intellectual beauty inspires in the persona of Shelley's "Hymn to Intellectual Beauty." Shelley's "I," in asserting that the light of intellectual beauty gives "grace and truth to life's unquiet dream," (36) implies the capacity of the individual sensitive to intellectual beauty and to the spirit of beauty to distance himself from the vicissitudes of everyday mortality, if only temporarily. In dedicating himself to intellectual beauty Shelley's "I" has enhanced his creative vitality immeasurably—for he is able to "call the phantoms of a thousand hours / Each from his voiceless grave" (64-65). Although the "I" may not be able to transcend mortality completely he can achieve a sense of aesthetic viability and emotional-spiritual stability in the effulgent calm and autumnal harmony which the spirit of intellectual beauty may offer him. Such an effulgent serenity and radiant harmony is similar in intensity to the luminescent vision of Wordsworth's "I" in "I Wandered Lonely as a Cloud." The persona in each of these poems experiences a sanctuary of light and serenity which will perpetually nurture his spirit and soothe his soul.

A similarly intense experience of light and inner illumination appears in "My Heart Leaps Up When I Behold." In this short poem the persona asserts that when he sees a rainbow, his heart is enlivened. The heart and the soul of the persona, the poet, are inspired and soothed when he experiences a rainbow with its luminescent colors. Such scenes of light and radiance in a beautiful natural environment have a powerful emotional effect on the persona. As the poem continues the persona declares that such an appreciation of nature will motivate his entire existence. The persona concludes with an emphasis on the importance of achieving a sense of continuity: "And I could wish my days to be / Bound each to each by natural piety" (8-9). The persona, the poet, makes an implicit connection here between the beauty of luminescent visionary moments and the experience of a vital continuity of self, suggesting that such radiant moments can help generate and sustain a perpetually resilient continuity of self through different phases of life.

Wordsworth's "Ode: Intimations of Immortality from Recollections of Early Childhood" (written 1802-04) is about beauty, the beauty of nature, the importance of light, creative vitality, and how to make life enjoyable and pleasurable, if not inspirational, when that beauty begins to fade and when that creative vitality begins to diminish. One might also say that Wordsworth's poem deals with an eternal challenge to the human spirit—how to make life meaningful and worthwhile in a world that is fragile and mortal.

For Wordsworth the answer to this challenge, the inspiration to overcome this challenge, is to be found in the following: 1) in Nature, in the eternal, cyclical beauty and dynamism of the natural environment and in the poet's experience of an emotional and a spiritual unity and continuity with that environment; 2) in his own creative capacity as a poet, in his artistic vitality as a creator, which is strengthened as he matures and grows older; 3) in the importance of memory, in the rememberance of significant past personal events which are congenial enough to provide strength and confidence to confront the present and the future; and 4) in the importance of an emotional vitality, of a generous and magnanimous heart and spirit that would include in its perception and vision all aspects of the world (not only fountains, meadows, brooks, and clouds, but also the most inconspicuous flower).

Wordsworth's Immortality Ode begins with a lament about the inevitable passage of time. The first two stanzas reveal a sense of beauty in nature as well as an awareness of mortality, that these beautiful things will pass away. In stanza one the persona recalls observing in the past that various, or even all, aspects of nature were suffused with a "celestial light" (4), which he now no longer experiences. The first line of stanza two sets the tone for the rest of the stanza. That "The Rainbow comes and goes" (10) symbolizes and affirms the inevitable transience of beautiful aspects of nature.

The third stanza reinforces the persona's awareness of mortality and suggests that mortality may be transcended, if only temporarily, by the emotional-spiritual participation of the sensitive individual in the spatial magnanimity and permanence of nature. Although the beautiful in nature may pass away, there is a continuity, a cyclicality in the natural world which overcomes and intensifies the transience of its enchanted moments. The persona will also be revitalized by perceiving the joyousness and vernal vitality of nature.

The fourth stanza affirms initially the joyous aura of nature. In his capacity to appreciate the beauty of nature emotionally and spiritually, the persona enhances his own sense of bliss. Yet, in the midst of the beauty and vitality of nature the persona senses the inevitable flux of time which will ultimately bring about a change in his visionary power. The persona feels a sense of bliss, but is compelled by the subtle signs of mortality to wonder about the fading of the visionary gleam. As in the first two stanzas, the perception of the vital beauty of nature is linked to and challenged by an awareness of mortality, of the flux of time.

The isolated tree, the single field, and the pansy remind the persona of the transience of all animate creatures. The joyousness of the persona has been reduced by the end of the fourth stanza to two interrelated questions: "Whither is fled the visionary gleam? / Where is it now, the glory and the dream?" (56-57). In the first question the "I" seems to raise a concern about his own visionary capacity, as if such a capacity were adversely affected by the presence of images of transience. The second question intensifies the concern of the first. The intensification is made all the more poignant not only by the coupling of the two lines in end-rhyme, but also by the fact that the word "gleam" (56) seems to have energized the formation of "glory" (57) and "dream" (57) in the following line. The concern about the visionary capacity of the persona is transient, for the visionary gleam is revitalized in the last stanza of the poem, especially in the capability to appreciate a continuity of "spots of time" to make life meaningful.

Stanza five of the Immortality Ode glorifies the time of youth as having a heavenly aura. The child is depicted as being closer to nature emotionally and spiritually than individuals in later stages of life. He is closer to the pulse of nature, perhaps because of his pristine imagination and his capacity for wonder. One might think of Ruskin's statement that the genius is largely a child at heart, preserving a capacity for perpetual wonder. The youth is sustained by a positive and radiant vision of the beauty of nature—as long as he keeps the spirit of nature in his heart, he will be able to counter the vicissitudes of mortality. In the final two lines of stanza five Wordsworth's persona acknowledges that adulthood is not typically capable of sustaining the profoundly vital visions of youth which ultimately diminish, fade, and vanish. There is also a strong religious undertone in stanza five, for the persona asserts that "trailing clouds of glory do we come / From God, who is our home" (64-65). This statement could imply that the individual soul who comes from God and the divine realm will inevitably participate in the eternal cyclicality of life and return at the end of his life to this home, to this divine realm.

In stanza six Wordsworth suggests that nature, realizing the inevitable loss of emotional innocence and fall from a paradisical state of creative grace of humankind, produces her own delights to encourage the individual conscious of mortality to reflect less upon or to forget the glories of the past. Nature tries to exhort such an individual to believe in the present, in the fullness of nature's vitality in the present, in the spirit of the Augustinian trilogy of the Eternal present.

Augustine described past, present, and future not only as experiences relating to external space, but also as experiences within the mind of man: "Perhaps it might be said rightly that there are three times: a time present of things past; a time present of things present; and a time present of things future. For these three do coexist somehow in the soul" (324).

Stanza seven reveals Wordsworth's reflections on and thoughts about childhood and the creative urges developing in that phase of life. Wordsworth's persona implies an ingenuous, even profoundly naïve, creative capacity in the first stage of the growth process. The child learns through time, with the generous assistance of time, to fulfill the different and inevitable roles of human development. There seems to be an implication here that the persona, because he is cognizant of the generous assistance of time, cannot view time harshly—instead, the persona considers the negative dimension or facet of time, mortality, as inimical and hostile.

Perhaps the capacity to differentiate time and mortality is related to the acceptance by Harold Bloom in *The Visionary Company* of Wordsworth's belief in the potential for unity between mind and nature in the "autonomy of the poet's creative imagination" (79). Such a powerful union of vital reciprocity redeems the world of everyday reality and intimates, at least symbolically, an immortality of imaginative experience.

Stanza eight continues the apotheosis of youth unaffected by the rapacious flux of time. In his ingenuous creativity and profound simplicity the child is a philosopher and a prophet who is intuitively aware of the truths which the mature individual strives all his life to find. Like the Romantic painter John Constable, Wordsworth believes in the importance of the permanences of nature and the glory of childhood to encourage and inspire us and to give us a sense of continuity and transcendence, if only temporarily, over mortality.

Wordsworth's persona is poignantly aware in stanza eight of the ultimate power of mortality. In suggesting that the child provokes the passage of time, Wordsworth's persona seems to diminish the power of time, and by implication, the destructive presence of mortality. There is a heroic quality to this child who appears, in the spirit of Carlyle's hero in the essay "Heroes and Hero-Worship," to live in the inward sphere of things and to understand, if only intuitively, the divine idea of the universe. And yet, the use of the word "blindly" (125) implies that the child is unaware, perhaps because he is a "best Philosopher" (110) and "Mighty Prophet" (114) of time, that time cannot flow without his presence. It is noteworthy that the child is described as "glorious" (121) in a spatial context, in the freedom of the spirit which spatial magnanimity confers, perhaps to offset the inevitable flux of time.

With respect to the theme of mortality in the Immortality Ode, Cleanth Brooks asserts in *The Well Wrought Urn* that we must be aware of the importance of daylight, of sunlight. The climax of the process which is initiated in stanza two by the glorious birth of sunlight is the sunlight, "the light of common day" (76), of stanza five which "has here become the symbol for the prosaic and the common and the mortal" (223). Yet, there is another type of light in the poem which is revealed in the "innocent brightness of a new-born Day" (194). Although perhaps not as eternally radiant as the light in Bernini's *Ecstasy of St. Theresa*, this light of "innocent brightness" (194) illuminates the inner heart, the soul of softly ecstatic tenderness.

In stanza nine of the Immortality Ode Wordsworth's persona glorifies "those first affections" (148) which represent the sources of our creative and visionary capacity. Moreover, such affections, such "shadowy recollections" (149), have the power to transform the boisterous flux of mortality into epiphanically serene moments of eternal truth. By achieving a continuity of such dynamic moments, the creative self shapes a meaningful, vital life. The conception of eternity expressed in this stanza by Wordsworth's persona anticipates that of Hermann Hesse's Steppenwolf, who claims that "eternity was nothing else than the redemption of time, its return to innocence, so to speak, and its transformation again into space" (176). For Wordsworth, too, mortality is redeemed in the eternity of spatial permanences of pristine vitality.

The persona praises not only those "first affections" (148), which, like "spots of time," will illuminate and guide the rest of his life, but also the "obstinate questionings" (141) of his intellectual curiosity and the noble instincts which allow for the possibility of transcendence. A further development of the noble instincts is the visionary power of the persona at the end of stanza nine, who can not only see the "immortal sea" (163), but who can also participate in the presence of the shore of eternity.

In stanza five Wordsworth privileges the early stages of human development as being closer (or seeming to be closer) to heaven and to the divine—and yet, it is only through the passage of time, which takes us away from that child-like state of innocence and involves a sense of loss, that we can evolve a series of "spots of time" to be the perpetual "fountain-light of all our day" (151) and to make life worthwhile. Of this sense of loss necessitated by transience Durrant writes in *Wordsworth and the Great System*:

> The neo-Platonic notion of the world as a prison-house has served only to provide a provisional account of the loss of the primal joy of childhood. When the loss of that joy has been acknowledged and accepted, what remains is not the consolation of eternal life in a transcendental world, but a strong assertion that the world can be transformed and given life and meaning by the eye of experience—that innocence is not the only basis for joy. (122)

In articulating in the last stanzas of the Immortality Ode his vision of the eternal permanences of nature and of epiphanic moments of experience which may be reinforced and strengthened by participation in such eternal permanences, Wordsworth's persona intensifies the validity of the introductory three lines: "The Child is father of the Man; / And I could wish my days to be / Bound each to each by natural piety." By striving for a vital sense of continuity, by aspiring to achieve a strategy of continuity which emulates the eternal continuity of nature, Wordsworth's persona asserts that he has the potential to bind his days in a perpetually congenial association of natural piety.

Wordsworth's universe of temporal discourse and his quest for a sense of timeless recurrence are articulated in a language of exuberant spatiality. The permanences of nature provide a sense of joy. John Beer in *Wordsworth in Time* wonders whether Wordsworth's Immortality Ode is an Ode to Joy or an Ode to Nature:

> If Wordsworth had been called to the unwelcome task of identifying his purposes more closely, he would no doubt have been forced to say rather that he was invoking those elements in nature which gave evidence of joy. By addressing the happy shepherd-boys and the creatures of the spring, and by beginning even his last group of stiller natural presences with the word 'Fountains,' he is paying tribute to those unobtrusive vital forces in nature which keep alive the spirit of joy in the human observer. (111)

In stanza ten the persona wishes once again to revel in the effusive dynamism of nature—yet, this is not an ingenuous activity, but rather one infused with an awareness of mortality, an awareness informed and shaped by consistently assiduous questionings. Unlike the earlier phase of the persona in stanza three who overcomes his thought of grief merely by expressing it and exhorting the "Child of Joy" (34) to shout merrily to distance any morose or mournful thoughts, the persona of stanza ten admits a poignant awareness of mortality. By this point in the development of the poem such an awareness of the inevitable passing of animate life no longer links with grief. The persona has achieved an emotional and an intellectual acceptance not only of the necessity or inevitability of mortality, but also of his capacity to participate in the dynamic cyclicality of nature to transform or transcend such transience.

In the last lines of this stanza the persona responds to his poignant and thoughtful awareness of mortality by asserting that he will find hope and strength in what remains behind after the splendor of the past is gone:

> We will grieve not, rather find
> Strength in what remains behind;
> In the primal sympathy
> Which having been must ever be;
> In the soothing thoughts that spring
> Out of human suffering;
> In the faith that looks through death,
> In years that bring the philosophic mind. (179-86)

Is not what the persona finds in the present as powerful as or even more powerful than what he experienced in the past? He will find strength in a "timeless" present of things past, things present, and things future. In fusing these qualities in the "faith that looks through death" (186), the persona implies his capacity to participate in and to shape an expansive sense of time.

In stanza ten especially Wordsworth's persona attains intimations of immortality not only through the joy of nature, by participating instinctively and vitally in the eternal beauty and dynamic joyousness of nature, but also through his experience of the primal sympathy and the philosophic mind and through his own creativity. In articulating the notion of "the primal sympathy," the poet implies that he is an integral part of the harmonious whole which is the universe. He uses the language of that universe (tangible objects, specific aspects of nature) to describe his place in it and even to suggest a sense of transcendence. Wordsworth's philosophy of nature and his belief in the harmonious wholeness of the universe is similar to the belief of the idealistic philosopher Friedrich Wilhelm Schelling that the universe is an organic, living whole permeated by a unified, vital spirit and that the natural environment represents visible spirit, a manifestation of the spirit of the universe.

We might call Wordsworth an organo-centric poet, for whatever he chooses to describe or present is a whole or a semblance of the whole, and not a part. Even when he is describing a part of the natural environment, a feature of this universe, for example, the brooks or the clouds, the poet has the whole in mind. The "soothing thoughts" of this stanza signify not only the poem itself, but also Wordsworth's creativity as an artist. The philosophic mind represents the mature understanding of Nature linked to the visionary sense of faith which is analogous to the "faith in life endless, the sustaining thought / Of human Being, Eternity, and God" (*The Prelude*, 14.204-05). Wordsworth anticipates here the prospect of a perpetually vital future for humanity as eternal as that of God or a divine force in the universe.

The tone of these lines, and indeed of the entire Immortality Ode, reminds one of the tone of praise, hope, and faith despite mortality and suffering which emerges so strongly in Rilke's *Sonnets to Orpheus*. Wordsworth and Rilke both celebrate the importance of nature for the creative self and believe in the supreme vitality of eternal silences of truth and of beautiful spaces.

Wordsworth speaks in stanza nine of the Immortality Ode of the eternal silence which nurtures and stimulates "truths that wake / To perish never" (155–56). In Sonnet 1, X to Orpheus Rilke presents a similarly vital silence of eternal resonance:

> There rose a tree. O pure transcendency!
>
> O Orpheus singing! O tall tree in the ear!
>
> And all was silent. Yet even in the silence
>
> New beginning, beckoning, change went on. (17)

In Sonnet 2, XXI to Orpheus the poet exhorts himself to sing of incomparable gardens which he only knows intuitively, gardens which symbolize not only the aesthetic richness of creative vitality but also the tapestry of life. This sonnet is, like the Immortality Ode, a Promethean paean to the eternal permanence of beautiful natural spaces which may soothe and inspire the persona, and to feeling, to the importance of an orphically vital feeling which revels in the mysteries of life and appreciates the lyrical beauty of everyday existence.

At the end of the Immortality Ode, Wordsworth's persona claims that he now loves the brooks even more than when he appreciated them in a state of emotional, intellectual innocence. Although he has gained a lyrical and a philosophical knowledge of the human condition, in conjunction with the melancholy and profound reflectiveness such knowledge is often infused with and inseparable from, he can still appreciate "the innocent brightness of a new-born Day" (194). The final image of nature in the poem is, perhaps not surprisingly (especially considering the importance of "the light of setting suns" from "Tintern Abbey") an image of evening, which heightens the presence and the awareness of mortality. Yet, the light of the setting sun in Wordsworth's Immortality Ode seems as radiantly bright as the light in Van Gogh's *Sower with Setting Sun* (1888).

For what Wordsworth's persona has learned by the end of the poem, expressed so effectively in lines 6 and 7 of the last stanza, is that he has come to appreciate and love Nature even more through his mortality, through his awareness of the inevitable flux of time and animate life, than he did in his earlier, child-like, seemingly immortal state. Only through the passage of time which takes us away and displaces us from that child-like state can we develop a series of "spots of time" (as described in stanza nine) to make life meaningful and worthwhile. And it is only through the passage of time that Wordsworth's persona can achieve a mature understanding and vision of Nature. Such a mature understanding and vision of Nature involves realizing the importance of the spatial permanences of nature, the significance of beautiful and sacred natural spaces. By believing in and participating in the eternal cyclicality of the spatial permanences of nature and in beautiful and sacred natural spaces of light and expansiveness which may result in a sensation of "innocent brightness" or in "Thoughts that do often lie too deep for tears" (203), the persona may achieve a dynamic continuity of self. Such a sensitive, perceptive, and intuitive persona gains not only a sense of the expansiveness of space and time but also participates in the radiant vitality of the lovely natural spaces which illuminate and soothe the mind and the soul.

The emphasis on participating in the cyclicality of nature is important in the poetry of Wordsworth, as it is in the work of Percy Shelley, especially in Shelley's "Ode to the West Wind." The persona in the Immortality Ode and the persona in "Ode to the West Wind" are concerned about time and mortality. Wordsworth's persona is interested in achieving a continuity of self to counter the flux of mortality. He participates in the eternal cyclicality of nature while maintaining his own integrity, the integrity of his aesthetic and creative self. Shelley's persona tries to transcend mortality by being infused with the dynamism of nature. In "Ode to the West Wind," as in "The Cloud," Shelley's persona reveals a romantic longing to be an integral part of nature's spirit. The persona transforms himself into a significant dimension of the natural environment, of the eternal cyclicality of nature, so that he can transcend, if only for an epiphanic moment, the vicissitudes of mortal existence. And similarly, as Harold Bloom effectively points out in *Shelley's*

Mythmaking, the "I" in this poem wants the spirit of the west wind to become and revitalize his spirit: "Let your spirit be my spirit is the prayer . . . so that your impetuosity, your energy, and life may also be mine, and that your message may be my message. The need here is mutual: poet needs Spirit but Spirit as desperately needs poet" (87).

Harold Bloom's argument that "Ode to the West Wind" is a poem about the process of making myths, "a poem whose subject is the nature and function of the nabi and his relation to his own prophecies" (*Shelley's Mythmaking* 67) is important because it emphasizes the prophetic power of Shelley's persona. By asserting his prophetic capacity and his ability to achieve a vital personal relation to the spirit of the west wind and of nature Shelley's persona strengthens his potential to achieve a strategy of transcendence. By participating in the cyclicality of nature, by becoming an integral part of that cyclicality, by using the cyclicality to claim his own creative power, by defining the importance of that cyclicality to some extent through his own artistic energy and prowess, by sharing his own creative energy to nurture the vitality of nature, and by implying his capacity for prophetic visionary experiences, the persona in "Ode to the West Wind" strives to transcend mortality. The final question of the poem is not so much a sentimental yearning for spring as an assertion, as implicit as it is explicit, of the persona's power to participate in the cyclicality, the seasonal inevitability of the natural process. It is the persona's affirmation of his own capacity to appreciate intuitively the integrity of natural processes and to participate sensitively and vibrantly in the eternal cyclicality of nature.

The poet Johann Wolfgang von Goethe wrote in a poem entitled "Natur und Kunst" ("Nature and Art") the memorable lines: "In der Beschränkung zeigt sich erst der Meister, / Und das Gesetz nur kann uns Freiheit geben." The individual who would master his existential circumstances must prove himself first in the context of limitation and restraint. Only a devotion to "law" and order can give us a true sense of freedom. Only in the context of laws which guide and motivate the inner, private self in conjunction with the public, external self can the individual develop a viable sense of freedom.

William Wordsworth's "Nuns Fret Not at Their Convent's Narrow Room" describes and interprets a thematic situation similar to that in Goethe's poem. Wordsworth's poem deals with the possibility of finding personal happiness and satisfaction in the spatially and temporally determined context of one's own life, as confining and limiting as such a context may seem to others, or even occasionally or consistently to oneself. This poem reveals an attempt to transcend time through the strategy of a hermetic spatiality, in contrast to Rilke's "Sonnet 2, XXI to Orpheus" which endeavors to overcome the constraints of mortality by stressing an orphic spatiality.

In the first quatrain of Wordsworth's sonnet various activities are characterized and qualified by an element of restraint. The choice of nuns and hermits as the character-types to initiate the poetic argument is significant because these are individuals typically associated with centripetal philosophies of life which are directed away from the exuberance and abundance of experience in everyday reality. Nuns and hermits typically lead relatively solitary, existentially and spatially relatively confined lives.

Yet, the nuns do not fret. And the hermits are contented. The nuns do not fret about the apparent spatial limitations of their immediate environment because the convent and its narrow rooms represent an ambience conducive to prayer, to calm devotion, to the constructively serene and spiritual communion of the "wisely passive" individual with the divine. This is also a sanctuary of radiance, of inner luminescence and of divine radiance which permeates and inspires the individual soul. This environment allows the nuns to express themselves most eloquently and imaginatively in their religious devotions and spiritual exercises.

The hermits, like the nuns, exist contentedly in their spatially confined environment (that is, an environment which might seem spatially restricting to an outsider, but which is suitable, if not desirable, for the hermits). The students, like the hermits, are happy with the ambience of their "pensive citadels" (3). For both, as for the nuns, such existential contexts are very conducive to, and most desirable for, a productive and vital self-fulfillment.

In contrast, Byron, in "Childe Harold's Pilgrimage" and in "Don Juan," for example, is interested not in a timeless spatiality or in a spatial, or spacious timelessness, but rather in a temporal, a vitally temporal spatiality, in an exuberantly spacious temporality in which he can revel effusively and profusely. He is interested not in competing against, but in competing with time. Byron wishes not to overcome time, but to become its metaphysical complement.

The fourth line of Wordsworth's poem, the last line of the first quatrain, introduces a new semantic tone in the poem. For the first three lines describe groups of individuals who are distanced from or seemingly separate from the hectic pace and chaotic clamor of everyday reality. Line four of this poem describes groups of individuals who belong to and contribute to society directly and who are most productive personally and professionally within the cultural and social framework of that society. The maids work the wheel and the weaver his loom primarily to earn a living: they must confront the demands and the exigencies of everyday life with an inevitable immediacy.

These two groups, the nuns, hermits, and students on the one hand, and the maids and weavers on the other, are further distinguished by the fact that the first group is portrayed in spatial terms, whereas the second is depicted in a temporally-determined and temporally-motivated context. There is a sense of timelessness, of timeless luminescence in the narrow rooms of the convent, in the cells of the hermits, and in the pensive citadels of the students which is challenged by the images of the wheel and the loom, which are objects functioning in and dependent on time.

One might perhaps argue that the use of the alliterative sequence "convent's"-"contented"-"cells"-"citadels" reinforces the semantic coherence of the first three lines. The alliteration "nuns"-"narrow" in line one is balanced by the "wheel"-"weaver" alliteration in line four. Moreover, the abba rhyme scheme of the first quatrain intensifies the theme of isolation and seclusion which dominates the initial three lines.

The use of the word "sit" at the beginning of line five diminishes the emphasis on time which dominates the two complementary images in line four and presents for the first time a concrete verb in contrast to the more abstract verbs in the first three lines. Yet, in using "sit," the poet also suggests a spatial correlation between the nuns, hermits, and students on the one hand, and the maids and weavers on the other. For "sit" implies an existence within a distinct spatial context with its own unique physical and emotional parameters.

In describing the emotional and psychological attitude of the maids and the weavers toward their work as "blithe" (5) and "happy" (5), the persona of the poem seems to suggest that they are happier than the more temporally and spatially free (as spatially confined as they may seem to be to the average observer) individuals who fret not and are contented with their immediate environment. There seems to be a greater emotional intensity in the response of the maids and the weavers to life, to the obligations and rewards of everyday reality. Perhaps this emotional intensity is necessitated by the fact that these individuals do not have the same heightened sense of timelessness and inner luminescence which motivates and strengthens the ethereal calm and serenity of the nuns and the hermits.

After the semi-colon, line five continues with a focus on animate nature. The persona describes soaring bees, that is, bees which are not spatially confined or restricted and which can soar as high as they desire. The bees, given such freedom of movement, will soar as "high as the highest Peak of

Furness-fells" (6). And yet, such bees, the persona implies, are at least equally contented and blithe when they can "murmur by the hour in foxglove bells" (7). The phrase "by the hour" is especially interesting not only because it insinuates a sense of temporal regularity in the context of the bees' spatial confinement within the foxglove bells, but also because it represents the first concrete manifestation of time in the poem. One might describe the phrase "by the hour" as spatially confined in the ambience of the poem—it is a phrase symbolically imprisoned in the linguistic structure of the poem. Depending on one's perspective, the effect of its temporal vitality could either be strengthened or diminished by its phonological linkage with "murmur," which connotes an activity of timeless repetition or regularity with only a mild, or even subconscious, awareness of the flux of time.

The alliterative arrangements in lines five through seven are highly significant. First, the consonance of "blithe"-"bees"-"bloom" in line five links the worlds of humankind and nature, if only symbolically. The alliterative associations "bees"-"bloom"-"bells", "high"-"highest"-"hour" and "Furness-fells"-"foxglove" all affirm and strengthen the formal and semantic coherence of the second quatrain of the poem.

There is also an interesting interrelation of form and meaning in the association of lines two and three with lines six and seven (the b-rhymes of the octet). The outer lines of this arrangement, lines two and seven, end in words which suggest an earth-bound ambience. The inner lines of this chiastic arrangement, lines three and six, have line-end words which emphasize a heaven-directed aura. The bracketing of the heaven-directed by the earth-directed ambience reinforces the theme of spatial confinement or restriction (which may lead to, inspire, or strengthen a transcendent sense of timelessness) which generates the beginning of the poem.

Despite the semantic chiasmus produced by the bracketing of lines three and six by lines two and seven, it is noteworthy that the line-final words of these lines rhyme with one another. That these different spatial locations rhyme with one another perhaps acknowledges and affirms the argument of the poet that whether the locus of one's intellectual, spiritual, or artistic activity is a religious cell, citadel, Furness-fell, or bell, one can achieve a sense of fulfillment, either blissful or contentedly serene, in such activity.

The beginning of line eight shifts the semantic focus from the concrete world of nature, of external reality, to the more abstract environment of reflection, meditation, and thought. The persona expresses a broad philosophical insight which is given the prominence of an eternal truth in the context of the poem: "In truth the prison, unto which we doom / Ourselves, no prison is" (8-9). This statement is also important because it upholds formally the semantic argument of the poet in the enjambement from line eight to line nine. That line eight flows into line nine without formal break or pause asserts structurally and symbolically that what seems to be a prison is not really a prison at all. Or, one might claim that what seems to be spatial confinement is actually the vital medium, the inevitable and necessary means, to achieve a transcendent sense of being.

Wordsworth's visionary power signifies the vitality, the creative eternity of the Orphic Aion. In his strategy of hermetic spatiality Wordsworth's persona in "Nuns Fret Not" and in the Immortality Ode transforms "kairos" to "Aion" and in so doing achieves a sense of aesthetic and emotional, if not spiritual, transcendence. Yet, "Aion" does not carry with it an inevitable implication of ever-resurging youthfulness, as John Beer in *Wordsworth in Time* points out with respect to a passage in Wordsworth's *The Prelude*: "The suggestion of 'aion' in the image of the mountain-top, the word 'golden' and the temporary assurance of rebirth are undermined only by the suggestion that the 'top' might be that not of a mountain but of a wheel" (68). Beer further suggests that the hours might not be "the dancing graces of classical mythology but the inevitable circling and reversals of time" (68). In the experience of "Aion" the persona is so captivated by the inward imagination, by his own sanctuary of creative luminescence and vitality, that he feels no sense of transience in the flow of time.

The culminating moment and the concluding argument of the poem relates, not surprisingly and very naturally, to the poet's own creative enterprise. From line 10 to line 14 the persona speaks of his own literary expression using the form of the sonnet. This poetic form is characterized by and celebrated for certain distinctive rules as well as notable considerations of form and space. The poet writing a sonnet works in a formally somewhat "regulated" and linguistically somewhat "confined" space. But within this context, and perhaps even because of the formal "confinement" (or the appearance of such), the poet creates a work of art, an aesthetically interesting, emotionally pleasing, and intellectually stimulating artistic achievement. The poet shows by example, by the example of his own imaginative vitality, that formal or spatial restriction (or apparent formal or spatial restriction) can generate a constructive and interesting work.

The caesura in line nine functions like the one in line five to separate complementary dimensions of the poetic argument. In line nine the caesura signals the shift from theoretical statement to personal expression, from the general to the specific. The poet, the "I" of the poem, who expresses himself directly in the poem for the first time at the end of line nine, states that he considers it a "pastime" (10) to work within "the Sonnet's scanty plot of ground" (11). The use of the word "bound" (10) is noteworthy because it complements the use of "prison" (8) to emphasize ironically the notion of physical confinement. That the "I" metaphorizes the ambience of his sonnet as a "scanty plot of ground" (11) might also be said to strengthen the increasing emphasis in the poem on earth-bound and earth-directed as opposed to heaven-directed activity.

The poet, like the other subjects in the poem (though perhaps with a different degree or kind of contentment or satisfaction) is pleased with his poetic labor in the "Sonnet's scanty plot of ground" (11). Yet, his sense of pleasure and accomplishment is not merely self-directed. Not only does he aim to find personal solace and satisfaction in his work, but he also wishes to provide comfort and inspiration for others, especially for those who have been burdened by an excess of liberty. Although such souls may not "murmur by the hour in foxglove bells" (7), they may achieve a sense of comfort and aesthetic enrichment, whether brief or more sustained.

There is an aura of timelessness in this brevity which embodies the imaginative force and creative vitality of the initial lines of Blake's "Auguries of Innocence":

To see a World in a Grain of Sand

And a Heaven in a Wild Flower,

Hold Infinity in the palm of your hand

And Eternity in an hour. (1-4)

For the existential context of the convent's narrow room, as that of the student's citadel, as that of the foxglove bell, as that of the sonnet itself, signifies its own world as well as the aesthetic, emotional, intellectual, and spiritual dimensions of that distinctive and unique world. In the imaginative experience of such a world, as self-defined and self-generated as it seems to be, one may experience a vital sense of sanctuary and a sense of timelessness, of timeless spatiality. In the sensitive appreciation and thoughtful understanding of the creative endeavor of the "Sonnet's scanty plot of ground," which is really an abundantly fertile locale, one may attain a solace transcending earthly concerns and also hold infinity in the palm of one's hands and eternity in an hour.

Before discussing *The Prelude* as a sanctuary of light and as an ambience of timeless spatiality, I would like to consider several other poems by Wordsworth, all of which offer a vision of an expansive sense of light and space. In "Ode: 1814" there is a vision of a beautiful landscape in sleep, a dynamic vision of England. The persona seems to suggest that the people of the isle of England have the capacity to challenge and transform the negative aims of mortality. In "Vernal Ode" a solitary individual, a stranger, stands alone in a majestic landscape. This unusual individual sings as he plays a golden harp. He sings of a landscape of absolute serenity which is free from decline and decay. The poem concludes with a holistic vision of the world in which earth and stars are complementary dimensions of a universal heaven.

In "Composed upon an Evening of Extraordinary Splendour and Beauty" an effulgent sunset encourages the poet to proclaim that the power of this beautiful natural setting can sanctify the day. In this poem the persona offers a luminescent vision of profound harmony and tranquility which can revitalize the individual struggling against the vicissitudes of mortality. The persona even suggests that the grace of the divine power, the presence of which he senses and feels, can remind him of the light, the radiance, which was experienced earlier in life and has since been diminished or lost. The persona concludes by saying that his soul feels so revitalized that he delights in a second birth. Yet, at the end of the poem the vision appears to fade as the night approaches.

In "Inscriptions Supposed to Be Found in or Near a Hermit's Cell" the persona speaks of the vagaries and vicissitudes of everyday mortality. Glory, pride, truth, and all of life are transient and transitory. The only enduring value is faith in a "Gracious God." At the end of the poem the hermit prays to God and asks for a sense of blissful peace, which he receives.

The yew-tree in "Yew-Trees" signifies a natural analogue to the monastic individual in the human domain. This special yew-tree, which stands single and alone in a dark environment, displays a "form and aspect too magnificent / To be destroyed" (12-13). The poem "Yew-Trees" proceeds to describe a grove of four trees in a solemn setting. This grove even seems to represent "a natural temple scattered o'er / With altars undisturbed of mossy stone" (29-30). In this very isolated and secluded spot spectral forms may meet. The solemnity and twilight sanctity of this hermetic setting is reinforced by the nature of the forms which the persona imagines would be interested in convening or would dare to gather in such a dusk-filled ambience: "Fear and Trembling Hope, / Silence and Foresight; Death the Skeleton / And Time the Shadow" (26-28).

In various passages of "The Excursion" Wordsworth stresses the vital presence of light, harmony, and tranquillity in the natural environment. For example, in describing the twin peaks of the valley, the persona suggests that various aspects of nature from the sunlight to the mist to the moonlight all contribute to the harmonious ambience. The light of this natural space is extraordinary for not only is the twilight radiance of the sun impressive here, but the stars at night sparkle in the same place with a conspicuous brilliance.

In the "Prospectus" of "The Excursion" the persona stresses that the sublime and the beautiful can be found in everyday life and activity. As the "Prospectus" continues, the persona asks the "prophetic spirit" (83), which has the power to inspire "The human soul of universal earth" (84), to give him genuine insight so that his "Song / With star-like virtue in its place may shine" (88-89). His song, his poetry, will then exert a benign and a positive influence over his immediate environment and over the world which represents the focus of his creation.

The second book of "The Excursion" delineates the mist as well as a golden light in the hills. At a particular moment, the mist clears and the person views a spectacular panorama:

Fabric it seemed of diamond and of gold,

With alabaster domes, and silver spires,

And blazing terrace upon terrace, high

Uplifted; here, serene pavilions bright.... (839-42)

The omnipresence of a powerful radiance is reinforced in the following lines: "towers begirt / With battlements that on their restless fronts / Bore stars— illumination of all gems!" (843-45)

This is a dynamically vital light which encompasses multiple aspects of the natural environment and the human domain and creates an all-embracing luminescence of universal brilliance. Such luminescence ultimately reveals "an object like a throne / Under a shining canopy of state" (862-63). The exceptional radiance permeates the natural ambience and creates an otherworldly aura. The persona is so impressed and awed by this vision that he represents it as "the revealed abode / Of Spirits in beatitude" (873-74).

In the poem "Composed upon an Evening of Extraordinary Splendour and Beauty" the persona depicts a similarly vital presence and experience of profound peace, supreme harmony, and a powerful radiance. This is a momentary sanctuary of lovely, dynamic, and inspirational light. Unlike the perpetual aura of sanctuary in "The Excursion," the luminescent and visionary splendor of this moment in "Composed upon an Evening of Extraordinary Splendour and Beauty" is not sustained, as it ultimately diminishes and vanishes in the shades of the night.

Book Third of "The Excursion" depicts a place of profound tranquility which ultimately reveals the presence of Heaven, of a divine realm. This is a sanctuary pervaded by an inner divine light where hope and memory signify a unity of mind and heart. Such a secluded and blissfully serene sanctuary of light is also characterized by the presence of the immortal soul which appreciates and values the importance of quiet meditation, reflection, and the heavenly ambience. The ethereal tranquillity of this divine sanctuary is comparable to the aura of profound serenity in a more secular setting delineated in "Composed by the Side of Grasmere Lake" at the end of which Pan himself whispers: "Be thankful, thou; for, if unholy deeds / Ravage the world, tranquility is here!" (13–14).

In Book Fourth of "The Excursion" Wordsworth makes an interesting parallel between the rising and radiant light of the moon in a particular grove, which sheds a powerful light over the natural world, and the development of virtue in the "celestial spirit" of an individual. When such a power of goodness emerges, it grows and magnifies itself, filling the world around it with an inspirational goodness and an extraordinary light. As the moon "Burns, like an unconsuming fire of light, / In the green trees" (1065–66) and spreads an abundance of light and radiance over the natural landscape, so the individual possessing a celestial spirit encourages and inspires the presence and the development of virtue and goodness with a "calm, a beautiful, and silent fire" (1073). The unity of the natural environment and the human domain is reinforced by the presence of a dynamic and vital luminescence in both and by a shared belief in the supreme importance of a golden and an inspirational light.

In achieving a continuity of self and an appreciation of the importance of such a celestial spirit and a vital luminescence, Wordsworth's persona in *The Prelude* (1850 version) attains a diastolic sense of time. The persona who can converse with past, present, and future generations of humankind is the one who fulfills the challenge and the promise of the introductory lines of the Immortality Ode. Not only has this persona bound his days together in a continuity of natural piety, but he has transcended the sense of the existence of days by asserting that he envisions the end of time.

The importance of continuity is emphasized throughout *The Prelude*. In Book 14, for example, the persona speaks of the capacity of higher minds to approach the universe in a magnanimous spirit of inquiry and sensitivity. They have the potential to emanate from themselves "kindred mutations" (14.94). Through communicating with a series of kindred mutations, which are revelations and elaborations of the creative self, the persona achieves a dynamic continuity of self.

Robert Langbaum suggests in *The Mysteries of Identity* that whereas Hume considers continuity a fiction, for Wordsworth "continuity is the fundamental reality" (29). Langbaum proceeds to claim that "for Wordsworth, Keats and the other romanticists, continuity is dynamic" (29). It is such a continuity of growth which allows us to absorb "individual perceptions into an intuited whole" (29). Through this dynamic sense of continuity, Wordsworth's "majestic intellect" (14.67) is ultimately able to encompass diverse "spots of time" into a vibrant, organically developing whole.

The crucial difference between the strategy of the personae with respect to the theme of continuity in the Immortality Ode and in *The Prelude* is marked by a shift from a relatively passive to a consistently active tone. In the Immortality Ode, the persona wishes that his days could be bound to each other by natural piety. In *The Prelude*, the persona signifies the higher mind which creates and shapes its own continuity of existence.

Harold Bloom writes that "the Nature of *The Prelude* is what Wordsworth was to become, a great teacher" (5). He proceeds to say that Nature is so powerful a teacher "that it must first teach itself the lesson of restraint, to convert its immediacy into a presence only lest it overpower its human receiver" (5). Through the inspirational mediating presence of nature Wordsworth's persona will achieve not only a dynamic continuity of self but also a unified, visionary "majestic intellect" (14.67).

Mary Jacobus, in "Apostrophe and Lyric Voice in The Prelude," says that "the poet himself, Wordsworth implies, is not only murmurous but has inward ears that can hear; this is what makes him a poet" (156). Jacobus goes on to say that "imagined sound becomes a way to repress or deny writing and undo death" (156). Jacobus proceeds to assert that if "a monument marks the site of a grave, voice—'breathings for incommunicable powers'—gives evidence of a poet's enduring life" (156). Such a powerfully vital creative persona not only sees "the emblem of a mind / That feeds upon infinity" (14.70–71) but also hears "Its voices issuing forth to silent light / In one continuous stream" (14.73–74). This is a sublime mind which has the capacity to create its own vital and harmonious sanctuary of light to sustain and affirm the continuity of the self.

For Jacobus, visionary power is a heightened sense of hearing which makes language into "something ghostly, nonreferential, ancient, and without origin, like the homeless voice of waters in the Snowdon episode" (156). This power of hearing is an integral aspect of the majestic intellect who would converse with the spiritual world in an aura of timeless voices.

The aspiration to achieve a vital continuity of self begins with the concern to attain a dynamic and an open-ended sense of space. For only when the persona has gained a powerful sense of space can he devote himself to the quest for a continuity of self and the concomitant diastolic sense of time. The importance of this sense of space appears already at the beginning of *The Prelude*. In the first ten to fifteen lines of Book 1 the persona asserts the significance for his own emotional, aesthetic, and intellectual vitality of an open sense of space which encompasses multiple dimensions and features of nature. Not only does the persona describe himself as being "free as a bird to settle where I will" (1.9), but he proclaims that the earth is before him, that he may participate in any spatial aura of nature which innately attracts him.

Having liberated himself from the city where he remained a "discontented sojourner" (1.8), the persona suggests that the renewed sense of diastolic space which he experiences allows him to breathe again. The intensity of the language the persona uses to describe his feeling for the spaciousness of nature and the contrast between the liberation of self in nature as opposed to the limitation of self in the city implies that the persona's experience of a sense of space is crucial to his existence.

Once he has asserted the importance of space, the persona introduces the element of time into his language, speaking of "long months of peace" (1.24) and "long months of ease" (1.26). Yet, at this initial stage of the work the temporal is less an independent entity than an outgrowth of or supplement to the spatial. Time is conceived of in terms of space—for the persona says that the long months of peace are his in prospect, which is a spatial construction.

The potential continuity of the self is developed and enhanced throughout *The Prelude* by the sense of continuity of the self and nature. In Book 1, for example, the persona speaks of feeling not only the breath of heaven blowing on his body, but also a correspondent breeze within the self, which, though seemingly tempestuous, is essential to activating the creative energy of the self.

As the opening book of *The Prelude* progresses, the persona affirms the importance of space by saying that he poured out his soul to the open fields. In this ambience of diastolic space the persona realizes the importance not only of spontaneous expression, but also of the capacity of nature to revitalize the self. The open sense of space is defined and strengthened by the existence of special places, each a locus amoenus, which generate the aesthetic and spiritual power of the natural space. One such distinctive space is the "green shady place" (1.62) or "the sheltered and the sheltering grove" (1.69) which the persona discovers. The renovating power of this experience of nature is enhanced by its being characterized by an aura of perfect stillness.

Wordsworth's quest for the liberation of the self from the spirit, but not the substance, of everyday mortality derives its philosophical foundation from several eighteenth-century notions of the imagination which assert the capacity of the creatively vital self to participate in the expansiveness of time and space.

For example, John Baillie in his *An Essay on the Sublime* proclaims that "every Person upon seeing a grand object is affected with something which as it were extends his very Being, and expands it to a kind of Immensity" (4). Baillie goes on to suggest that the soul is elevated in viewing the heavens and expanded in considering extended natural prospects. Joseph Priestly affirms this sense of the potential expansiveness of the soul in his statement: "The mind . . . conforming and adapting itself to the objects to which its attention is engaged, must, as it were, enlarge itself, to conceive a great object" (151). Alexander Gerard, in his *An Essay on Taste*, suggests that "we always contemplate objects and ideas with a disposition similar to their nature" (12). Gerard proceeds to say that when a sizeable object is presented, "the mind expands itself to the extent of that object, and is filled with one grand sensation" (12).

Albert Wlecke in *Wordsworth and the Sublime* argues that, in considering such conceptions of spatial extension, one should not "take literally these metaphors of the expanding space of mind" (51), for "they are intended to describe not the nature of the mind but the experience of consciousness when consciousness is directed towards the 'larger Scenes and more extended Prospects' of nature" (51). In this experience of sublime consciousness "insofar as the mind is felt to expand, it is sensed as possessing an increasing amount of extension, as spreading itself outward into space" (52).

The possibility of unifying mind and nature becomes clear, suggests Wlecke, if we keep in mind that "the extension of the mind throughout space tends to become infinite insofar as the 'grand Object,' to which consciousness is struggling to accommodate its capacity, is in itself unbounded" (52). Wlecke proceeds to make the interesting point that the mind, in confronting sublimity, may become lost: "It almost seems as if the very intensity of the sense of spatialization of the mind carries within itself a potential sense of a kind of 'aspatiality,' of passing over into a dimension of being where no localization of the self is possible" (53).

Wlecke distinguishes between Cartesian space (the extension of which allows for the determination and localization of the object) and sublime space (the space that is produced by the mind's sense of itself expanding outward with the concomitant potential for the subject's sense of transcendence or of dislocation of the self). He also suggests that when the sense of dislocation or uncertainty of the self becomes too vivid and immediate, the subject may move towards a sense of transcendence. This point is similar to Hartman's claim that Wordsworth's expansive imagination exposes him to the terrors of "apocalypse," to the possibility of the destruction and loss of his world. To counter this potential, Wordsworth, argues Wlecke, aims to "lodge his mind in nature's phenomena" so that he can localize a consciousness that will ultimately tend towards a sense of transport (54).

To challenge further the anguish and intensity of the dislocating experience, the persona may suggest an identity or unity of creator and created in a higher state of consciousness. The belief in a sublime consciousness becomes a continuation of some eighteenth-century notions of divinity, positing the mind as a creating divinity. This uplifting of the soul in contemplation of the majestic or magnificent, in the spirit of Longinus, culminates in an extension of the sublime consciousness, in an expansion of the mind and its own powers.

This quest for an openness of space is intimately linked not only to the emotional and spiritual regeneration of the persona but also to the preservation and the revitalization of his creative faculties. In Book 1 the persona says that the serenity he experiences becomes a longing to be active, which is further transformed to a desire to endow some airy phantasies with outward life. Although the persona admits that he struggles to write because of internal and external impediments (interestingly enough, the external ones are presented in the language of time), he asserts as well an implicit confidence in his creative capacity. In saying that he has a vital soul the persona prepares the way for his ultimate claim in Book 14 that he represents not only "a mind sustained / By recognitions of transcendent power" (14.74–75), but also one that can create kindred mutations and "hold fit converse with the spiritual world" (14.108).

The tension between space and time at this stage of the work is illustrated also in this contemplation about creative vitality. When speaking of the lofty and variegated story which he would like to create, the persona says that the sun, symbol of light, warmth, and regeneration as well as of time's fluidity, brightens and melts its unsubstantial structure. This ultimately negative aspect of time contrasts in the same passage with the security and stability which a sense of space offers, signified in the lines "With meditations passionate from deep / Recesses in man's heart, immortal verse" (1.231–32). The linkage of space, of the space of an inner expansiveness of self, and immortality prefigures the ultimate conception of a diastolic sense of space and a diastolic sense of time.

Despite the importance of space at this point of the narrative, the persona feels listless and unproductive. Yet, he believes that he was early in life chosen to be a creator, that the voices and images of nature were directed, at least partially, at him, that he was selected (perhaps by the divinity in nature) to be a sensitive interpreter of the beauty and the variety of the natural environment. The persona suggests that he may overcome this listlessness by wandering through various aspects of nature without any concern about the passage of time. The restlessness of the poetic persona is also soothed by his rememberance of the foretaste of calm which he had gleaned from nature, which had permeated his soul in the presence of nature. The calm "That Nature breathes among the hills and groves" (1.281) is orphic, not hermetic—it is an outward-directed tranquility which parallels and reinforces the openness of space.

In Book 1 of *The Prelude* Wordsworth (aware of the sense of duality in the early self, represented by the simultaneous presence of beauty and fear) proceeds to assert an awareness of mortality in the lines "dust as we are" (1.340) coupled with a sense that the immortal spirit within reveals and strengthens an aura of harmony, that the immortal spirit within the creatively vital self may reconcile discordant elements in a dynamic fusion of light and space.

The persona in Book 1 stresses his quest for expanding spaces and extended boundaries, especially for "the horizon's utmost boundary" (1.371). Lines 376–80 seem to suggest, the motion of the boat notwithstanding, that the persona shows the power of a visionary imagination here. Nature seems to be especially alive on the summer evening when the persona ventures with the little boat onto the silent lake above which towered a dark and giant peak. This image of the dark side of nature is not as congenial and comforting to the persona as the many other experiences of nature typically are. And yet such a bleak and lonely image is part of the expanse of nature which the persona tries so intimately and thoughtfully to understand.

In the next section Wordsworth continues to reflect on the power of nature as a living presence in his life. Here Wordsworth's persona speaks of the soul of nature as the wisdom and spirit of the universe. The soul of nature represents the "eternity of thought" (1.402) which gives life to and perpetually regenerates the multiplicity of forms and images, both light and dark, picturesque and sublime, in the natural environment. Nature has inspired the persona to strive beyond "the mean and vulgar works of man" (1.408) and to aspire to be a part of the "enduring things" (1.409), in the process of which the elements of feeling and thought are purified. By experiencing a range of emotions, from delight to fear and from bliss to anxiety, in the presence of various features of nature, the persona prepares himself to sense a "grandeur in the beatings of the heart" (1.414). Such an extraordinary capacity to appreciate and to understand the nuances and subtleties of nature as well as her various moods and seasons was only properly developed and nurtured from childhood and youth. Wordsworth felt not only in his childhood and youth but throughout his life a consistently vital emotional and spiritual intimacy with the "Presence of Nature in the sky / And on the earth!" (1.464-65).

Book 1 of *The Prelude* offers a considerable foreshadowing of Book 14. In describing his adventure with the little boat in Book 1, Wordsworth presents elements which are essential to the central visionary experience of Book 14—the moon with its wide swath of light, the mountain and its aura of majesty, and the tension between the limitation and the expansiveness of space in nature. One might perhaps view the incident in Book 1 as a challenge to the poetic persona which he will eventually confront more vitally and overcome effectively in the final book. Wordsworth's early awareness of the presences (or Presences) of nature influencing his childhood thoughts and feelings ensures that the constraint of Book 1 will ultimately be transcended. By nurturing a sensitivity to nature in his childhood Wordsworth prepares himself to experience early in his life a sense of the expansiveness of space in a lovely natural environment.

The intensity of Wordsworth's feeling for nature as a child is exemplified by the passage when he speaks of holding "unconscious intercourse with beauty / Old as creation" (1.562-63). The persona feels a deep emotional pleasure in the beauty of nature. Moreover, this sense of nature is not spatially fixed or limited. In describing "the silver wreaths / Of curling mist" (1.564-65) and the interaction of water and clouds, the persona implies a dynamic fluidity, a Turneresque fluidity, in nature which affirms the expansiveness of natural spaces. In defining his vision of nature with images that rise and soar, Wordsworth suggests that his relation to nature is characterized by and reaffirmed by an innately dynamic expansiveness of space. In the spirit of this emphasis on a dynamic fluidity in the nature of the poem Herbert Lindenberger observes that the dominant images of *The Prelude* are "wind and water, images which by their very nature . . . allow the poet free range between the observable world and the higher transcendental reality which he wishes to make visible to us" (71). Lindenberger concludes this point by saying that their "chief function is to act as intermediaries between the two worlds" (71).

In Book 2 Wordsworth reinforces the sense of space which was developed in Book 1. He describes, for example, the temple or holy scene which has the hermetically orphic aura expressed by the sonnet "Nuns Fret Not." The essential feature of such a place is its profound tranquility as well as the "safeguard for repose" (2.114) which it provides. As a corollary to the description of the holy calm spreading over his soul Wordsworth's persona proceeds several lines later to assert that because he has received so much from nature, all his thoughts are "steeped in feeling" (2.399).

Through his sensitive appreciation of the beauty, truth, and vitality of nature the persona felt "the sentiment of Being spread / O'er all that moves and all that seemeth still" (2.401-02). Through his connectedness to this "sentiment of Being" Wordsworth's persona achieves an expansive sense of emotional, spiritual communion with various aspects of the beautiful natural environment.

Wordsworth also speaks of his growing affection for the sun, not only as the magnanimous light of life, but also as a light of expansive spatiality. The image of the sun spreads "His beauty on the morning hills" (2.184) as well as touching the western mountains at sunset—this presents the sun as a signifier of diastolic spatiality. The persona, by perceiving the sun's capacity, participates in this expansive spatiality as well. The sun spreading its effulgent radiance upon the morning hills represents a vital sanctuary of light which comforts and inspires the soul of the persona. The expansive brightness of the sun and the sense of sanctuary and spatial expansiveness of the soul which it provides are seen with equivalent vitality in John Constable's *Wivenhoe Park* and *View of Dedham*. *Wivenhoe Park*, in particular, reveals a blissfully serene and luminescent landscape in which the array of clouds reaffirms the peaceful harmony of the natural environment. In the light of the evening sun the persona also feels a sense of sanctuary, a sense of contentedness and delight which permeates his soul. The sun represents a sense of continuity with which the persona wants to infuse his own personal and creative life. John Wootton's *Classical Landscape: Evening*, Thomas Gainsborough's *Rest by the Way*, and Joseph Wright's *Matlock Tor by Moonlight* exemplify the presence and the spirit of a sanctuary in the evening or at night, a sanctuary of potently tranquil light which permeates the soul of the persona and suffuses the landscape.

One of the ways in which the aura of continuity, despite the apparent flux of mortality, can be achieved is by attaining a pervasive sense of tranquility which reinforces the expansiveness of space. For example, when speaking of the Vale in Book 2, the persona describes the utter solitude of the Vale in the early morning, a solitude which implies the expansiveness of nature and of the self through the aura of calm it nurtures.

One of the central issues of Book 3 is the inspiration which nature affords when the crowds and buildings of Cambridge had ceased to motivate the persona. In his solitary ramble Wordsworth's persona searches for universal or universally important images and objects. After communing with the earth and the sky which reveal to him a sense of the first paradise and a semblance of heaven, respectively, the persona's mind turns inward. Interestingly, the inward-turning gesture of the mind is described in spatially expansive terms—"spread my thoughts / And spread them with a wider creeping" (3.117-18)—which parallel the spatial expansiveness of the environment through which the persona is walking.

In turning inward, Wordsworth's persona experiences "visitings / Of the Upholder of the tranquil soul" (3.119-20), that is, an awareness of a divine force in the universe which acknowledges the inevitability of mortality while asserting the capability of eternity and of the eternal soul ultimately to vanquish time. As this section continues, the persona not only proclaims that he believes that various aspects of nature can feel, but also presents himself as a "kindred mutation" of the "Upholder of the tranquil soul" (3.120). The persona proceeds to suggest that he has in some sense imaginatively created the emotional, spiritual vitality of his immediate natural environment. Such an emphasis on the imaginative vitality of the persona is manifest especially in the following lines of Book 3: "I had a world about me—'t was my own; / I made it, for it only lived to me, / And to the God who sees into the heart" (3.144-46).

Book 3 emphasizes the capacity of the individual, inspired by the diastolic spatiality of nature, to achieve an expansiveness of self. In implying the power of his own imagination the persona reveals the open-ended spatiality of the eye which may shift its attention from the earth to the ocean to the heavens, yet ultimately "could find no surface where its power might sleep" (3.166). Such is the imaginative eye which will develop itself by Book 14 into the majestic mind which transforms an expansive spatiality into a diastolic temporality.

Wordsworth suggests in Book 3 that he is less interested in an expansive spatiality of endless solitude than in an expansive spatiality characterized by human endeavor. Such a philosophy of space is in keeping with Wordsworth's argument in the Preface to *Lyrical Ballads* that the poet should be ultimately concerned with the world of human thoughts, actions, and feelings. In speaking of his experience of the human sphere, the persona uses the metaphor of the museum. This is interesting not only because such a site suggests literally a closed sense of space in contrast to the open sense of space in nature, but also because it underscores the element of change which seems to pervade this existence. The profound tranquility and holy calm of nature is not present, at least at this point of the persona's perceptual and conceptual development, in the world of human endeavor.

At the beginning of Book 4 Wordsworth's persona has a vision of expansive space as he stands alone overlooking "the bed of Windermere" (4.5). In this context the sun has a radiantly positive aura because it affirms the openness of the watery space through the expansiveness of its light. This epiphanic moment, signified by the revelation of these forms "with instantaneous burst" (4.10), represents one of the most vital conceptions of space in the early chapters of *The Prelude* because it is generated by a vision of "A universe of Nature's fairest forms" (4.9). The beauty of this seemingly unlimited display of nature's aspects is made more visible and more beautiful through the light of the sun. This natural area signifies a lovely sanctuary of light which inspires and soothes the persona intellectually and emotionally.

Occasionally, Wordsworth's persona will imply or proclaim the diastolic nature of time or his conception of the diastolic capacity of time. In Book 4, for example, in talking about the happiness he enjoyed in making "the circuit of our little lake" (4.138), the persona asserts that "That day consummate happiness was mine / Wide-spreading, steady, calm, contemplative" (4.140-41). Whether these four adjectives are used to characterize the atmosphere of the day or the happiness which the persona feels on this particular day, they are primarily, keeping in mind their use so far in the poem, aspects and dimensions of space, of the expansiveness of space. Jane Eyre experiences a similar sense of the expansiveness of space in the initial phase of her life at Thornfield. The autumn sun shines serenely on the lovely property around the mansion and the "calm prospect" (102) which the scene offers.

This is one of the first moments in the poem when the persona adopts the language of space to present the image of time and where the persona foreshadows his ultimate assertion in Book 14 of the diastolic nature of space and time. It is noteworthy here that the presentation of space once again precedes the discussion of time.

As this section of the poem continues Wordsworth describes an inspirational "spot of time" in his experience of walking through a natural landscape in the evening. He senses how the immortal soul "with God-like power / Informs, creates, and thaws the deepest sleep / That time can lay upon her" (4. 166-68). This vision of and faith in eternity, in the eternity of the soul, is conjoined with a conviction in the capacity of the vital mind and noble spirit to exert a profound influence on everyday life, on the world of mortality.

Several stanzas later in Book 4 the persona affirms the revitalizing power of solitude to counteract the anguish and hardship of everyday mortality. This sense of solitude is described as being "Most potent when impressed upon the mind / With an appropriate human centre" (4.359-60). What unites, in the mind of the persona, the three examplars he offers of this sense of solitude—hermit, votary, and watchman—is their similar experience of an expansive sense of space. Solitude, at this point of *The Prelude* and throughout most of the rest of the work as well, is defined through the qualities of a spatial expansiveness and a profound tranquility.

The wilderness and the unknown in which these characters participate in their solitude is not inherently tempestuous or violent. Rather, the solitude of the wilderness and the unknown is gracious and benign, perhaps because of the innately serene character of these individuals. There is something here of the strategy of "half-creating, half-perceiving" from "Tintern Abbey"—it is through the imagination of the persona, and through the corresponding vision of the characters he envisions in a solitary existential condition, that the solitude may assume "A character of quiet more profound / Than pathless wastes" (4.369-70).

In the next passage of Book 4 there is an episode which prefigures, at least partially, the mountain vision in Book 14. The persona speaks of experiencing a long ascent, the powerful presence of the moon, the stream of water, and a sense of tranquility—all of these features will be regenerated in the Mt. Snowdon vision in Book 14. Perhaps one might argue that the presence of the tall man in Book 4 is comparable to the rift of waters in Book 14 which disturbs the quietude of the scene. Yet the man, unlike the rift, ultimately blends into the silence of the surrounding nature.

In Book 5 the expansiveness of space is revealed even in dream. The persona, seated in a sea-side cave reading the adventures of Don Quixote, dreams of "a boundless plain / Of sandy wilderness" (5.71-72). The desolation of this solitude is made the more frightening by the appearance, as in the previously mentioned episode in Book 4, of a stranger. This "uncouth shape" (5.75) gives the persona a shell which reveals to him the harmony and dissolution of humankind. Listening to the shell provides the same kind of visionary sense of the future as does the experience of the majestic intellect in Book 14 which can look to the end of time. The crucial difference between the two visions is that the one in Book 5 depicting a destructive end of temporality is motivated by an external source, whereas the one in Book 14 signifying the capacity of the creatively vital mind to envision a positive end of temporality is generated from within.

The two books of which the Arab speaks are of special interest for this discussion of space, time, and light in *The Prelude*. The first book is undisturbed by space or time; the second has a multiplicity of voices and existential forms. Both of these are qualities which will reappear in Book 14 with a dynamic intensity in the individual of majestic mind. The capacity to hold acquaintance with the stars will become the mind which feeds upon infinity and which converses with the spiritual world. The dimension of wedding soul to soul in purest bond of reason will become the powerfully creative mind that can send from itself kindred mutations and that can aspire to create an ecumenical vision from its magnanimous spirit.

At the end of his encounter with the Arab rider the persona sees "a bed of glittering light" (5.129) over half the wilderness. That his companion explains this as "the waters of the deep / Gathering upon us" (5.130-31) prefigures the "roar of waters" (14.59). The destructive imminence of the deluge is only assuaged when the persona suddenly awakes to find himself back in his room.

Bloom argues that "the soul in solitude moves outward by encountering other solitaries" (10). As Wordsworth writes in Book 4, solitude is most powerful when impressed upon the mind with an appropriate human center. This sense of the importance of human reciprocity, as Bloom calls it, intensifies in Book 5 when Wordsworth encounters the Arab who tells him that the stone he carries is "Euclid's Elements" (5.88) and that the shell is "something of more worth" (5.89), that is, poetry.

Wordsworth's persona finds certain similarities between his own existence and the life of the Arab. Not only does he have the aura of a Don Quixote, but he is "crazed / By love and feeling and internal thought / Protracted among endless solitudes" (5.145-47). Bloom suggests that such "is a fate that Wordsworth feared for himself, had his sensibility taken too strong control of his reason" (11).

Bloom proceeds to claim that "the Arab's mission, though the poet calls it mad, is very like Wordsworth's own in *The Prelude*" (11), for both aim "to save Imagination from the abyss of desert and ocean" (11). Whereas the quest of the Arab appears hopeless before the imminent deluge, "Wordsworth hopes that his own quest will bring the healing waters down, as he pursues his slow, flowing course toward his present freedom" (11).

In Book 6 Wordsworth speaks of his intellectual contemplations at Cambridge leading him to realize the presence of the "one / Supreme Existence" (6.133–34) which is beyond the exigencies of space and time and beyond the vicissitudes of mortality. Such meditation on the existence of "God" (6.139) gives the persona a sense of "transcendent peace" (6.139) which prefigures the serene wisdom of the majestic intellect of Book 14.

After leaving Cambridge for his adventure in continental Europe, Wordsworth describes his experience of nature as vitally dynamic. He moves forward on the streams of the Saone and the Rhone with majestic ease. By participating in the fluidity of nature the persona enhances his sense of the expansiveness of space—indeed, his carefree movement on the stream enables him to experience the surrounding natural environment as a "succession without end / Of deep and stately vales" (6.383–84). Spatial expansiveness is linked here with spatial infinitude.

The powerful sense of solitude which the persona has previously achieved and proclaimed the importance of is heightened in his alpine adventure in the ambience of the Convent of Chartreuse. As Wordsworth's persona approaches the Convent of Chartreuse he hears the voice of Nature, which reverberates in from the past to the present, asserting that this special place should be devoted to eternity, indeed, that it should be considered unique in its devotion to eternity. This is a place of primarily expansive spatiality and diastolic temporality which represents a significant precursor to the later vision on Mt. Snowdon.

Wordsworth's description of the spatiality of La Grande Chartreuse, the chief monastery of the Carthusian order in the mountains near Grenoble, exemplified by the idea that entering this domain "leaves far behind life's treacherous vanities" (6.453), reveals an aura similar to that of Arnold's depiction of the atmosphere of the Grande Chartreuse in his poem "Stanzas from the Grande Chartreuse" and similar to that of Shangri-La in James Hilton's *Lost Horizon*. Arnold's and Hilton's spatially hermetic spaces are devoted to eternity as well, although Arnold's is more emotively oriented and Hilton's more aesthetic and cultural.

The aura of the Grande Chartreuse, a sublime cathedral of light and radiance, is similar to the sense of sanctuary expressed in Wordsworth's "Inscriptions Supposed to Be Found In and Near a Hermit's Cell":

> I bent before Thy gracious throne,
> And asked for peace on suppliant knee;

And peace was given,--nor peace alone,

But faith sublimed to ecstasy! (IV, 17-20)

In this poem the persona describes a sanctuary of faith, serenity, and peacefulness. The persona states that all aspects of human experience and life are fleeting and transient except for a sense of faith and the devotion to the divine.

As the vision on Mt. Snowdon of the majestic intellect is a threshold experience generated by the tension between the roar of waters and the starry heavens and reinforced by the existence of the mind that feeds upon infinity at the edge of the abyss, so the aura, the vitality, of the Chartreuse monastery is defined by its distinctive threshold nature. At the interface of earth and heaven, the monastery is also contiguous with "the sister streams of Life and Death" (6.439). That both streams are described as murmuring gives the entire scene a dynamism and an expansiveness which transforms the hermetic tone to one of orphic, outward-directed energy.

As Shangri-La in Hilton's *Lost Horizon*, this environment is one pervaded by the "great spirit of human knowledge" (6.450). The crucial difference between the two is that the temporal emphasis in Shangri-La is on the present and the future in contrast to the spirit of knowledge at this point of *The Prelude* being vitalized by the past and the future. Yet, both spaces preserve the capacity to suspend the flux of mortality or to transcend, if only temporarily, mortality.

After leaving the Convent of Chartreuse, Wordsworth's persona proceeds to describe various noteworthy and salient spaces, including the summit of Mont Blanc and the Vale of Chamouny stretching far below. The expansiveness of this vale, now impressive less by its absolute fluidity than by its crystalline, motionless capacity, leads the persona to contemplate the everyday vitality of multiple dimensions of nature. The expansiveness of space generates not only an expansiveness of soul, but also a sense of the diversity and multiplicity of nature.

After crossing the Alps Wordsworth reflects on the power of the imagination which inspires the poetic persona to realize the vital importance of the statement: "Our destiny, our being's heart and home / Is with infinitude, and only there" (6.604-05). It is through an inward-turning gesture of epiphanic vitality, "when the light of sense / Goes out" (6.600-01), that Wordsworth's persona senses his participation in the diastolic vitality of time. In this passage, a sanctuary of light, a moment of brilliant radiance, is described. For when the light of sense vanishes, there is a "flash that has revealed / The invisible world" (6.601–02). This sense of temporal infinitude links to a belief in eternal hope, effort, expectation, and desire. This passage apotheosizes the creative mind which is powerful in itself and which does not need external praise. Such a mind that is "blest in thoughts / That are their own perfection and reward" (6.611–612) is the precursor of the majestic intellect of Book 14.

In suggesting several lines later that the various aspects of nature in this mountain landscape, whether the "giddy prospect of the raving stream" (6.633), the "unfettered clouds" (6.634), or the "Tumult and peace, the darkness and the light" (6.635), were "all like workings of one mind" (6.636) the persona again anticipates or foreshadows the ultimate vision in *The Prelude* of the mind that is "sustained / By recognitions of transcendent power" (14.74–75) and that may converse with past, present, and future generations of humankind "till Time shall be no more" (14.111). The essential difference between the mind of Book 6 and the majestic intellect of Book 14 is that the latter is more consciously aware of his visionary capacity to communicate with the spiritual world and with multiple generations of humankind until the end of mortality. The self-confidence of the majestic intellect of Book 14 enables him to develop kindred mutations with a greater sense of serenity.

The capacity of signifying in one individual, of encompassing in one creative mind, diverse aspects of nature (a capacity shared by the mind of Book 6 and the majestic intellect of Book 14) is similar to the capability of the magnanimous protagonist in Hermann Hesse's *Siddhartha* to encompass in himself multiple dimensions of earthly existence beyond the constraints of space and time:

> He no longer saw the face of his friend Siddhartha. Instead he saw other faces, many faces, a long series, a continuous stream of faces—hundreds, thousands, which all came and disappeared and yet all seemed to be there at the same time, which all continuously changed and renewed themselves and which were yet all Siddhartha. (121)

Siddhartha, in his capacity to embrace all of these forms and to establish a continuity of kindred mutations, embodies the vitality of the creatively dynamic intellect of Wordsworth's persona as "a mind sustained / By recognitions of transcendent power / In sense conducting to ideal form" (14.74–76).

The mind of Book 6 of *The Prelude* assumes in itself "Characters of the great Apocalypse" (6.638) which are the "types and symbols of Eternity" (6.639) and shows the ability to fuse these complementary yet opposite experiences of "Apocalypse" and "Eternity" in a threshold realm of creative vitality. It is at this threshold moment, or threshold succession of moments, at the interface of the raving stream and the unfettered clouds, tumult and peace, darkness and light, apocalypse and eternity that the persona glimpses the diastolic, expansive nature of space and time. The cyclicality implied by line 640 in Book 6 ("Of first, and last, and midst, and without end") will be transformed into the cessation of Time in Book 14. The vision of the ultimate atemporality of Time reveals the extraordinary power and range of the majestic intellect which is only intuited in Book 6.

The capacity of Wordsworth's persona to encompass in himself diverse features of nature is reinforced by his desire to preserve and to strengthen a continuity of self and nature. The persona who says of the lake near the end of Book 6 that its beauty remains with him especially because he feels intimately connected to it believes in the importance of a continuity of self and nature. In conceiving of himself as a spiritual and physical dimension of the lake's domain in saying "Like a breeze / Or sunbeam over your domain I passed" (6.675-76), the persona affirms a sense of continuity with nature as powerful as it is serene.

In the last lines of Book 6 the light also plays an important role. Wordsworth's persona speaks of "golden days" (6.724) which he experienced and which filled his travels with a positive and blissful influence and presence. The importance of the light is also emphasized in lines 774-78 of Book 6— here the persona speaks of the universe as inspiring a sense of youthfulness and vitality as it reveals its glories and delights. The vernal blossoming of the powers of the universe is exemplified by the delights which "Spread round my steps like sunshine o'er green fields" (6.778). This is a perpetual sanctuary of light which energizes and inspires the persona in his creative and aesthetic endeavors.

In the passage starting with line 592, the persona suggests the inadequacy of language to capture and to express the power of the imagination. Yet, at the same time he asserts the dynamic vitality of the imagination. For the imagination of the creatively vital individual has the potential to experience epiphanic moments such as the revelations of the world of nature or the spirit beyond everyday mortality. At this moment the persona realizes that his destiny, the destiny of those sensitive and perceptive individuals infused with the power of the imagination, "is with infinitude and only there" (6.605).

In Book 7 Wordsworth not only stresses the continuity of the self with nature, but also reaffirms the importance of the threshold experience. After the hour of sunset one evening, at the threshold of light and darkness (both indoors and outside), Wordsworth's persona hears a lovely bird-song. He is inspired to go outside and observes a glow-worm beneath a plume of fern. In this twilight ambience Wordsworth experiences pristine qualities of sound and silence. The pristine aura of this profoundly serene moment enables him later to experience the threshold ambience of the majestic intellect as a timeless continuum of past, present, and future generations.

In Book 8 Wordsworth affirms the importance of Nature as his aesthetic guide and inspiration. Geoffrey Hartman writes in "The Romance of Nature and the Negative Way" that nature for Wordsworth "is not an 'object' but a presence and a power; a motion and a spirit; not something to be worshiped and consumed, but always a guide leading beyond itself" (60). In saying that his heart was first opened to the sense of natural beauty in the "domains of rural peace" (8.73), Wordsworth is once again not only privileging the dimension of space but also critiquing the incapacity of the urban environment and its turbulence to arouse the same aesthetic vitality in him. He speaks of his home environment as a "tract more exquisitely fair / Than that famed paradise of ten thousand trees" (8.75-76). As beautiful as this "sumptuous dream of flowery lawns, with domes / Of pleasure sprinkled over" (8.84-85) is, the paradise of his home is far more beautiful.

Such a vital devotion to the landscape of youth is found with similar intensity in the affection of John Constable for the landscape and the natural environment of his childhood. Indeed, Constable's creation of the aesthetic, spiritual aura of the Stour River valley is comparable to Wordsworth's imaginative rendering of the aesthetic, spiritual aura of the Lake District of England. Wordsworth's recollection, as Constable's, of the paradise landscape of youth is not merely a praise of nature—it is also a praise of the individual laborer, of the man working for himself in a state of relative independence.

John Constable's response to nature reveals a sensitive appreciation of its various moods and scenes. Constable writes of his love of diverse features of the natural environment, from the sound of water escaping from mill-dams and waterways which gave him pleasure in his early youth to the lovely clouds, the sweep of cloud shadows across the sky, and transient gleams of light. Constable's objective in painting is very similar to Wordsworth's in poetry. In his preface to the Second Edition of *Lyrical Ballads*, published in 1800, which Constable read and admired, Wordsworth wrote:

> The principal object, then, proposed in these Poems was to choose incidents and situations from common life, and to relate or describe them, throughout, as far as was possible, in a selection of language really used by men, and, at the same time, to throw over them a certain colouring of imagination, whereby ordinary

things should be presented to the mind in an unusual aspect . . . . Humble and rustic life was generally chosen, because in that condition, the essential passions of the heart find a better soil in which they can attain their maturity.

Wordsworth and Constable also share a sense of the potentially vital importance of the landscape of one's own youth for one's artistic development. Of the significance of such a familiar environment Constable wrote: "But I should paint my own places best—Painting is but another word for feeling. I associate my 'careless boyhood' to all that lies on the banks of the Stour. They made me a painter." Several of Constable's paintings which exemplify a Wordsworthian aura and nature-sensibility are *The Hay Wain, The Cornfield, The White Horse, Flatford Mill, and Hampstead Heath.* Constable, as Wordsworth, shows a profound nature-sensibility and an exceptional sensitivity for the nuances and subtleties of the natural environment from the interplay of light and darkness to the epiphanic vitality of radiances within shadows as well as an aesthetic concern to ensure that there is a human presence in a wide array of nature scenes.

This section of *The Prelude* culminates in Wordsworth's praise of the shepherd who, in representing the noblest qualities of the human spirit, becomes an integral part of nature. In the midst of this praise of the shepherd Wordsworth lauds as well the openness and the expansiveness of space to inspire and soothe the shepherd. In presenting various aspects of nature such as moors, mountains, and vales, Wordsworth implies the capacity of the openness of space in the natural environment to generate and to reinforce the sense of freedom of the shepherd. As earlier in *The Prelude*, so in this context the openness of space is used to challenge or counteract the seemingly inevitable flux of time. For example, to elude the "lingering dews of morn / Smoke around him" (8.244-45) the shepherd wanders from hill to hill. Through the medium of space the shepherd seeks not only an escape from the exigencies of mortality, but also a transformation of time.

Perhaps because he is beset by various dangers of the solitudes through which he wanders as "a freeman, wedded to his life of hope / And hazard" (8.253.54), the shepherd is granted a nobility of stature by Wordsworth's critical eye. Not only does the presence of the shepherd exert a dynamic emotional-spiritual influence over his immediate natural environment, but he appears as a giant in the mist with "his sheep like Greenland bears" (8.267). The power of the shepherd's presence is amplified or intensified by the surrounding nature. For example, as he steps "beyond the boundary line of some hill-shadow" (8.268), the form of the shepherd is illuminated by the setting sun. The figure of the shepherd participates in a sanctuary of light, although momentary, which reaffirms his important presence in the world of nature.

Such a moment of radiance seems to be an aspect of the sense sublime "Whose dwelling is the light of setting suns" (97) that Wordsworth describes in "Tintern Abbey." In concluding this section by depicting another appearance of the shepherd as "a solitary object and sublime" (8.272), Wordsworth presents him as a figure with the stature of the persona in C. D. Friedrich's *Traveller Looking Over a Sea of Fog* (1815). The similarity of these conceptions is reinforced by the shared conviction of Wordsworth and Friedrich in the capacity of such creative and thoughtful individuals who are so sensitively aware of the beauty and the vitality of the natural environment to signify the "sanctity of Nature given to man" (8.295).

The portrayal of the shepherd in this section is also important because it reveals qualities which will later be emphasized as essential for the majestic intellect of Book 14. The shepherd is by his creatively vital and thoughtful nature the precursor and the harbinger of the majestic intellect not only with respect to his magnanimous soul and his capacity to "send abroad / Kindred mutations" (14.93–94) into his immediate natural environment, but also in light of the sense of freedom which he represents. The nobility of the shepherd, as of the majestic intellect of Book 14, ultimately leads Wordsworth to reaffirm his "faith in life endless, the sustaining thought / Of human Being, Eternity, and God" (14.204–05).

The potential of a special natural space to exert a consistently affirmative influence on the persona is proclaimed in Book 8 in the depiction of the grove "whose boughs / Stretch from the western marge of Thurston-mere" (8.458–59). As in various previous passages of *The Prelude* it is the golden light of the setting sun which inspires and motivates the emotional and spiritual energy of the moment. As the golden light of the setting sun rests in silent beauty on the ridge of a high hill, the persona declares that wherever the future will take him he will always think back on the extraordinary beauty of this special natural domain, of this lovely natural sanctuary, to encourage and inspire him.

This devotion to special and distinctive natural places which will guide the persona congenially through the flux of mortality is expressed with similar conviction and intensity in the poetry of the nineteenth-century German Romantic Joseph von Eichendorff. For example, in Eichendorff's poem "Abschied" ("Farewell") the persona, in departing from a beautiful natural space of the kind of personal importance that Wordsworth and Constable ascribe to their childhood places, asserts that his heart will never grow old in his wanderings through the vicissitudes of the world of mortality as long as he may reflect upon the emotional, spiritual, and aesthetic beauty of his beloved forest.

Wordsworth distinguishes between at least two complementary, if not essentially antithetical, dimensions of time. In contrast to mortality, to the evanescence of animate life, thought, and action, there is Time, which is a sense of mortality raised to a higher power, to a condition of apparent atemporality. In Book 8 when Wordsworth speaks of memory as divinity he describes the latter dimension of time: "All that took place within me came and went / As in a moment; yet with Time it dwells / And grateful memory, as a thing divine" (8.557-59). This sense of Time is both mortal and atemporal; in signifying memory as a divine condition it seems to anticipate the sense of timelessness in Book 14, but it is still more closely linked to evanescence than to permanence. The third dimension of Time is seen in Book 14 when the persona anticipates an existential condition when "Time shall be no more" (14.111). This sense of time is a timeless, atemporal time beyond the temporal mortality and the atemporal mortality of Book 8.

Herbert Lindenberger writes in "The Structural Unit: 'Spots of Time'" that the personal past, "the quest for which is the substance of *The Prelude*, is not recreated in and for itself, but only within the perspective of the present, through which alone it derives meaning" (77-78). It is the timeless, or atemporal, present which encompasses the past in an existential condition of epiphanic vitality, as the majestic intellect of Book 14 embraces in himself kindred manifestations of nature.

From Book 9 to Book 11 of *The Prelude* Wordsworth speaks of his experiences in France, especially during the time of the French Revolution. One of his first critiques of the excesses of the revolution is that an atmosphere of terrible agitation and strife was produced. Wordsworth describes in Book 9 this unquiet commotion as a mockery "Of history, the past and that to come" (9.169). In light of this statement, which is presented in temporal terms, perhaps one could argue that Wordsworth is so interested in space because he views it as a means of ameliorating or transforming the anguish of mortality. Yet, the kind of space that he ultimately needs is not the flatland, which he describes in the passage as "the land all swarmed with passion, like a plain / Devoured by locusts" (9.175-76), but a place that affords a certain physical distance from and a novel emotional and intellectual perspective on the context of the unquiet commotion and hectic activity.

Raymond Williams speaks in *Culture and Society: 1780-1950* of the vital influence which the French Revolution had on its contemporary political and social context, suggesting that the hope, energy, and vision accompanying the

French Revolution was not merely background material but "the mould in which general experience was cast" (30-31). This sense of the positive influence of the French Revolution is shared by Wordsworth's contemporary, William Hazlitt, who asserted in *The Spirit of the Age* that the innovations in Wordsworth's poetry derived from the spirit of the sentiments and opinions that produced the French Revolution. J. S. Mill shared Hazlitt's conviction, stressing in his essays on *The Spirit of the Age* the animating, revolutionary spirit of the age which was inspiring and stimulating a more vital literary expression.

The negative influence of the French Revolution on Wordsworth, an influence which lasted through the rest of his life, is already seen in 1792 in his awareness of the horrific violence which permeated the revolutionary ambience. As late as 1840 Wordsworth told Thomas Carlyle that he had witnessed the execution on October 7, 1793, of the journalist Gorsas, an event equally disturbing because it raised the question "Where will it end, when you have set an example in this kind" (Hanley 47)?

Wordsworth's quest for the magic mountain is a quest for a sanctuary of luminescent serenity, for a profoundly tranquil space beyond the atmosphere of terror and violence of such events as the French Revolution and beyond the social unrest in England, while at the same time preserving the humanitarian dimension of the revolutionary spirit. Wordsworth's persona on Mt. Snowdon aspires to achieve the revolution of a humanely sensitive consciousness in the spirit of Friedrich Schelling's assertion of the purpose of his philosophy "to point out to the human spirit a new road, to give bruised and battered spirits courage and inner strength" (Abrams 26).

In portraying the unique officer whom he meets in France, Wordsworth presents an individual who is at least to some extent a precursor of the majestic intellect of Book 14. This individual is depicted as a man of noble spirit, generous heart, humane soul, and wise intellect. His death, fighting for liberty and against the inhumanity, thoughtlessness, and violence of contemporary society is a great loss for Wordsworth. Yet, the memory of his nobility of soul is preserved in the creative persona of Book 14. Wordsworth shared his friend's idealistic conviction that a better, more humane world would emerge in the near future.

In the essay "The Revolutionary 'I': Wordsworth and the Politics of Self-Presentation" A. Nichols argues that the Wordsworthian first person develops out of the interaction of "complementary and conflicting discourses: the rhetoric of the French Revolution, eighteenth-century ideas about the profession of authorship, and Wordsworth's need to create an identity whose apparent center is at once poetical and philosophical" (66). In suggesting that what is revolutionary in the lyrical sources and lyrics of *The Prelude* is "their evolution of a new version of the autobiographical 'I'" (66), Nichols claims that in Goslar, where Wordsworth produced the lyrical fragments that eventually became the source texts for *The Prelude*, he "does not start telling the story of his past life so much as he begins writing a version of his life that can become his story" (67).

Nichols says that "by the time he returned from Goslar, Wordsworth had begun to connect his poetics as social practice with a specific view of his profession as a calling" (76). Nichols proceeds to suggest that, in the spirit of Wordsworth's statement in the Preface to *The Excursion* of how its author had returned to his native mountains, "retirement became Wordsworth's means of beginning a career" (76). In creating an identity whose center is simultaneously poetical and philosophical Wordsworth's persona prepares himself to achieve ultimately the stature of the majestic intellect who can encompass various dimensions of the world in the holistically unified aura of the creative self.

In Book 10 Wordsworth gradually regains his faith in humanity and in justice as some of the perpetrators of the excesses of the French Revolution lose their authority. At the beginning of Book 11 Wordsworth is confident that a sense of renovation will proceed, for "Authority in France / Put on a milder face" (11.1-2) and "Terror had ceased" (11.2). The glorious renovation will be more vital if it learns from and derives its power and wisdom at least to some extent from the "One great society alone on earth: / The noble Living and the noble Dead" (11.394-95). For these are the majestic intellects of the world, the souls of magnanimous spirit and of more than mortal privilege.

In Book 12 of *The Prelude* Wordsworth affirms that nature may comfort and encourage him vitally when the world of everyday mortality becomes oppressive or painful. As in Thomas Gainsborough's *Wooded Landscape with a Cottage, Sheep, and a Reclining Shepherd* (1747), John Constable's *The Hay Wain* (1821) or in C. D. Friedrich's *The Solitary Tree* (1822) it is a vital sense of natural space (the sense of space the protagonist gains through a sensitive appreciation of nature) that gives the persona emotional inspiration and aesthetic-spiritual stimulation.

In roaming "from hill to hill, from rock to rock" (12.143) in search of new forms, Wordsworth's persona is also questing for a "wider empire for the sight" (12.145). One is reminded of Jane Eyre's belief in the importance of the horizon in developing her visionary imagination. As this passage progresses Wordsworth describes "a maid / A young enthusiast" (12.151-52) who was attuned "by her benign simplicity" (12.161) and by her "perfect happiness of soul" (12.162) to every scene that presented itself to her view. Similarly, the personae in Constable's *The Hay Wain* and Friedrich's *The Solitary Tree* savor the relatively enclosed and hermetic space in which they exist. Wordsworth's persona, although appreciating the beauty of hermetic spaces, implies that he is not truly content with this strategy. His creativity derives to a considerable extent from a complementary awareness both of the beauty of hermetic spaces and the grandeur and sublimity of diastolic spaces.

As in the Immortality Ode, Wordsworth speaks in *The Prelude* of the significance of "spots of time" (12.208) that may nourish and invisibly repair our minds beset by the cares and obstacles of everyday mortality and locates the source of the "spots of time" in childhood. Wordsworth suggests that while these profound, regenerative moments of emotional, intellectual, or spiritual vitality may occur at any time in our lives, they derive especially from the landscape and experience of childhood and youth. Bloom asserts that "the function of the spots of time is to enshrine the spirit of the past for future restoration" (21). The "spots of time" are moments of heightened emotional, intellectual, or spiritual awareness similar in intensity to W. Pater's moments of "quickened, multiplied consciousness." Whereas for Pater in *The Renaissance* to achieve the most intense impression possible was the great objective of living and to seize and transfix this moment became an aesthetic duty, for Wordsworth in *The Prelude* the recovery of the past might enable the poet, the artist, who is most able to appreciate these "spots of time," to achieve a faith in the integrity of the self to prepare him for the future.

One such epiphanic moment which Wordsworth describes is an experience on the eve of the Christmas holiday when he, in an anguished state of mind, went forth into the fields. In anticipation or foreshadowing of his adventure on Mt. Snowdon in Book 14, Wordsworth speaks of his ascending a crag and experiencing a misty, wild atmosphere. In this threshold experience the persona on the crag is sheltered or trapped between images of light and darkness (it is day, yet it is a tempestuous, dark day) and life and death (on his right hand a single sheep, on his left hand blasted hawthorn).

Moreover, the image of being shrouded by mist which only occasionally diminishes or evaporates to provide glimpses "of the copse / And plain beneath" (12.304-05) suggests a threshold experience of emotional and spiritual intensity—this is affirmed in the death of his father soon after. This threshold epiphany becomes meaningful for Wordsworth when he observes the seemingly antithetical features as complementary dimensions of an existential whole. He speaks of the diverse elements, the wind and rain, the sheep and the hawthorn, as "kindred spectacles and sounds" (12.324). By assimilating the conflicting aspects of this moment into a harmonious whole, by viewing them as a unified vision, Wordsworth is able to overcome the existential fragility and despair which might otherwise ensue. Wordsworth suggests further that his creativity is most stimulated at such a threshold moment.

David Simpson in "The Spots of Time: Spaces for Refiguring" claims that the spots of time, especially the poet coming upon the gibbet in early childhood and the poet climbing to the top of a crag to try to observe the horses which are to carry him home, "seem to involve a recognition and acceptance of the notion that the figurings of the moment are always displaced, often painfully, into subsequent and ongoing refiguring" (142). Simpson proceeds to describe these refiguring as forms that "are not prefigured by others, and are integrally educative rather than merely habit-forming" (142). In its emphasis on a continuous growth process, this capacity for refiguring affirms the persona's potential for participating in and shaping an expansive sense of time.

Herbert Lindenberger speaks of the "spots of time" as progressing "from a world of transitory things to intimations of a more eternal realm" (146). In one of his chapters on time-consciousness, Lindenberger writes that "Wordsworth grounds his image of a timeless realm in the natural world, above all, in the lakes and hills with which he portrays the self in interaction" (178). Lindenberger proceeds to assert that for Wordsworth, as for "Rousseau nature acts as a kind of catalyst to lead him into a contemplative state whereby he is gradually removed from the distractions of the temporal realm" (178).

In Book 13 Wordsworth's persona prepares himself increasingly more for his ultimate vision in the final book. He proclaims nature to be the source not only of his creative power, the "energy by which he seeks the truth" (13.8), but also of the profound tranquility which pervades the genial spirit. In enlarging the horizon of his mind, the persona declares that he devoted himself to the intellectual eye in his quest for great truths. Although the persona admits that other environments may be a source for such truths, he concludes by asserting that there is no ambience as inspirational, as enriching, and as illuminating as that of Nature.

The image of the path leading towards the horizon signifies one of Wordworth's perpetual spots of time. As familiar as the "windings of a public way" (13.143) may be, they have exerted and still exert a powerful stimulus on the persona's imagination. The sense of expansive windings, representing "an invitation into space / Boundless, or guide into eternity" (13.150-51), affirms the diastolic spatiality which energizes the persona.

Wordsworth continues this thoughtful argument by claiming that the "wanderers of the earth" (13.155) have always possessed a certain emotional-spiritual grandeur in his mind. Wordsworth concludes this passage by implying that those individuals who have a diastolic sense of space (and who believe in the importance of an expansive space) are able to see into the depths of human souls. Through his diastolic experience of space the persona heightens and enriches his burgeoning understanding of the universal heart, of the human condition. Gill stresses the importance of the complementarity of imagination and love for the creative self to achieve such an understanding of the human condition: "Imagination is presented as the power that enables Man to convert into knowledge that which he perceives, to shape his world. In alliance with Love it binds him to his fellow beings" (239).

An interesting passage about the complementarity of space and time occurs when the persona proclaims that his youthful spirit was raised when he was once among the wilds of Sarum's Plain. As the persona wanders across the pastoral dawns, as he experiences an expansive spatiality and an increasing solitude, he also attains an expanding sense of time, a vision of the past as "Time with his retinue of ages fled / Backwards" (13.318–19). In observing the ancient past of England, an ambience of the living and the dead, the persona anticipates the capacity of the majestic intellect in the final book to communicate with past generations of humankind.

As this vision of the past continues, Wordsworth's persona sees the stone work of the Druids, representing their knowledge of the heavens, and observes the "long-bearded teachers, with white wands / Uplifted" (13.345–46) pointing towards the starry sky and the plain in a melodious moment of universal harmony. Not only does the persona envision the past in this threshold experience as dynamic as the previous threshold moments at the interface of light and darkness, the living and the dead, but he participates in its vitality. The persona in this passage strengthens his visionary imagination as well by aspiring to achieve a creative and enduring work which may become a "Power like one of Nature's" (13.312).

In Book 13 Wordsworth's persona asserts the importance of a sensitive emotional vitality, especially an emotional vitality connected with wisdom, by stressing the significance of the "feeling intellect." It is this "feeling intellect" which can express a genuinely fraternal love in a spirit of humanitarian vitality. In distinguishing his approach from the strategy of the historians who are interested in describing "power and energy detached / From moral purpose" (13.43–44), Wordsworth's persona suggests the significance of looking upon the world and especially upon the "unassuming things that hold

/ A silent station in this beauteous world" (13.46–47) with a sense of appreciative love. As the circumference of his imagination is enlarged by thoughts of ever new delight, the persona becomes more desirous of participating in the "energy by which he seeks the truth" (13.8) and which derives from the vitality of nature.

M.H. Abrams describes Book 14 of *The Prelude* as opening "with a literal walk which translates itself into a metaphor for the climactic stage both of the journey of life and of the imaginative journey which is the poem itself" (Gill 217). Abrams proceeds to argue that ". . . the walk is not a movement along an open plain but the ascent of a mountain, the traditional place for definitive visions since Moses had climbed Mt. Sinai" (Gill 217).

In Book 14 of *The Prelude* Wordsworth's persona experiences the epiphanically vital vision on Mt. Snowdon. The stream of moonlight combined with "the roar of waters" (14.59) creates a moment of extraordinary sensory vitality. This experience of the dynamism and the power of nature suggests to Wordsworth's persona the presence of a "majestic intellect" (14.67), of a mind / That feeds upon infinity" (14.70–71). This majestic intellect is capable of experiencing both "kairos" and "Aion" and of transforming "kairos" to "Aion."

Panofsky says that in classical art Time was described either as fleeting Opportunity ("kairos") or creative Eternity ("Aion"). In the moment of fleeting opportunity the individual "feels himself to be actively and totally fitted to the world about him" (Beer 32). In the experience of "Aion" there is an influx of visionary power—the individual "is so possessed by inward imagination as to feel no transience in the passing of time" (Beer 32). The "spots of time" of Wordsworth's persona in *The Prelude* may signify either an experience of "kairos" or of "Aion," yet ultimately he transforms "kairos" into "Aion," for the majestic intellect represents an influx and a diffusion of visionary power.

The diastolic spatiality of "Tintern Abbey" and the Immortality Ode becomes the timeless space of Book 14 of *The Prelude*. This timeless space is both an expansive landscape of the mind and a dynamic landscape of nature. There is throughout *The Prelude* and in the last book in particular a correlation or reflection of mind and nature which enhances the power of both. In suggesting that the higher minds of the universe "can send abroad / Kindred mutations" (14.93–94) from their own vital selves, Wordsworth creates an existential aura which reaffirms the reflection of humankind and nature.

Such a capacity to "send abroad / Kindred mutations" (14.93–94) is also seen in Shelley's "The Cloud." Shelley's persona, the cloud, revitalizes the natural environment perpetually and plays a vital role in the eternal cyclicality of nature. By projecting himself into the figure and the aura of the cloud Shelley's persona, like Thoreau's in *Walden,* becomes an integral part of the significant features of the natural landscape he describes. Shelley's "I" becomes the cloud as the cloud becomes part of him just as Thoreau's "I" in *Walden* becomes the sun, the north star, the Mill Brook, a dandelion and they become part of him.

In stanza six of the poem, Shelley's "I" asserts his potential for a transcendence of mortality which is derived directly from his transformational vitality, from his capacity to assume different forms. In the lines "I pass through the pores of the ocean and shores: / I change, but I cannot die–" (75–76), Shelley's "I" argues for a transformational vitality of cyclically regenerative powers. That he can assume various shapes and forms and still maintain the integrity of his being gives Shelley's persona a strong semblance of immortality. This transformational strategy ultimately enables the persona to achieve a semblance of the inner harmony and peace which Wordsworth's "I" experiences in "Home at Grasmere." Yet, Shelley's persona, in laughing silently at his own cenotaph and then rising out of the caverns of rain to unbuild it again, reveals a creative self-confidence which enhances his transformational capacity. Moreover, the "I" affirms in the second-to-last line his ability to encompass the diversity and extremes of life and death in his dominion. One might even argue that the rhyme "womb"-"tomb" (83) suggests the capacity of the "I" to mediate between the realms of life and death. The image of genesis, of a cyclically recurring genesis, is important in the last stanza because it emphasizes the ability of the "I" to create a world of order, of internal harmony, out of the chaos of "the caverns of rain" (82).

The "faith that looks through death" (185) and the philosophic mind of the Immortality Ode become the powerful creative intellect of Book 14 of *The Prelude.* One of the most vital characteristics of this majestic intellect is its capacity "to hold fit converse with the spiritual world" (14.108) and with past, present, and future generations of humankind until time shall no longer exist. The realization of this capability is a dynamic sign of the success of the magic mountain adventure for this persona. Moreover, this is a mind that not only achieves the highest consciousness possible for a mortal being, but also seems to be motivated by and spiritually and intellectually connected to a divine force in the universe.

We have seen that the sense of space generates the sense of time in Wordsworth's work. In "Tintern Abbey" there is a diastolic sense of space and a sense of time that is both hermetic and orphic, hermetic in the sense that the persona is aware of mortality, orphic in the sense that the persona believes intuitively that an expansiveness of space may lead to a sense of expanding time. In "Nuns Fret Not" there is a hermetic sense of space that is really innately diastolic and expansive. The Immortality Ode offers a diastolic awareness of space that encompasses multiple dimensions of the natural environment and a sense of time founded on "the faith that looks through death" (185). The power of this diastolic sense of space and time is energized by the epiphanic vitality of "those first affections" (148) which "are yet the fountain-light of all our day" (151). The diastolic sense of space is affirmed in the image of the "immortal sea" (163), the vision of which will perpetually revitalize the persona.

One may describe the epiphanic vitality of those "first affections" (148) and "shadowy recollections" (149) as moments in the dynamic present of things past. In contrast to Book 14 of *The Prelude*, which motivates its expansive sense of space and time by an emphasis on the present of things present complemented by the present of things past and future, the Immortality Ode stresses the supremely influential role of significant past moments to inspire and sustain the persona.

The motion and the spirit that move through all things which the persona senses in "Tintern Abbey" are comparable to the image of the "Kindred mutations" (14.94) in *The Prelude*. The difference between the two contexts is that in "Tintern Abbey" the persona senses the motion and the spirit that permeates all things but is not necessarily the agent of that motion. On the other hand, in Book 14 of *The Prelude* the majestic intellect which is revealed to the persona and which is a manifestation of the persona's own mind, acts as the generating spirit which "can send abroad / Kindred mutations" (14.93–94) and may actively shape the spirit that moves through all things.

Jonathan Wordsworth suggests in "The Image of a Mighty Mind" that what makes the achievement of the climbing of Mt. Snowdon so notable is that it fuses two dimensions of the imagination which have existed throughout *The Prelude*: ". . . the shaping force that is perceived as an external agency, and has been responsible for restorative . . . impressions upon the mind, and the power that is felt to well up from underlying sources within the individual" (Gill 243–44).

As in the previous poems by Wordsworth which have been discussed in this essay, so in *The Prelude* a sense of space generates or leads to a sense of time. The persona in Book 14 has a vision of the light of the moon spreading over the "billowy ocean" (14.55) and of the "roar of waters" (14.59) emerging from the rift before he expresses a sense of time. The vision of the light in this scenario is another important sanctuary of light in *The Prelude*, a sanctuary which inspires and strengthens the persona emotionally and intellectually. It is also noteworthy that the persona experiences the expansiveness of light and space before he envisions the mind "that feeds upon infinity" (14.71).

Alan Liu describes the expansiveness of the self in *The Prelude* as "Wordsworth's moment of Absolute Knowledge" (447) which involves "the knowledge of many things" (447). Liu proceeds to argue effectively that "Snowdon is a vision of poetic Imagination that has 'usurped' upon the world in which actual usurpers rise to power" (447).

The capacity of the majestic intellect to create and to participate in an expansiveness of self, space, and time is affirmed in the lines that stress the significance of the "mind sustained / By recognitions of transcendent power" (14.74–75). In the following line, "In sense conducting to ideal form," the persona implies the potential of the majestic intellect to be an active part of an ambience of spatial expansiveness, an ambience aspiring to encompass ideal forms. Line 77, "In soul of more than mortal privilege," suggests the capacity of the majestic intellect to challenge and transcend mortality. These few lines are important not only because they delineate qualities of the majestic intellect, but also because, in representing a thematic unity, they affirm the interrelation of space and time.

In Book 14 the persona suggests that the individual who has achieved a diastolic sense of space and time, who has participated in an aura of the expansiveness of space and time, has attained a condition of genuine liberty. An essential, perhaps the essential, dimension of this sense of liberty is the development of the imagination which Wordsworth characterizes in Book 14 as "but another name for absolute power / And clearest insight, amplitude of mind / And reason in her most exalted mood" (14.190–92). The phrase "amplitude of mind" (14.191) especially reaffirms the importance of a diastolically vital imagination, the development and strengthening of which leads to the powerful faith in humanity, eternity, and the divine.

In aspiring to achieve and preserve a diastolic, an expansive, sense of space and time, the individual of majestic intellect develops a dynamic faith, a faith which unifies the strivings of humanity, time and the divine for eternity. Through his experience of this faith on the mountain the creatively vital persona shapes the diastolic sense of space into a simultaneously dynamic awareness of the expansiveness of time.

Wordsworth's "Preface to the Second Edition of the Lyrical Ballads" (1800) offers several interesting statements focusing on the themes of space and eternity. Wordsworth even uses the language of space to describe the goal of the poet. Despite geographical, cultural, and historical differences in the world of humankind, "the Poet binds together by passion and knowledge the vast empire of human society, as it is spread over the whole earth, and over all time." Not only does the poet have this special capacity to connect in his literary vitality images and forms of the past, present, and future, but he is also attuned to and aware of various aspects of the world around him.

The spatial and temporal expansiveness of the poet's vision is reinforced in such statements as "Poetry is the breath and finer spirit of all knowledge" and "Poetry is the first and last of all knowledge—it is as immortal as the heart of man." While the former above quoted statement suggests that poetry suffuses all knowledge with its power and represents the eternal spirit of such knowledge, the latter above quoted statement implies the eternal presence of poetry—as long as humankind will exist, poetry will be present to affirm the spirit of humanity and the greatness and significance of emotionally and intellectually vital perceptions and visions of the world.

Wordsworth's definition of the poet also mentions several issues of special relevance for the present discussion. In describing the poet as having a more lively sensibility, a greater knowledge of human nature, and a more comprehensive soul than other individuals, Wordsworth attributes to such a creative figure an expansiveness of the mind and spirit which complements and parallels the expansiveness of space and time which are often integral dimensions of the poet's vision of the world. In saying of the poet what Shakespeare said of man, namely, that "he looks before and after," Wordsworth affirms such an expansiveness of mind and soul and anticipates the capacity of the majestic intellect in *The Prelude* to "hold fit converse with the spiritual world" (14.108) and with past, present, and future generations and stages of humankind until time in the form of mortality shall no longer exist.

The Prelude, as Wlecke and others have argued, can be seen as representing the development of a sublime consciousness in the spirit of Longinus' sense of the sublime as signifying an uplifting of the soul and an expansion of the mind and its powers. R. P. Knight in an *Analytical Inquiry into the Principles of Taste* emphasizes this essential feature of the theory of the sublime of Longinus: "Longinus observes that the effect of the sublime is to lift up the soul; to exalt it into ecstasy; so that, participating . . . of the splendors of the divinity it becomes filled with joy and exultation" (329). This sense of "participating of the splendors of the divinity" is essential not only to Wordsworth's majestic intellect of *The Prelude* but also to various other similarly motivated characters in world literature, such as those in James

Hilton's *Lost Horizon*, who appreciate and value the sublime serenity of Shangri-La.

Wordsworth's capacity to appreciate the sublime develops in his youth, for he speaks of the vitality which was conferred by early converse with the works of the divine. After emphasizing the pure grandeur of the mind which confronts habitually the majesty of nature, Wlecke asserts that "through constant 'converse' with these hills, through a deepening comprehension of their eternity" (61), the mind develops a strong sense "of how indeed the 'soul' has a 'prospect' of 'majesty' precisely because the mind is eternal" (61). The sublime consciousness which Wordsworth develops is affirmed in his intuition, expressed in Book 2 of *The Prelude*, for example, of the one life in all things. The expansiveness of self through space and time is reinforced not only in the experience of continuity through natural piety in the spirit of the introductory lines of the Immortality Ode, but also in the sentiment of Being in which the persona of sublime consciousness participates and which permeates and unifies the phenomenal world.

Of Book 14 of *The Prelude* Geoffrey Hartman writes in *The Unremarkable Wordsworth* that "Snowdon is a vision of mastery, though a peculiar one" (103), especially in the sense that "there is no single locus of majesty or mastery" (103). Perhaps there seems to be an absence of a cosmological or ontological position to resolve the tension between the powers of sound and light, nature and mind, because this position exists in the expansive mind of the creative persona who encompasses the disparate elements in his dynamic self.

Hartman argues further that the ascent of Snowdon "presents a sequence of two moments curiously harmonized" (172), the fusion of sight and sound, the light of the moon and the roar of waters. Of this moment Hartman writes: "Spotting the moon fulfills his hope in an unexpected way, which also foreshortens time. The mind of the poet is disoriented; but the time is lengthened as the sight of the moonstruck scene takes over in a kind of silent harmonization" (172). Through the aura of silent harmonization such a lengthening of time affirms the spatial and temporal expansiveness of the creative self. Such a "silent harmonization" creates and reinforces the experience of a sanctuary of light.

The Prelude contains various sanctuaries of light, both fleeting and sustained, spatially and temporally generated, radiantly luminescent and more subtly radiant. One of the most vital sanctuaries of light in *The Prelude* is the epiphanic moment of Wordsworth's experience of the Convent of Chartreuse in Book 6. The voice of nature which the persona hears in Book 6 proclaims that this monastery should be one special and unique space on earth "devoted to eternity" (6.35). Wordsworth's experience of the Convent of Chartreuse in Book 6 of *The Prelude* is comparable to Arnold's depiction of the same monastery, the Grande Chartreuse, in his poem "Stanzas from the Grande Chartreuse."

In both poetic portraits of the monastery there is an emphasis on the capacity of the persona to achieve a serene wisdom and a spiritual tranquility in this space of hermetic vitality. In both poetic scenarios there is a fusion of the picturesque and the sublime in the depiction of the natural environment surrounding the monastery. J. M. W. Turner's watercolor *Lake Lucerne: the Bay of Uri from above Brunnen* (1842) reveals an ambience similar to the one described in the poetic versions by Wordsworth and Arnold. The cauldron of vapors in the middle of the watercolor, suffusing both the lake and the mountain, clears slightly at the edge of land and sea to affirm a moment of tranquility. A perfect painterly analogue to the final stage of the ascent experienced by Wordsworth's persona and by Arnold's persona in this environment is signified by J. M. W. Turner's engraving *Llanthony Abbey* (1836) which reveals a seemingly spectral or unearthly edifice beyond the mountain precipice and torrents. The pervasively misty aura of this work is not present in Turner's 1794 watercolor of Llanthony Abbey. In this work the abbey, though a ruin, appears beyond the lingering clouds and vapors of the heights as a sublime revelation in the mountain landscape. Turner's Llanthony Abbey and the Grande Chartreuse depicted by Wordsworth and Arnold are permeated by an ethereal serenity which generates and sustains the vitality not only of the architectural creation itself but also of the surrounding landscape.

The positive attributes which Wordsworth ascribes to the Grande Chartreuse and the spiritual ambience of the monastery are reflected in Arnold's poem as well. In Arnold's poem, although the courts are silent, they do contain "splashing icy fountains," which could be considered as a source of the mountain torrents. The silent courts of the monastery in Arnold's poem, as the "courts of mystery" (6.451) in Wordsworth's version and as the individuals in Wordsworth's "Nuns Fret Not at Their Convent's Narrow Room," are content to represent a hermetic sense of space and do not strive to expand into another sphere of existence. The silent courts in Arnold's poem are pleased to participate in a cyclical ritual in which the icy fountains splash water into their stone-carved basins. This ritual, which occurs day and night, represents a seemingly perpetual cycle of renewal and also implies the presence of an inherent capacity to transcend the constraints of everyday mortality.

Another of the most impressive sanctuaries of light in the entire work is the description of the majestic intellect in Book 14. In the ascent of Mt. Snowdon, Wordsworth's persona has a vision of an extraordinary mind that "feeds upon infinity" (14.71) and is "intent to hear / Its voices issuing forth to silent light / In one continuous stream" (14.72–74). As the "Snow" episode in Thomas Mann's *The Magic Mountain* leads to an effusion of light, so this scenario in Book 14 of Wordsworth's *The Prelude* signifies a dynamic luminescence. The presence of the phrase "continuous stream" might even suggest that this sanctuary of light is so vital that it is self-regenerating and self-perpetuating.

The organic nature of Wordsworth's thought and his subjectivity, in which, Hartman argues, "the starting point for authentic reflection is placed in the individual consciousness" (9), enable and stimulate the consciousness of the creative self to burgeon expansively. Such an organically developing consciousness encompasses not only a process of self-revitalization which signifies the dynamic continuity of the self but also a capacity to appreciate and understand the expansiveness of space and time.

In the spirit of his emphasis on the organically developing nature of the majestic intellect, Hartman asserts that *The Prelude* is "a 'Bildungsroman' that takes the child from solipsism to society and from his unconsciously apocalyptic mind, dreaming of an utterly different world, to a sense of realities" (16). Hartman proceeds to describe *The Prelude* as "the epic of civilization, the epic of the emergence of an individual consciousness out of a field of forces that includes imagination, nature, and society" (16). Yet the consciousness that will ultimately come to a sense of realities is still capable of dreaming of utterly different worlds which may border on, interact with, and encompass eternity, the eternal permanences of nature, as well as infinity.

✳ Ernst Theodor Amadeus Hoffmann

In the stories of E. T. A. Hoffmann, one of the most creative and brilliant writers of the nineteenth century, there is a continual interplay of dream and reality, light and darkness, and a vibrant emphasis on the importance of creativity which generates and is influenced by this interplay. Hoffmann, as some other Romantic writers, was interested in portraying a world in which the ordinary and the everyday are connected to and imbued with the extraordinary and the supernatural. The versatility of Hoffmann's own professional experience as a writer, musician, composer, orchestra conductor, lawyer, painter, and essayist is reflected in the polymathic vitality of some of the protagonists in his dynamic stories.

One of Hoffmann's most interesting stories is "Ritter Gluck," which was first published in 1809 in the *Allgemeine musikalische Zeitung* and marked the auspicious beginning of the author's literary career. The person whom the narrator encounters at the beginning of the story asserts that while many people aim to be or strive to be composers, only a few actually achieve such a distinction and enter the kingdom of dreams. And only a small group of those persevere and navigate through the kingdom of dreams to discover truth or the essential truth. This is a not an uncommon claim among genuinely devoted artists and writers of various cultural eras and historical periods that only a few people in society are true artists and creators. Some "artists" are mere entertainers while others are motivated primarily by commercial and financial interests and inclinations. Only a few select and extraordinary individuals are genuine artists and creators who are committed to their work in the spirit of Rilke's statement that an artist should show an absolute devotion and dedication to his creative endeavors.

Hoffmann's "Ritter Gluck" is a narrative about the imaginative interplay of dream and reality, about the possibility of the simultaneous coexistence of multiple, different "realities," about the consecration and devotion of the artist to his creative vision, and about the transcendent power of the imagination. "Ritter Gluck" also celebrates the importance of light and luminescence.

At the beginning of "Ritter Gluck" the narrator admits that he likes to sit in a part of one of the cafes in Berlin which offers him a good view of the people and of the activities while keeping him at a distance (or allowing him to maintain a distance) from the "cacophonic" music of a nearby orchestra. As he sits here the narrator likes to indulge in reveries in which congenial characters appear with whom he can talk about art and life. In this reflective condition, the narrator is undisturbed by the flow and the commotion of the people around him. For him the only agitation is caused by the poorly performed (or less than perfectly performed) music in the vicinity.

As the narrator is musing about the world around him he suddenly notices that there is someone sitting next to him. The narrator shows an immediate and intense interest in this individual. One might wonder whether this person is one of the imaginary companions to which the narrator had just alluded or whether this is a reflection of the self of the narrator. However one interprets this figure, he is certainly a kindred spirit of the narrator. There seems to be an instinctive emotional and intellectual kinship and connectedness between the narrator and the person who has just sat down at the table next to him.

The other individual abruptly goes up to the musicians and asks them to play the overture to *Iphigenia in Aulis*. That he shows considerable respect towards the musicians whom he addresses suggests that this individual has a great admiration for the world of music. As the orchestra plays this individual seems to know the music intimately and perfectly—he acts like the "Kapellmeister" who guides and leads the orchestra. For example, in tapping his left foot, he signals the entrance of the voices; and when he drops his right hand, the allegro begins. This individual, who is clearly an artist of considerable sensitivity, lives and breathes the music. This figure makes the music come alive; he animates the music and creates the musical intensity of the moment.

James McGlathery in his book *E. T. A. Hoffmann* describes the musical enthusiast whom the narrator encounters in "Ritter Gluck" as "deranged" (59). Moreover, McGlathery declares that "the stranger's description of his discovery of truth suggests that his sojourn in the land of dreams was in reality a succumbing to benign madness" (59). While McGlathery's discussion of Hoffmann's work is generally very effective, the above statements seem rather too critical of this highly sensitive individual who certainly represents the artistic and creative elite in this society and in Hoffmann's work. The individual who is so creative in his depiction of how truth is revealed to him (through the bright eye which pours forth melodies) is also a very talented musician who knows the works of the composer Gluck intimately.

Perhaps this distinctive character seems somewhat "deranged" to the world of everyday reality. But in the context of the aesthetic world which Hoffmann creates, this individual is an eminent, though somewhat unusual, representative of artistic genius and creative capacity. Like the Archivist Lindhorst in Hoffmann's "The Golden Pot," this creative individual in "Ritter Gluck," who claims ultimately that he is Gluck, is an extraordinarily imaginative and aesthetically vital person. The point which "Ritter Gluck" ultimately makes (and which is equally relevant for the situation of the Archivist Lindhorst in "The Golden Pot"), and with which the author appears instinctively to agree, is that he only seems crazy or mad to a society which does not have a generally sensitive appreciation for and understanding of music and art.

As this artistic individual in "Ritter Gluck" is guiding the orchestra, his dynamic emotional connection to the music is clearly evident. This is reinforced by the emotionally intense language which is used throughout this passage. For example, a richly burning glow flushed his cheeks and a dynamic inner storm kindled his wild expression. As the music of the orchestra concludes, the artistic individual is described as seeming to awaken from a dream. The dream was the intense musical moment which this individual experienced as he subtly and dynamically guided the orchestra.

When this artistic individual and the narrator go into a room to talk further, the former opens his outer coat revealing somewhat old-fashioned clothing beneath. The old-fashioned clothing reinforces the unusual nature of this individual and suggests that he belongs to another time period. The description of this old-fashioned dress of Gluck is similar in importance to the depiction of the antiquated clothes of Hendrick Hudson and his exploring party in Washington Irving's "Rip Van Winkle." One might even claim that both Ritter Gluck in "Ritter Gluck" and Hendrick Hudson in "Rip Van Winkle" are returning to their former haunts and familiar places to make sure that their past efforts are being appreciated. Ritter Gluck wants to feel that his beautiful music is still valued. Hendrick Hudson aims to feel that his lovely Hudson River valley is being properly cared for and appreciated.

After a short conversational exchange between the narrator and his companion in "Ritter Gluck," the latter, an exemplary artistic individual (who is only directly revealed at the end of the story as the composer Gluck) gets up and sings a passage from *Iphigenia in Tauris* in a very innovative and novel manner. The narrator is very impressed and realizes that his companion possesses an extraordinary musical ability.

In the ensuing conversation the artistic individual speaks of his devotion to music and suggests that true musical talents are rare. When he says that only a few people ever see the special ivory gate of the kingdom of dreams and that even fewer are able to pass through, he implies the uniqueness of a genuine consecration to a life of music. The artistic individual, Ritter Gluck, culminates his argument by declaring that only a few genuinely vital creators experience the kingdom of dreams and attain a vision of the truth and of eternity. The intensity of this statement is reminiscent of Percy Shelley's assertion in "A Defence of Poetry" (which was written in 1821 and published in 1840) that a poet "participates in the eternal, the infinite, the one" (Perkins 1073). Gluck proceeds to suggest that the individual who achieves this sense of the eternal and the ineffable experiences a moment of considerable illumination in which his soul is bathed with a vital radiance. Such a glorious sanctuary of light perpetually energizes and soothes the soul of the artistic individual.

Ritter Gluck then describes a surrealistic adventure which he had in the kingdom of dreams. Tortured by various pains, he observes rays of light shooting through the darkness—and ultimately he realizes that these rays of light are musical tones which envelop him delightfully. When he awakes from his sufferings he sees a large eye from which tones and melodies are shimmering and streaming forth. The eye sustains him above the swift stream of these melodies so he is not drowned. Gluck says that he saw this eye again at a later time. He was once more in the kingdom of dreams and was listening to the flowers singing together. When a sunflower, who was initially silent, suddenly raised her head, the calyx opened and shone towards him. As rays of light flowed from Gluck to the sunflower, the leaves grew ever bigger and encompassed him in an ecstasy of light. Gluck had found great solace and comfort in nature and in the brilliant radiance of various aspects of the natural environment. Such an aesthetically vital moment represents a sanctuary of light for this individual. This luminescent moment in the kingdom of dreams protects and shelters the artistically sensitive and thoughtful individual from the world of everyday mortality and reality.

This passage in "Ritter Gluck" about the importance of light and about the existence of a sanctuary of light is somewhat reminiscent of the intensity and radiance of the light which is described in the final canto of Dante's *The Divine Comedy*. Like Hoffmann, Dante stresses the rejuvenating power of the light. At one point he writes that he would have been lost if it had not been for the power of the light. Several lines later Dante speaks of a profound and shining depth of light and of the presence of a fiery radiance. While Dante and Hoffmann share a similarly intense linguistic description of the light and of the power of the light, there is a noticeable difference in their luminescent visions. Whereas Dante speaks of the unchanging glory of the triune Deity, Hoffmann offers a more Heraclitean vision of the world, a vision generated and sustained by changing forms and by the transformational vitality of the light.

When the narrator in "Ritter Gluck" encounters the composer a little later near the Brandenburg Gate, he says that he is condemned to wander as his personal destiny and torment. Everyday life in the past has been barren for him because he has been searching for a kindred spirit without apparent success. When the narrator raises the possibility of Gluck's finding a kindred spirit among contemporary artists and composers, Gluck responds that they spend too much time talking about art and do not show enough devotion to genuine creativity. In this passage as in others of the narrative Gluck reveals an intense dedication to his music and to creativity which is reminiscent of the statement by Rainer Maria Rilke that a true artist must consecrate himself or herself to his/her work with the greatest devotion.

Several months later the narrator passes by a theater where Gluck's *Armida* is being performed. By the window of the theater there is a soliloquy in which one individual (none other than Gluck himself) carefully describes to himself significant moments of the musical drama as they are performed. The narrator and Gluck reestablish their acquaintance and proceed to Gluck's house (for he implies that as a spirit he cannot go into the house of another). The exploration of the house to find Gluck's room is analogous to the exploration of the self—this is a symbolic journey through the darkness to a space of inner light. The old-fashioned aspect of Gluck's clothing is reinforced by the antiquated dimension of the household furnishings. Such distinctive furnishings are comprised of old-fashioned chairs, a wall clock with a gilded case, and a broad, heavy mirror which exudes the aura of a past splendor.

As the narrator glances at the piano in the middle of the room he observes further evidence of decay and disuse, for the paper on the stand has become yellow and the inkstand is covered with spiderwebs. Ritter Gluck pulls aside a curtain in a corner of the room and reveals a row of books with golden letters—these are all of Gluck's masterworks. This special room in and of itself (and because of its seclusion and the difficulty of finding it) represents a sanctuary away from the vicissitudes of everyday reality. That the curtain within the room exists to separate the beautiful musical works even further from the world of everyday mortality affirms that this is a very private and special inner sanctum.

The spirit of this pulling aside of the curtain to reveal an inner treasure is comparable to a similar statement in Percy Shelley's "A Defence of Poetry." Shelley writes that poetry "lifts the veil from the hidden beauty of the world" (Perkins 1076). Moreover, "it reproduces all that it represents, and the impersonations clothed in its Elysian light stand thenceforward in the minds of those who have once contemplated them, as memorials of that gentle and exalted content . . . ." The array of Gluck's masterworks do represent the "hidden beauty of the world" which are bathed symbolically, if not literally, in an Elysian light.

In response to the narrator's ejaculation that his companion has Gluck's complete works, the companion merely smiles in a strange manner as the play of muscles in his cheeks distorts his face to that of a subtly frightening mask. Such a mask could reinforce the notion of concealing his identity or it could perhaps represent a mask of death. He takes one of the books, *Armida*, goes to the piano and starts playing the work, even though no notes are written on the pages. Gluck plays his work with great virtuosity and innovative dynamism. When Gluck finishes playing, he is weary and his eyes are closed, as if he is in the kingdom of dreams or in a symbolic death-like state.

Ritter Gluck proceeds to confess to the narrator (to whom he has still not directly revealed his identity) the reason for his existential condition as a wandering spirit. He proclaims that when he came from the kingdom of dreams, from the world of artistic creation he betrayed that which is holy to the unholy and was therefore condemned to wander among the unholy like a departed spirit. In trying to encourage, as many other vital artists have done, some people to appreciate his work who ultimately did not do so and perhaps disdained it, Gluck suffered. Yet, despite this suffering which certainly still plagues his spirit, Gluck shows a remarkable and a resilient musical genius and artistic vitality.

For example, the narrator points out that although 'the allegro' of *Armida* as played by his extraordinary companion had Gluck's main thoughts in it, the companion was exceedingly innovative and introduced new variations and modulations of the original. And when his artistic companion plays the final scene of *Armida* so poignantly, he does so by deviating considerably from the original; yet, the transformed music was the Gluck scene with greater potency. As this exceptionally talented musician plays, he captures the spectrum, the heights and the depths, of human emotion most sensitively. The narrator even feels that the voice of his companion suddenly seems to be that of a young man. This is a very important moment because it suggests that Gluck has found a kindred spirit who appreciated his work and has thereby achieved the renaissance of self for which he was longing and striving. This is the moment when the sunflower raises Ritter Gluck to the eternal and he is emotionally and spiritually revitalized.

In *Hoffmanns Erzählungen: Eine Einführung in das Werk E. T. A. Hoffmanns* Klaus Deterding asserts appropriately that Hoffmann's "Ritter Gluck" contains all of the important themes and issues of his creative work except for the magical. Deterding proceeds to say that a viable appreciation of the story depends on an understanding of the character of Ritter Gluck as "eine Erscheinung, und zwar von etwas—nicht dieses Etwas selbst. . . . Gluck ist 'Erscheinung,' Inkarnation, des Geistes der Musik und der Kunst" (23). Some critics might interpret the figure of Gluck as a real person of mythical vitality who has returned to a world of music to see if his works are still being appreciated and to find a kindred spirit. Other critics might view the figure of Gluck as a specific symbol of the composer Christoph Willibald Gluck who feels intensely and passionately about his work and returns to hear his own work in particular. Still others might consider the figure of Gluck as a symbol of the artist in general who wants to feel that the contemporary society is developing a genuine and a thoughtful appreciation and understanding of significant works of music and art. One might even interpret the figure of Gluck in the story as a manifestation or a hallucination of the narrator who sits at the café in Berlin watching the passersby and listening to the afternoon concert.

At the very end of the story the individual who played *Armida* so beautifully and hauntingly vanishes momentarily. When he reappears he is dressed in rich, old-fashioned garments and says, as he smiles, that he is Ritter Gluck. The smile of Gluck at this moment of personal revelation is profoundly similar to the smile and laughter of the Immortals as described in Hermann Hesse's *Steppenwolf*. The composer Gluck, as many similar artists, creators, and writers in the era of romanticism and in other cultural periods when there has existed a conflict or tension between the artist and the bourgeois, is typically undervalued and devalued by the society in which he lives and works. Such an individual sometimes returns, as does Hendrick Hudson in Washington Irving's "Rip Van Winkle," to a familiar or a beloved landscape or place to try to find a sympathetic soul or kindred spirit who can appreciate and understand his work. Gluck reveals his identity at the end of the narrative because he believes that he has truly discovered such a kindred spirit in the narrator.

The intensity of musical expression and the devotion to musical vitality which are so important in "Ritter Gluck" are of comparable significance in

Hoffmann's "Rat Krespel" ("Councillor Krespel"). Krespel is a multitalented and multifaceted individual who exhibits an extraordinary creative vitality. Musician, violin-maker, architect, creator of miraculous and everyday objects, Krespel has the aura of a creative genius about him. As Cardillac in Hoffmann's "Mademoiselle de Scudery" who finds it difficult to give away lovely and precious jewels which he has made, so Krespel shows a strong inclination to create a beautiful object, a violin, play it for a while, and then put it away so that neither he nor anyone else can touch it. According to the professor, Krespel is also known to take apart special violins to examine their inner structure—if he does not locate what he is looking for, presumably an indication or a sign of the beautiful inner structure or an innovative detail of the inner workings of the instrument, then he casts the pieces into a chest which contains the fragments of other similarly examined musical instruments. Like Cardillac, Krespel is exceedingly devoted to and passionate about his work.

Krespel's daughter, Antonia, as Cardillac's daughter, Madelon, is described as being an angel and as having a seraphic and a lovely character. Antonia is further distinguished for her beautiful voice. At one point in "Rat Krespel" Antonia's voice is depicted as being exceptional and unique, sometimes sounding like the breath of an Aeolian harp and sometimes even like the warbling of a nightingale. However, as delightful as Antonia's voice is, there is sadly a physical danger for her in her singing activity. As with some other Romantic artists, Antonia's artistic vitality is intimately connected to a physical condition which has the potential to threaten her life. For Antonia has an organic weakness in her chest which gives her voice not only its wonderful power but also its transcendent tone and vital resonance. Because of this tragic connection, at one point in the narrative Antonia is warned by her doctor that if she continues to sing, she will die within several months. The beauty of Antonia's voice shapes a temporary sanctuary of gorgeous music and an inner radiance of delightful melodies which illuminate and soothe the soul; sadly, such a sanctuary is only transient because of the physical condition which endangers Antonia's existence and eventually causes her demise.

E. T. A. Hoffmann characterized seven of his stories as *Märchen* or fairy tales. Two of the most prominent and famous of these *Märchen* are "Der goldene Topf" ("The Golden Pot") and "Nussknacker und Mausekönig" ("The Nutcracker"). Hoffmann's "Der goldene Topf" was completed in March, 1814 and published in the autumn of 1814 as the third of four volumes of *Fantasiestücke*. It has been argued effectively by McGlathery and others that the "magical realm" in this story is "that found in Fouqué's *Undine*, namely the realm of elemental spirits" (114-15). In "Der goldene Topf" the world of the artist, represented by the Archivist Lindhorst, Serpentina, and ultimately by Anselmus as well, is contrasted to the world of the bourgeois, represented by Vice-Principal Paulmann, his daughter, Veronica, and others. There exists also a persistent conflict in the story between the Archivist Lindhorst, signifying the realm of elemental and pristine spirits, of goodness, and of light and Frau Rauerin, the old woman peddler, signifying a domain of darkness and evil.

In "Der goldene Topf" ("The Golden Pot") there are numerous references to light and to the importance of light and radiance to counter the forces of darkness and evil. The Archivist Lindhorst and Anselmus are two characters who instinctively and vitally represent goodness and light. Their antithesis is the old woman peddler from the Black Gate who is a character who signifies evil and darkness. From the very first paragraph of "Der goldene Topf" it is evident that one of the major and constant themes of the narrative is the interaction of light and darkness, the conflict between good and evil.

At the beginning of the First Vigil of the narrative Anselmus accidentally runs into a basket of apples and cakes which the old woman is selling at the Black Gate. That Anselmus gives an involuntary shudder as he leaves the immediate vicinity of the accident or incident suggests that he intuitively knows that this woman is a problematic figure and not a representative of goodness and light. Anselmus is saddened by the incident because he had wanted to celebrate Ascension Day with innocent fun.

The light of the surrounding natural environment is radiant, for the waves of the River Elbe are described as golden yellow, while the city of Dresden beyond reveals glistening spires. Despite the presence of this radiance Anselmus laments his fate and his apparent social awkwardness which lead him into various unfortunate mistakes and circumstances. At this moment of self-critical despair, when Anselmus interestingly enough even says that the devil himself had compelled him to run into the accursed apple-basket, he suddenly hears a rustling and a whispering in the leaves of the elder-tree above him.

In listening more intently Anselmus even senses that the sounds are transformed into words. As "a triple harmony of clear crystal bells" (4) seemed to peal above his head, Anselmus sees three little snakes "glittering with green and gold . . . and stretching out their heads to the evening sun" (4). The movements of the three glimmering snakes makes the elder-tree seem as if it represented a profusion of sparkling emeralds. Even before the direct appearance of the snakes, this moment is one of considerable radiance. For the initial words of the snakes suggest that they are slithering through the sunshine while the evening sun glistens over this space.

While Anselmus gazes into the beautiful eyes which look at him with considerable yearning, he is enveloped by the lovely peals of the crystal bells and by the "glittering emeralds . . . flickering around him in a thousand sparkles and sporting in resplendent threads of gold" (5). This is a moment of intense luminescence which fills the soul of Anselmus with a radiant happiness and yearning. This experience is synaesthetic and encompasses multiple senses in an effusion of light and sound: "Flowers and blossoms shed their odours round him, and their odour was like the lordly singing of a thousand softest voices" (5). Their song is born away by the evening clouds as they move towards distant lands. As the light of day vanishes at the end of the First Vigil the three snakes are called away by a voice to return to the Elbe River.

In the Second Vigil of the narrative, Anselmus is crossing the Elbe in a boat when he thinks that he sees the three little snakes swimming in the river and seems to lunge towards them as he asks them to sing once more for him as they did so melodiously when he was under the elder-tree. This abrupt action causes consternation in the boat, and the other parties present are astonished at Anselmus for such seemingly erratic behavior. The Second Vigil displays the conflict between the world of the artist and the world of the bourgeois, between imagination and reality in the being and the soul of Anselmus.

Anselmus believes that he sees the three golden snakes in the waves whispering softly to him. The other people in the boat, Mr. Paulmann and his daughters and Mr. Heerbrand, represent the bourgeois world of everyday reality which challenges, undermines, and undervalues the domain of the imagination and of the artist. In the presence of such conspicuous and stalwart representatives of the bourgeois world, Anselmus is encouraged to believe that what he thought were the precious green snakes in the waves whispering gently to him are really only gleams from the windows of nearby houses. Paulmann and Heerbrand try to assert a rational and realistic explanation for such imaginative wonders as those which Anselmus believes that he experiences emotionally and spiritually.

At the end of the Second Vigil Mr. Heerbrand informs Anselmus of a job opportunity with the Archivist Lindhorst which involves the copying of manuscripts. As Anselmus has an excellent hand and copies documents carefully and skillfully, he is very interested in the position and appears at Lindhorst's door the next day at the appointed hour. However, just as

Anselmus is about to use the doorknocker at Lindhorst's house, it is abruptly transformed into the face of the old woman from the Black Gate who shrieks at him in such a terrifying manner that he swoons and is unable to enter. This episode reinforces the point that the life of Anselmus signifies a struggle between the forces of good and evil: one might even say that the dimensions of good and evil, of light and darkness, are striving consistently and intensively to attain the soul of Anselmus.

At the beginning of the Third Vigil of "The Golden Pot" the Archivist Lindhorst tells a story about his ancestry which pulsates with light and with love. In the story, for example, when the youth Phosphorus enters a vale, his presence is described as a brilliant and vital light. And when Phosphorus kisses the lily, she becomes a flame and seems filled with an effusively radiant light. At the end of Lindhorst's story when the lily is freed, Phosphorus embraces her, and she becomes the queen of the vale. This vale represents a sanctuary of considerable radiance. Most of the other individuals who are at the narrative presentation by Lindhorst laugh at the distinctive and seemingly incredible details in disbelief. However, Anselmus responds differently and more thoughtfully, suggesting that he, unlike the others, has a poetic and a sensitive soul as well as an instinctive appreciation of the unusual circumstances which the Archivist Lindhorst relates. At the end of the Third Vigil, Anselmus is officially introduced to the Archivist Lindhorst as the individual who would be willing to copy his rare manuscripts.

In the Fourth Vigil, the author addresses the reader and encourages him to realize the truth of the notion (and to respect the notion) that he is "in the faery region of glorious wonders, where both rapture and horror may be evoked" (18). Hoffmann suggests that such a fairy realm is often revealed to us in our dreams. He even proceeds to say that such an extraordinary realm is really closer to us than we might normally think or imagine. Such a thought is very similar to the idea expressed by Nathaniel Hawthorne in "Rappacini's Daughter" that truth is often revealed to us in our dreams and reveries.

After the meeting with the Archivist Lindhorst, Anselmus becomes somewhat estranged from everyday reality and its demands and expectations, for he feels a strange force within him. In one of his wanderings Anselmus happens to return to the elder-bush which had previously spawned such interesting images and delightful visions. As he sits under the tree, the visions of previous bliss and ecstasy are revived. Anselmus proceeds to embrace the tree and to express his ardent love for the lovely snake. Even though Anselmus proclaims his love for Serpentina in the most vital and effusive manner, there is no audible or perceptible response except for the rustling of the leaves.

Anselmus continues to return to the elder-bush at other times to express his deep love for the beautiful little golden snake. The use of the word "golden" as an attribute for the snake, for Serpentina, could suggest that she signifies a sanctuary of light and beauty in and of herself. Serpentina as an individual animate being has the capacity to represent a sanctuary of lovely luminescence which may enrapture and delight Anselmus.

On one particular occasion when Anselmus addresses the elder-bush in a very loving and emotionally dynamic manner he is met by the Archivist Lindhorst. When Lindhorst inquires why Anselmus has not come to his house to copy any manuscripts, Anselmus reveals the profound and abiding love which he has for the green and gold snake, the eternal beloved of his soul. In expressing the intensity of his love for the snake and in narrating the events for Lindhorst which had happened on Ascension Day, Anselmus makes a point of saying that he does not care whether the Archivist thinks him sane or not. This is a sign that the artistic side of Anselmus triumphs in this scenario—he will be devoted to love, beauty, and truth regardless of the response or reaction of the everyday world. Of course, at this point in the narrative Anselmus does not yet realize that the Archivist Lindhorst is an eminent representative of and supreme symbol of the artistic world.

The Archivist Lindhorst responds that the gold-green snakes are his three daughters and that he already knew that Anselmus was in love with Serpentina, who is his youngest daughter. At this point in the narrative there is the suggestion that Anselmus felt as though he instinctively knew this already. This implies a subtle connection between Anselmus and the Lindhorst family. Such a connection, of a strong sense of connectedness, is further reinforced when Lindhorst holds a gleaming stone before Anselmus. The radiant stone becomes a mirror which reveals the three gold-green snakes dancing and twisting around in an array of glittering forms and crystalline tones. One of the snakes, with her dark-blue eyes seemingly full of desire, speaks to Anselmus and asks him if he believes in her. After Anselmus responds briefly with a depth of emotion, Lindhorst breathes on the mirror and the image ceases. Lindhorst also declares that Anselmus may see his daughter often enough if he comes to work for him and copy the manuscripts carefully and diligently.

As the Archivist and Anselmus say farewell for the evening, the Archivist suggests that the woman from Black Gate is a hostile figure and his nemesis. Lindhorst proceeds to give Anselmus a bottle of a yellow liquid which he can use on the door-knocker if it appears again as the face of the woman from the Black Gate and tries to scare him away from his sacred work and obligation.

The interest of Anselmus in working for the Archivist to copy the precious manuscripts is intensified not only because he is fascinated by the copying of rare manuscripts but especially because he knows that it is probable that he will encounter Serpentina in the sanctuary of the Archivist Lindhorst's house.

In the Fifth Vigil, there is a noteworthy conversation between Mr. Paulmann and Mr. Heerbrand about Anselmus and his future prospects. Paulmann, while acknowledging that Anselmus is a talented classical scholar, declares that he is disappointed because he does not apply himself properly and does not follow his advice. Heerbrand, on the other hand, defends Anselmus, suggesting that he might even become a Court Councillor someday. Veronica, Paulmann's daughter, happens to overhear this conversation and is quietly thrilled by the prediction of a very positive future for Anselmus. Veronica imagines that Anselmus will be a Councillor someday and that she will be the Councillor's wife. Veronica even admits to the Frau Rauerin, the old woman of the Black Gate, that she loves Anselmus. The woman, a dabbler in black magic who would do anything to injure or undermine the Archivist Lindhorst, promises to help Veronica vanquish Archivist Lindhorst and the green snake and to enable her to enchant Anselmus so that she will become his wife.

In the Sixth Vigil Anselmus begins his important work with the Archivist Lindhorst. It is noteworthy that Anselmus feels instinctively that if he performs his work proficiently for Lindhorst then he will be rewarded with the love of Lindhorst's daughter, Serpentina. After Anselmus enters the house of Lindhorst he is taken to a gorgeous conservatory which has an aura of spatial expansiveness and sensory exuberance about it. Moreover, the conservatory is filled with a lovely radiance. The magical light of this beautiful sanctuary seems to arise from this extraordinary space for there is no window present which can allow the entrance of light from the outside. Anselmus experiences a sense of spatial expansiveness in this environment when he observes the bushes and trees, for "long avenues appeared to open into remote distance" (31). The sensory abundance of the moment is manifest in the fact that Anselmus not only views beautiful objects (from marble fountains to the fire-lilies) and listens to delightful murmurs of unusual voices but also is enchanted by exotic fragrances.

The house of the Archivist Lindhorst is a paradise of gorgeous flowers, plants, objects, fragrances, and melodies. One might say that the house itself is characterized by an inner sense or aura of spatial expansiveness. For when the Archivist Lindhorst shows Anselmus more of the house after the sojourn in the conservatory, he is described as going through many more rooms with exquisite and aesthetically interesting and stimulating colors and decorations. In one distinctive room, in particular, there were "gold-bronze trunks of high palm-trees" (32) rising from the walls and weaving "their colossal leaves, glittering like bright emeralds" (32) towards the ceiling. In the middle of this room is the golden pot.

The golden pot, which rests on a porphyry plate on three bronze Egyptian lions, is an extraordinarily beautiful and luminescent object which seems to contain on its surface of polished gold "a thousand gleaming reflections" (32) of various shapes. Anselmus even believes that he observes Serpentina in the radiant reflections gazing at him. However, Lindhorst appears to deflect such intensive observation by saying that Serpentina is actually in another part of the house practicing on the harpsichord.

The Archivist Lindhorst then proceeds to take Anselmus to a library in the house where he will copy the precious manuscripts. As Anselmus works on the manuscript which the Archivist gives him to copy, he feels increasingly more at home in the isolated room. The diligence and careful work of Anselmus is motivated by his love for Serpentina and by her faith in him. For as Anselmus copies the manuscript, he believes that he hears a crystal murmuring in the room which encourages him to be steadfast and to believe that he is being assisted in his labors by the spiritual presence of Serpentina.

When Lindhorst addresses Anselmus at the end of the Sixth Vigil, he speaks of the love which Serpentina has for Anselmus, of the destiny which he and Serpentina appear to share and which will be fulfilled in the future, and of his ultimate reception of the golden pot, which is her dowry. The Archivist also emphasizes that Anselmus is confronted by evil forces and can only survive if he believes in his own inner strength and in the love which he shares with Serpentina. One of the most important concluding points which Lindhorst makes is that if Anselmus carries the love and spirit of Serpentina within his heart and soul, he will overcome all of the negative forces around him and will ultimately achieve eternal happiness. The Archivist also asserts that Anselmus will experience the wonders of the golden pot if he develops and strengthens his love for Serpentina. As Anselmus leaves the house of Lindhorst at the end of the day, he admits to himself that he has the most profound love for Serpentina and will do everything he can to fulfill his commitment and devotion to her.

In the Seventh Vigil, the image of the light is a negative one. For the light in this instance is a ring of fire which has been conjured by Frau Rauerin, the woman from the Black Gate, who is assisting Veronica to cast a spell on Anselmus. Of course, this woman from the Black Gate, who is presented as an evil being, is also trying to use Veronica's interest in Anselmus to further her own destructive plans against the Archivist Lindhorst. The small mirror which Veronica receives from Frau Rauerin also streams forth "fiery beams" (41). These are beams which only give the illusion of genuine light and warmth, but which are innately cold sources of light, motivated by an inner darkness and emptiness of soul.

At the beginning of the Eighth Vigil, the considerable happiness and bliss of Anselmus is described. Anselmus admits that the several days during which he has been working on manuscripts at the house of the Archivist Lindhorst and during which he has consistently heard the consoling words of Serpentina and occasionally felt her gentle breath have been the happiest of his entire life. Anselmus even feels as if he does not have any notable concerns or worries in his everyday life. Moreover, he senses that a new life is beginning for him, a new life which is characterized by an aura of "serene sunny splendour" (42) and which reveals to him the secrets of a higher world.

It is interesting that the Archivist Lindhorst appears just at the moment when Anselmus finishes the final character of a manuscript so that he may give him another to copy. This event could suggest an instinctive connectedness between Lindhorst and Anselmus; it could even imply that Lindhorst is always aware of the progress which Anselmus makes in copying the manuscripts and is perhaps even actively guiding the process. It is noteworthy that Lindhorst typically wears a dressing-gown filled with images of brilliant flowers, so that he becomes a symbol of vernal dynamism and colorful energy.

On one particular day, the Archivist takes Anselmus once again through the halls and chambers which he had seen on his first visit. As before, Anselmus is amazed at the great beauty of the garden and of various objects and images in this lovely place. The themes of visual clarity, of visual integrity, and of visual illusion are all important in this scenario, for Anselmus now observes that many of the objects which he thought were flowers are actually insects gleaming with glorious colors. Moreover, Anselmus also observes that some of the beings which he thought were birds are actually beautiful flowers spreading their lovely fragrances over the entire space and inspiring in him an insatiable longing. The Archivist then takes Anselmus into the azure chamber, which now contains, instead of the golden pot and its porphyry stand, a special table in velvet where Anselmus will work on a new manuscript. The Archivist Lindhorst praises the work which Anselmus has done so far and now gives him a new and even more demanding challenge. The new work for

Anselmus deals with the "transcribing or rather painting of certain works, written in a peculiar character" (43).

Lindhorst stresses the necessity of absolute precision and meticulous attentiveness in this task. For if Anselmus makes the slightest mistake he will experience considerable misfortune. However, Lindhorst also encourages Anselmus to realize that if he has faith in his love for Serpentina, he will prevail in this daunting task. Anselmus feels inspired by the music of the garden, for he hears the same crystal tones which he did before on Ascension Day when he first encountered Serpentina in the elder-bush. These crystal tones are a sign of the presence of Serpentina, who encourages and motivates Anselmus in his work—Serpentina tells him that he will win her through his faith and devoted love. Serpentina also mentions that when she brings him the golden pot, they will be forever happy in a sanctuary of luminescent bliss.

Anselmus is as entranced by Serpentina as ever and exclaims that as long as he has her love he does not care about the everyday world. The love which Serpentina and Anselmus share is reminiscent of the intensity and vitality of the love expressed in Elizabeth Barrett Browning's poem "How Do I Love Thee." The powerful, pure, unconditional, and eternal love which E. B. Browning portrays in her poem captures perfectly the spirit and the depth of the love between Anselmus and Serpentina. In listening intently to every word which Serpentina expresses in this Vigil Anselmus feels revitalized for each word seems to fill his soul with a ray of light. Listening to Serpentina and taking in and accepting the light of her being and her words transforms Anselmus himself into a sanctuary of light. One might even say that both Serpentina and Anselmus represent two animate sanctuaries of light which ultimately coalesce into one beautifully melodious and aesthetically cohesive luminescent vision.

Serpentina proceeds to tell the story of her father and of the race of salamanders from which he is descended. In her narrative Serpentina articulates the importance of the kind of character of her beloved, which Prince Phosphorus proclaimed should be a condition of marriage to her and to both of her sisters. Serpentina describes this special individual as having a "child-like poetic character" (47), a noble heart, a capacity to understand her romantic song, and a capacity to appreciate the extraordinary and the uncommon in everyday life. The ultimate reward for the individual who has these qualities and who loves Serpentina will be a life of sustained happiness and bliss in Atlantis. Serpentina also warns Anselmus against the treacherousness and maliciousness of the old woman from the Black Gate, who is a hostile spirit and the nemesis of the Archivist Lindhorst and who is trying to gain possession of the golden pot. It is noteworthy that Serpentina emphasizes to Anselmus that his commitment to their love and his child-like poetic character will sustain him against the destructive and evil tendencies of Frau Rauerin, the woman from the Black Gate.

Anselmus is enraptured by the delightful, melodious presence of Serpentina. Whether Anselmus actually experiences the presence of Serpentina in this episode or merely dreams vitally and exuberantly of her presence is not clear. For when Anselmus awakes as if from a dream, Serpentina is no longer there. Anselmus is especially anxious because he suddenly realizes that he has not copied a single character on this occasion. The emotional and spiritual closeness of Anselmus to Serpentina and to Lindhorst is exemplified by the fact that even though Anselmus has not copied anything (or feels that he has not copied anything) on this occasion, the manuscript has been completely finished. The manuscript which Anselmus had to copy was the story which Serpentina related about her father, her mother, herself, and her sisters. By listening so attentively, so sensitively, and so thoughtfully and by loving Serpentina and by believing so devotedly in his love for her, Anselmus has completed the necessary work.

In the initial part of the Ninth Vigil, Anselmus is described as having withdrawn from the concerns and demands of everyday life and of being devoted to Serpentina and to the magical kingdom which the Archivist Lindhorst created. However, suddenly Anselmus begins thinking rather actively about Veronica and his feelings for her—in his "dream" of her she discourages him from being lured by fantastic visions. Conrector Paulmann invites Anselmus to come to his house where his daughter, Veronica, is fashionably dressed and very welcoming. In the alluring and especially attractive presence of Veronica, Anselmus is encouraged to forget about Serpentina. There is a strident conflict within Anselmus, a virulent struggle between the love of Serpentina and the allure of Veronica. In this scenario, Veronica triumphs by her physical attractiveness and by her conspicuous coquettishness to such an extent that Anselmus senses that he has only really loved Veronica and not Serpentina. The clash in the soul of Anselmus between the romantic and the realistic, between the artist and the bourgeois, temporarily shows the triumph of the latter. As Anselmus looks into the eyes of Veronica, which are full of love and yearning, he imagines that he will marry her someday.

After consuming some of the punch which was just prepared Anselmus experiences distinctive visions reflecting recent events—for example, he sees Lindhorst, in his dressing gown glistening like phosphorus, in the lovely azure chamber in his house and thinks about Serpentina. Anselmus even proclaims to Paulmann and Heerbrand that the Archivist Lindhorst is really a salamander who lives here in Dresden with his three daughters, the three gold-green snakes who try to lure young people "like so many sirens" (52). This statement is interesting because it suggests that in the presence of Veronica and in a resolutely bourgeois ambience such as the house of Conrector Paulmann, the love and devotion of Serpentina will inevitably be misinterpreted and misunderstood. Anselmus, who formerly spoke of Serpentina and of his love for her in glowing terms, now describes such love as lust and deceptive enchantment. It is interesting that Heerbrand affirms the claim of Anselmus that Lindhorst is a salamander with a capacity for creating light and fire, suggesting that he is more imaginatively inclined and not as bound to the bourgeois realm as Paulmann certainly is. Conrector Paulmann is distressfully astonished at the comments by Anselmus and Heerbrand about the Archivist Lindhorst and his strange capacities and believes that they are both raving mad. It is noteworthy that in the course of this conversation Anselmus even describes his love for Serpentina and his disdain for Liese, the Frau Rauerin, as an evil force. Veronica is, of course, very displeased to hear such comments and tries to challenge them vehemently. At the end of this conversational exchange, the intensity and creativity of which is at least partially kindled by the alcoholic essences and vapors, Anselmus returns home in the belief that he will marry Veronica in the near future. Despite his occasional reflections about Serpentina in the course of the evening and despite the apparent presence, whether literal or symbolic, of Lindhorst at this conversation in the punch bowl and in the form of the little manikin who reminds Anselmus to come to work for Lindhorst again tomorrow, the allure and enchantment of Veronica seems to have triumphed, at least temporarily.

When Anselmus returns to the house of the Archivist Lindhorst the next day to continue his copying of manuscripts, everything appears different, more ordinary, and less magical than before. The objects are less interesting, the colors less radiant, and the rooms much less captivating than they were on previous occasions. Presumably, the contact with Veronica, her world of bourgeois reality and everyday concerns, on the previous day has encroached upon Anselmus' sense of the magical aspect of the inner, aesthetically beautiful space of the house of Lindhorst. Aware of the struggle within the soul of Anselmus between his love for Serpentina and his interest in Veronica, the Archivist Lindhorst proclaims to his young protégé that he was actually sitting for a while in the punch bowl yesterday evening. Lindhorst wants to make Anselmus aware of the fact that he is watching and trying to guide him in his love for Serpentina, that he is trying to protect him from the guiles and allurements of Veronica and her world. However, Anselmus is not buying into Lindhorst's assertions in this episode, and he has seemingly entered the house today with a diminished love for Serpentina. The crucial indication of a diminished love for Serpentina and a diminished appreciation of Lindhorst is that Anselmus is not as careful with the copying as he should be and allows a blot of ink, despite the severe admonitions of his employer, to fall upon the original. Such a conspicuous mistake, which signifies the fact that the love and devotion of Anselmus is not completely directed towards Serpentina, causes an uproar and a clash of diametrically opposed forces in the room. As a result of this turbulence, at the end of the Ninth Vigil Anselmus finds himself trapped in a crystal bottle on a shelf of Lindhorst's library.

In the Tenth Vigil, Anselmus, imprisoned in the bottle, gains a sense of hope and faith when he believes that he hears the voice of Serpentina speaking to him and encouraging him to persevere. Then there is a dynamic and ferocious struggle between the Archivist Lindhorst and the woman from the Black Gate, who has managed to enter the premises. At the end of the Tenth Vigil, the Archivist generously says to Anselmus that his loss of faith, exemplified by his sudden interest in Veronica, was not his fault but was instead a sign of the influence of destructive and negative forces. The Archivist Lindhorst is pleased with Anselmus and declares that he has proved his loyalty to Serpentina through this ordeal and is now free and no longer trapped. In the last paragraph of the Tenth Vigil, the happiness of Anselmus and Serpentina is restored. Anselmus hears a melodious ringing of bells, after which the glass which encloses him is broken and he is able to embrace Serpentina.

In the Eleventh Vigil Veronica, while admitting that she had once entertained an affection for Anselmus, decides to accept the marriage proposal of Heerbrand, who has been made a Hofrat, or Counsellor. Both Veronica and the now Counsellor Heerbrand wish Anselmus well, but they both realize that they belong instinctively to another world and to another realm of existence. At the end of the Eleventh Vigil, Veronica has accomplished her dream—she is sitting at the window of her new home watching the passersby and being admired by them in return. Veronica desired a life of superficial elegance and glittering superficiality, which she has now attained.

At the beginning of the Twelfth Vigil, the narrator acknowledges the difficulty of articulating the wonderful experiences and the shared happiness of Anselmus and Serpentina. The narrator does not feel that he can adequately describe in words the joyous new life of Anselmus and Serpentina in Atlantis. In a state of emotional turmoil and uncertainty about how to complete his work, the narrator receives a note from the Archivist Lindhorst who says that he can assist him in the final stages of his literary endeavor. When the narrator meets with Lindhorst he is given a special elixir after which he develops a heightened sensitivity for the various objects and colors in the room and experiences a radiant vision.

The narrator believes that the emerald leaves of the palm trees in the room are whispering of wonders which are also expressed in the distant melodies of a harp. The narrator also perceives the dynamic azure of the walls mingling with and interspersed by glorious rays of light which ultimately reveals a grove in which one sees Anselmus. The beautiful flowers (hyacinths, tulips, and roses), bushes, and trees are effulgently vital. Serpentina appears carrying the golden pot "from which a bright lily has sprung" (68–69). As Serpentina and Anselmus embrace lovingly, they are enveloped by a dynamic luminescence which permeates all of the surrounding natural environment. This moment is a sanctuary of glorious radiance and effulgent light which energizes and enlivens various aspects of the natural environment: for example, the leaves of the trees rustle more vigorously and the brooks babble more melodically. This is a sanctuary of luminescent vitality, harmony, and peacefulness.

Armand de Loecker asserts in *Zwischen Atlantis und Frankfurt: Märchendichtung und Goldenes Zeitalter bei E. T. A. Hoffmann* that the inner development of Anselmus and the array of his experiences "führen im Schlusskapitel zu einer Apotheose hin" (62). De Loecker proclaims that the end of the narrative represents "die eigentliche Erfüllung der Sehnsucht, das Zusammensein von Anselmus und Serpentina in Atlantis" (66). The end of the story signifies the fulfillment of the longing which Anselmus and Serpentina reveal and affirms their eternal union in Atlantis. The "goldenes Zeitalter" (66) is discovered in "dem poetischen Erleben dieser Welt als kosmische Harmonie" (66). The poetic and imaginative conception of the world affirms the presence of a golden age of existence permeated by a sense of luminescent vitality and cosmic harmony.

K. Deterding describes in *Hoffmanns Erzählungen: Eine Einführung in das Werk E. T. A. Hoffmanns* the narrator's observation of Anselmus in this blissful paradise very effectively: "In einer rauschhaften Synästhesie von Farben, Duften, Pflanzen, Tieren, Sonne, und Wasser spricht die Natur nun mit dem, der sie durchwandelt: mit Anselmus" (59). Deterding proceeds to make the following interesting observation about the ending of the narrative: "Im Einswerden der Töne . . . , der Pflanzen, Dinge, und Wesen in dem wundersamen Garten von Atlantis werden auch die Liebenden eins . . . . Das steigert bis zur 'Verklärung' des Anselmus im 'Strahlenglanz'" (80). The existence which Anselmus and Serpentina enjoy in Atlantis is in the spirit of a Garden of Eden. There is a golden atmosphere, an atmosphere of golden light, here which suffuses this blissful domain and perpetually revitalizes the spirit of love and faith.

In addressing Serpentina at this moment of colorful and sensory exuberance, Anselmus expresses the depth of his love for her: "Belief in you, love of you has unfolded to my soul the inmost spirit of nature" (69). Anselmus proceeds to say that Serpentina brought him the lily "which sprang from gold, from the primeval force of the world" (69) which represents "knowledge of the sacred harmony of all beings" (69). In proclaiming his ardent love for Serpentina, Anselmus also asserts the importance of the knowledge which the lily brings and which the presence of the lily enables him to achieve. Anselmus even states that his eternal happiness will be motivated by the knowledge which the lily brings. Such an awareness signifies a sensitive appreciation and understanding of the beautiful natural environment. This condition of love and knowledge is presented as a perpetual sanctuary of light, for Anselmus proclaims that the golden blossoms of the lily will never fade.

In E. T. A. Hoffmann: Der goldene Topf Paul-Wolfgang Wührl offers an interesting discussion about the mythological dimensions of Hoffmann's "Der goldene Topf." Wührl views Hoffmann's story in the context of other mythological conceptions of romantic writers. One of the central issues for some of these writers was an attempt to create or recreate a golden age. Of Hoffmann's interest in this Wührl writes: "Als isolierte Erzählschicht gesehen, nehmen die Einschube in die dritte, achte, und zwölfte Vigilie die von den Frühromantikern hochgeschätzte antike Utopie von der Rückkehr ins Goldene Zeitalter auf, die Platon in seiner Erzählung von Atlantis in die Mythologie eingeführt hatte" (74). Wührl also suggests that Anselmus celebrates a "mystische Hochzeit" (75), a mystical marriage, with Serpentina in Atlantis, an event which has a symbolic significance as representing the sacred harmony of all things.

Wührl also points out interesting similarities and parallels between Hoffmann's "Der goldene Topf" and Novalis' Heinrich von Ofterdingen. Both Hoffmann and Novalis narrate the story of a young man who goes through different developmental stages before achieving the status of a creator or a poet. Wührl also states that the "Einweihung in die Dichtkunst" (75) in both works culminates in an apotheosis of poetry (75). Intimately connected with the protagonist's development of his creative vitality is a development of a heightened self-awareness and intuitive understanding of the world around him. Both Anselmus in "Der goldene Topf" and Heinrich in *Heinrich von Ofterdingen* ultimately transcend the constraints and limitations of everyday mortality and enter the "Reich der Poesie" at the end of their respective stories.

After such a blissful vision of the eternal happiness of Anselmus and Serpentina and of the lovely natural surroundings of their life together on their estate in Atlantis, the narrator returns to a sense of reality and laments that he will now have to confront the tribulations of everyday life. Lindhorst tries to give the narrator some encouraging advice by saying that as he has just been in Atlantis he should feel that he too has a piece of land there as the poetic property of his mind. The final statement of the narrative reaffirms that the happiness of Anselmus exists in poetry, in the power of the imagination, which reveals the sacred harmony of all things as a secret of nature. The radiant beauty and eternal loveliness of the estate of Serpentina and Anselmus is not diminished at all by the fact that it could be interpreted as a landscape of the mind. Atlantis is a sanctuary of light and love beyond the ravages and vicissitudes of everyday mortality and an inspirational and a suitable place for sensitive, artistic, poetic, and thoughtful souls.

In Hoffmann's "Der Sandmann" ("The Sandman," November, 1815; published in the autumn of 1816 in the first of the two volumes of *Nachtstücke*), the light plays a somewhat less prominent and less positive role than in the other stories discussed so far. For example, there is an abundance of light at Professor Spalanzani's party, where Olimpia makes her first public appearance and captivates the attention of Nathaniel. The lights are gleaming in the room—the glimmer of light seems to reinforce the superficial aspect of Olimpia, who is viewed by some of the people attending the party as stiff and mechanical. It is interesting that Nathaniel, looking at Olimpia playing the piano from the back of the room, cannot observe her features distinctly in the bright light of the candles. When Nathaniel shows his devotion to and adoration of Olimpia during the course of the evening, he notices that some individuals laugh at him, yet he ignores their derision and continues his considerable admiration of Olimpia and her consistently displayed characteristics.

Nathaniel is so enchanted with and by Olimpia that when one of his friends seems to criticize her on another occasion as being a wax doll, he is on the verge of becoming enraged, but controls himself, gaining solace in the fact that the friend is not a rival for the love of Olimpia. In defending his affection for Olimpia, Nathaniel proclaims that her gaze radiated through his heart and mind. Nathaniel is so enraptured by the thought and by the presence of Olimpia that he forgets about Clara and his family and friends and concentrates his energies on her and his love for her.

One day, Nathaniel finds a special ring which he wants to give to Olimpia as a sign of his devotion. When Nathaniel enters Spalanzani's house he hears a violent conflict between Spalanzani and Coppelius regarding a female figure. As Coppelius/Coppola leaves the room with the figure of Olimpia over his shoulder and her feet dangling, Nathaniel notices her lifeless eyes and realizes that she is merely a doll. Spalanzani even laments in the presence of Nathaniel that Coppola has stolen his best automaton. After the distraught Spalanzani throws the eyes of the doll against the chest of Nathaniel, he is in utter despair and appears to be mad. The story ends with the tragic demise of the unhappy and tormented Nathaniel, who was enchanted by the glitter and superficial radiance of a lifeless doll.

At the end of "The Sandman" Nathaniel tragically jumps off the city hall tower before his marriage to Clara. McGlathery effectively describes the ill-fated existence of Nathaniel, saying that "Nathaniel's planned marriage to Clara is subverted by his involvement with a sinister alchemist and builder of robots named Coppelius" (71). Coppelius is an evil character, or perhaps one should say a character with an evil aura about him, who interferes diabolically with Nathaniel's life and "engineers his infatuation with a robot named Olimpia that he and Nathaniel's physics professor pass off as the professor's daughter" (71). The especially sinister nature of Coppelius is apparent as Nathaniel associates him with the Sandman, who aims to steal children's eyes, as he was told in his childhood. To steal the eyes of children is to deprive them of their radiance and to abscond with their souls, an aspiration which various fiendish or devil-like characters certainly may be said to have and to cherish.

Hoffmann's "Nussknacker und Mausekönig" ("The Nutcracker and the King of Mice," completed November, 1816; published in the autumn of 1816 in a collection of fairy tales by Fouque, Hoffmann, and Contessa; then published in *Die Serapionsbrüder*, Volume 1) reveals various interesting similarities to such fairy tales as "Sleeping Beauty" and "Beauty and the Beast." In one part of Hoffmann's story a handsome young man is changed into a physically ugly nutcracker doll by a woman seeking revenge on a royal personage with a lovely daughter. The young man can only be returned to his former physical appearance by the supreme devotion and attentiveness of a person who can vanquish the vengeful woman's problematic son. In "Sleeping Beauty," there is the theme of a woman acting in a vengeful and negative manner towards the king of a beautiful daughter; in "Beauty and the Beast," the young woman develops an affection for the "beast" despite his physically unappealing appearance.

James McGlathery makes the excellent point that one key difference between Hoffmann's nutcracker story and literary fairy tales is that in the former "the central figure receives an explanation of the magical realm's entry into his or her life from another character in the story" (118-19). The young Marie Stahlbaum hears the fairy tale about the hard nut from her godfather Drosselmeier when she is recovering from her unfortunate injury. Marie tries to distinguish herself from the Princess Pirlipat by saying that she, unlike the Princess, would not reject a young man if he were not physically handsome. When Marie proclaims her love for the ugly nutcracker doll, the young Drosselmeier appears at the front door. For with Marie's lovely comment he has been released from his enchantment.

Music played a very important role in Hoffmann's life and art. Hoffmann is especially interested in music which is inspired by and reflects the vitality of nature's mysticism. Hoffmann believed that some of the most powerful music of Haydn, Mozart, and Beethoven was inspired by "a wondrous striving to discern the governing force of the enlivening spirit of nature, indeed our existence in that spirit, our superterrestrial spiritual homeland" (McGlathery 39).

At the beginning of Hoffmann's "The Nutcracker" it is Christmas eve at the home of the Stahlbaum family. The children of the family are not allowed to enter certain drawing-rooms in the house because of the festive preparations which are occurring there. In addition to the family members, Dr. Stahlbaum, his wife, and three children (Marie, Fritz, and Louise), Godpapa Drosselmeier is present for the holiday celebration. One of the first references in the narrative to a special place of light and natural beauty is Marie's statement on page 2 that Godpapa Drosselmeier told her about such a place. Marie says that he described "a beautiful garden with a great lake in it, and beautiful swans swimming about with great gold collars, singing lovely music" (72). There is also a lovely little girl in the scene who walks through the garden to the lake and feeds the swans. Marie's more realistic older brother, Fritz, tries to discourage her from thinking that the little girl in the story would have fed the swans cake and shortbread. However, Marie has a special innocence about her which nurtures a delightful imagination and enables her to believe such tales about the swans. At the end of the first section, entitled "Christmas Eve," silvery bells clang and the drawing-room doors are opened as a brilliant light shines from the room. This is the moment when the Stahlbaum children are invited to see their presents.

In the second section, "Christmas Presents," the beautiful Christmas tree is described as bearing "many apples of silver and gold" (73) as well as many other delightful items to eat and to admire. This splendid tree is presented as a tree of radiance, for "in all the recesses of its spreading branches hundreds of little tapers glittered like stars" (73). The gorgeous tree signifies a sanctuary of light which creates and sustains an atmosphere of festive illumination.

Godpapa Drosselmeier's Christmas present is also soon displayed. When a curtain is drawn, a "lordly castle with a great many shining windows and golden towers" (74) is revealed. In addition to the chime of bells which is heard, another notable feature is the considerable luminescence in the central hall. There are many small figures walking around in the castle environment. The scenario also contains a miniature version of Godpapa Drosselmeier.

In the next section, "Marie's Pet and Protégé," Marie notices the presence of a little man who seems very kind and benevolent and is dressed in the same manner as Godpapa Drosselmeier. It is explained to Marie that this little man beside the tree is "the Nutcracker." Marie seems especially interested in the Nutcracker and even addresses him as if he were an animate being. When the Nutcracker loses several teeth as he is trying to crack a very hard nut and looks at Marie mournfully, she shows genuine affection and concern for him and wants to protect him from further activity.

In the fourth section, entitled "Wonderful Events," Marie stays up especially late to play with her new doll and other gifts as well as to take care of the Nutcracker. Marie, while realizing that he is a wooden doll, promises the Nutcracker to nurse him until he is better. After Marie puts the bed with the Nutcracker in it on the top shelf of the special cupboard with various toys, a rustling and a whispering noise begins and increases rapidly. Marie is astonished and even frightened by this scenario, for the world of the Christmas toys comes alive. At one point Marie thinks that she sees many small lights glittering from out of the woodwork; however, these are actually only the eyes of little mice. Then an enormous mouse appears and frightens Marie considerably. A little later Marie hears a pretty peal of bells and sees a bright light in the cupboard revealing all of the toys and objects in motion. The vital sensory fusion of light and the peal of bells creates a sanctuary in which the Christmas toys come to life.

In the next section, "The Battle," the hussars, which Fritz had received as a gift, and the Nutcracker battle an army of mice. As the conflict proceeds, the Nutcracker is besieged by various mice. Marie tries to save him by throwing her shoe into the midst of the enemy. Suddenly, everything vanishes and only silence remains. Marie feels physically unwell and falls insensible to the floor.

In the first paragraph of the following section, section six, "The Invalid," Marie awakens after a deep sleep and is welcomed by the radiance of the sun, her mother, and the doctor. Marie tries to explain that there had been a terrible conflict between the toys and the mice and that she was trying to prevent the mice from making the Nutcracker their prisoner. At the end of this section Godpapa Drosselmeier appears to show Marie that he has healed the Nutcracker; he then proceeds to tell a story about how the Nutcracker came to have the physical appearance which he currently does. This is a wide-ranging narrative which is connected to the story about the Princess Pirlipat, the witch Mouserink, and the Watchmaker.

The narrative, "The Story of the Hard Nut," is a story within the section entitled "The Invalid." One notable and equally terrible event in this narrative is that the lovely Princess Pirlipat is transformed by the witch Mouserink from a beautiful young child into a bloated head and a deformed body. The court astronomer and the clockmaker, who was an ancestor of Godpapa Drosselmeier, developed the horoscope of the princess and discovered that she could only be healed from her enchantment by eating the kernel of the crackatook nut. The court astronomer and the clockmaker are then ordered by the king to travel throughout the world to find the crackatook nut.

Fifteen years later the court astronomer and the clockmaker are still wandering around the world in their diligent quest for the seemingly elusive crackatook nut. However, the clockmaker Drosselmeier desires to return to his native town of Nuremberg. In Nuremberg the clockmaker meets his cousin, the toymaker, whom he has not seen in years. This cousin says that he has the special nut which they are searching for. Moreover, his son is the one who will crack it so that the princess can consume the sweet kernel of the nut and vanquish the horrific curse which has been placed upon her.

When the Princess Pirlipat consumes the sweet kernel of the crackatook nut, she is transformed into a beautiful young woman. As the young Drosselmeier is walking across the floor, he unfortunately comes into contact with the witch Mouserink, who is trying to come up from beneath the floor. Young Drosselmeier is now transmuted into a nutcracker—instead of being welcomed by the princess, she refuses him because of his physical appearance and causes him to be sent away. The storyteller says that the physical deformity of this individual can only be corrected when the son of the mouse-witch is vanquished and when a woman falls in love with him despite his physical appearance. In addition, the court astronomer and the clockmaker are banished forever from the city because the king blames them for having proposed that the nutcracker marry his daughter. As the tale finishes, Marie is very disappointed in the harsh and ungrateful response of the Princess Pirlipat who sent her rescuer away because of his less than charming physical presence.

In the section "Uncle and Nephew," Marie realizes, or thinks that she realizes, that her nutcracker is Godpapa Drosselmeier's nephew and that Godpapa Drosselmeier is himself actually the clockmaker who was at the court of Pirlipat's father. At the end of this section Godpapa Drosselmeier says to Marie that she is a princess and that she reigns in a "bright beautiful country" (105). Moreover, he warns Marie that because of her attachment to the nutcracker she still has much to endure. But if she is faithful and true, she will be able to ward off evil, and especially the evil influence of the witch Mouserink. Such advice sounds strikingly similar to the advice which the Archivist Lindhorst gives to Anselmus in "The Golden Pot." For Anselmus, who like Marie possesses an innocence of character and a kindhearted outlook on life, must remain faithful and true to his love for Serpentina to overcome the destructive and negative influence of the Frau Rauerin.

In the following section, "Victory," Marie is awakened on a bright moonlight night by a noise in her bedroom. The mouse-king threatens to consume the nutcracker if Marie does not give him and his mice all of her candy. On the next night the mouse-king makes the same threat against the nutcracker unless Marie gives him and his mice all of her sugar toys. Marie's parents decide to use one of Drosselmeier's traps to catch the mice. At one point in this section the nutcracker suddenly comes to life and expresses his gratitude to Marie for her support of him and asks her to give him a sword to combat the mice menace. At the end of "Victory" Marie hears some commotion around midnight in the sitting-room. When she opens the door the nutcracker is present to thank her for inspiring him to show his knightly courage and valor and conquer the mouse-king. The nutcracker, who speaks with the voice of the young Drosselmeier, encourages Marie to follow him so that he can show her "glorious and beautiful things" (110).

In the next section, "Toyland," the nutcracker shows Marie a lovely, luminescent meadow called Candy Mead. He then proceeds to take her to various other lovely, colorful, deliciously radiant spaces such as Almond and Raisin Gate, Christmas Wood, Orange Brook, River Lemonade, Honey River, Bonbonville, and even a beautiful lake where "the loveliest swans were floating, white as silver, with collars of gold" (113). Marie remembers at this moment that Godpapa Drosselmeier had once told her that she would be the girl to play with the swans. All of the lakes and waters in Toyland are especially beautiful, vital, and luminescent. And the Christmas Wood represents a distinctive sanctuary of light and color, characterized by glittering and sparkling fruits in the trees. The gold and silver fruits chime softly in an effusion of light. As in other episodes in this and other Hoffmann stories such as "The Golden Pot" the fusion of radiant light and soft chimes creates a sanctuary away from the vicissitudes of everyday mortality.

In the next section, "Metropolis," which is also the second-to-last part of the narrative, Marie again experiences epiphanies and sanctuaries of light and color. For example, in "Comfit Grove" many objects glitter, glisten, and sparkle and their colors are very beautiful. In the metropolis Marie is amazed by the splendor of the entire ambience. Not only are there shining towers and gorgeous walls in the metropolis but there is an aesthetic sensibility here which manifests itself in various sculptured and artistically crafted nuances and subtleties. There is even a group of individuals who are portrayed as worshippers of the sun and of light.

At the end of "Metropolis" Marie is taken by the nutcracker to the Marzipan Castle, "a castle shining in roseate radiance, with a hundred beautiful towers" (117). The luminescent atmosphere of the castle is reinforced by the fact that the "great dome of the central building, as well as the pyramidal roofs of the towers, were all set over with thousands of sparkling gold and silver stars" (117). Such a radiant castle is reminiscent of the effulgent castle and architectural paradise which K. Schinkel created in several of his Romantic paintings such as *Castle along a River*. Other important images of light at the castle, this beautiful sanctuary of light and serenity, are the little pages with their "lighted clove-sticks" (117), the brilliantly attired ladies of the court, a hall "whose walls were composed of a sparkling crystal" (118), and the profusion of golden flowers in and around the exquisite furniture. Gradually, a silver mist appears to permeate these images and the experience of Marie at the Marzipan Castle, and she feels as if she, the nutcracker, and other individuals at the castle were floating and rising ever higher on a succession of waves.

In the "Conclusion," Marie suddenly awakens in broad daylight with her mother standing next to her bed. Her mother assures Marie that she has had an extraordinary dream and should now put all of those images out of her head. Her father also encourages her to stop what he considers to be foolish fancies. However, Marie continues dreaming in solitude of the beautiful and magnificent fairy realm. One day Marie even says to the wooden doll, the nutcracker, that she would not act as Princess Pirlipat had done and despise him if he were not handsome because he had had to suffer a physical transformation for her sake. Soon after this Godpapa Drosselmeier brings his young nephew to the Stahlbaum house and introduces him to Marie.

When young Drosselmeier and Marie are alone he thanks Marie for having rescued him from his enchantment. For when Marie said that she would not have despised him, as the princess had done, if he had been compelled to become physically unattractive for her sake, he ceased to be the wooden nutcracker and was transformed into his normal self. The young Drosselmeier proceeds to ask Marie to marry him and to share his kingdom at the Marzipan Castle, where he is now the king. Marie, although she is still very young, accepts the proposal, especially because he rules over such a delightful and alluringly radiant and colorful country. A year and a day later he took his beloved away in a golden coach to get married. The story ends with the assertion that Marie is "to this day the queen of a realm where all kinds of sparkling Christmas Woods, and transparent Marzipan Castles . . . are to be seen by those who have the eyes to see them" (123). This is a story which is permeated and generated by various vital moments of light and radiance and which culminates in a moment of supreme luminescence. For Marie, whether in reality or in the realm of her imagination, is the queen of a realm where beautiful and gorgeous objects exist, glisten, and sparkle. Marie is the queen of a realm which signifies a lovely sanctuary of light where peace and beauty reign supreme.

Another story by E. T. A. Hoffmann which contains various important images of light is "Princess Brambilla." In Chapter 1, after dressing Giacinta in the lovely gown, the old woman, Beatrice, wants to accentuate the young woman's beauty, so she surrounds her with numerous consecrated candles. The effect is magnificent, for Giacinta seems to have a regal presence in this aura of golden illumination. The rays of light highlight and reaffirm her physical beauty.

At the beginning of Chapter 2 Hoffmann addresses a similar issue, the capacity of a very sensitive and thoughtful observer and narrator of the human condition to perceive fairy-tale figures. He says that he has been able to view fairy-tale figures just at the moment when these ethereal images and visions were about to fade into nothingness and to describe them so that his readers can appreciate their existence as well. The narrator also asserts that he wants to encourage his readers to think beyond the limitations of everyday reality. Hoffmann continues to elaborate on this point by suggesting that we should be open to the possibility of magical events occurring in our everyday lives. When we are receptive to the possibility of the extraordinary, then we have the capacity to understand the universal spirit, the spirit which flows through and motivates the universe. In this section of Chapter 2 Hoffmann raises a question which is intimately connected to his argument about being open to the extraordinary and the unusual in life. In the spirit of other Romantic authors Hoffmann wonders whether the dream which one has represents true existence and whether the reality of everyday life is only the delusion or illusion of confused and jaded senses. This is a typical Romantic concern articulated with equal expressiveness and sensitivity by such writers as Novalis and Hawthorne.

In Chapter 3 the story of King Ophioch and Queen Liris is a narrative of light. After King Ophioch and Queen Liris have been in a death-like stupor and sleep for a long while suddenly the Magus Hermod appears on a fiery cloud, surrounded by various elemental spirits and powers. Above his head is a luminous star with an extremely powerful radiance. The Magus takes this star, which is actually a glorious prism, and lifts it into the air. As he does so, the prism melts and becomes a glittering stream of water which ultimately forms a delightful spring. After the elemental spirits have ceased their intense interaction, the place of their activity becomes a magnificent pool like a fluid mirror surrounded by gleaming stones and lovely flowers. A pristine spring gushes peacefully in the middle of the pool. This is a beautiful natural space, a sanctuary of light and serenity.

When the prism had dissolved to form the spring, King Ophioch and Queen Liris had awakened from their deathlike slumber and hurried to the beautiful pool. By gazing into the glistening waters, the king and queen are rejuvenated—they feel a new appreciation for the beauty of nature and a new and reenergized sense of self. Both individuals even feel so happy that they laugh to express their inner well-being. Other individuals as well from their kingdom who felt melancholy and very sad now feel much happier when they gaze into the lovely waters of the pool and the spring. In this natural sanctuary the sensitive observer of nature can feel rejuvenated and can feel that a new life is beginning.

In Chapter 4 Giacinta asserts that a young seamstress, who is, of course, herself, is a more wonderful individual than a young actor, who is Giglio, to whom she is talking. Giacinta describes a lovely young woman, elaborating on and subtly emphasizing her own youthful beauty and charm in a most expressive and sensitive manner. One of her most interesting and salient statements about this youthful figure is that she represents the mystery of feminine beauty which casts a spell over her admirers in an aura of colorful and gentle luminescence. As Giacinta continues her description of this lovely woman, she mentions directly the idea of a sanctuary. Giacinta says that for any individual the room of his or her lover is a verdant and a vibrant Arcadia which offers a refuge from the tribulations of everyday life and mortality. It is especially interesting that Giacinta portrays this lovely young woman in an atmosphere of radiance and illumination, in a sanctuary of light.

In Chapter 5 of "Princess Brambilla" Giglio discovers a hall of light. Wandering through the palace, Giglio is first made aware of this room by a gleaming ray of light which comes through the keyhole of the door. When Giglio enters, he realizes that this is a great hall with walls of purple-streaked marble. From the dome hangs a vital lamp which spreads a golden radiance throughout the room.

In Chapter 6 of this narrative the old Beatrice reads from a passage which describes a beautiful young woman sitting in a reflective manner and enjoying a splendid dream. The passage is very expressive and imaginative and suggests that the beautiful young woman is in a magical garden. This is a sanctuary of lovely light, images, and sound. For when the lace covering the shining bosom of this beautiful young woman swells like a flood of lilies and a roseate radiance gleams upon her cheeks, then the softly mysterious vitality of music awakens to reveal the supreme truth about the world.

In Chapter 8 of "Princess Brambilla" Prince Chiapperi and Princess Brambilla awake from their profound sleep and gaze into the mirror-like waters of the lake on the shore of which they find themselves. After seeing themselves in the lake, they look at each other and laugh in the same manner as King Ophioch and Queen Liris had laughed after experiencing a similar situation, before falling into each other's arms.

At the end of "Princess Brambilla" the Prince summarizes the moral of the narrative: namely, that all individuals may be considered to be happy and rich who have observed themselves, their lives, and their destinies in the beautiful sunlit mirror of the Lake of Urdar. As the other royal couples in the story, King Ophioch and Queen Liris and Prince Chiapperi and Princess Brambilla, so Giacinta and Giglio and any other similar couples may have the same wonderful experience. The Lake of Urdar represents a blissful sanctuary of light which illuminates the inner self of the individual and allows him or her to attain a more sensitive and profound self-awareness and understanding of the universe.

In Hoffmann's story, "Die Bergwerke zu Falun" ("The Mines at Falun," written in the winter 1818-1819 and published in *Die Serapionsbrüder*, Volume 1), a Swedish sailor, Elis Fröbom, decides to become a miner to satisfy an inner longing to explore the miraculous and to attain an intimate understanding of the supernatural depths of the mines, and of the queen of the mines, about whom he has dreamed. The first sentence of the story is resplendent with light, for it is a radiant, sunny July day when the crew of the East India company ship on which Fröbom has been sailing comes into Göteborg for a prominent feast. Fröbom, instinctively melancholy and unhappy with his life as a sailor, does not share in the general joyousness and merriment. At this moment of dissatisfaction Fröbom meets an old miner who tells him of the wonders of his career. He tells of the many glittering precious stones which he found in the mines; he even describes his experience in the mine as multiple enchanted wanderings through a magical garden. The rocks and stones beneath the earth glowed and sparkled. It is also noteworthy that as the miner describes these radiant adventures underground his eyes become increasingly brighter.

Fröbom is enraptured by the miner's description of his professional world. And yet, Fröbom feels not only as if he is already in the mines in spirit but also that he has been instinctively connected to the magic of this world since his boyhood. Elis Fröbom has a dream in which he believes that he is on a crystalline floor with various unusual and sparkling rocks and flowers around him. He also sees lovely maidens who smile at him pleasantly and melodiously. At one point in the dream, a profusion of light emerges from the depths in which Elis observes the physiognomy of a sizeable woman. Elis' perception of this figure includes ecstasy as well as fear. In this scenario Elis hears his dead mother's voice and the voice of a younger woman who tries to inspire him to enter her world. Elis also encounters the voice of the old miner who exhorts him to be true to the queen of the mines.

When the dream is over Elis wanders in the town but feels restless and full of longing for a new life, for a life among the glittering stones of the mine. Unable to participate in the festivities which everyone else is enjoying, Elis seems to hear an unknown voice whispering to him that the splendors for which he searches are to be found in the mine. After many days of walking Elis reaches Falun, which he believes is where destiny has been leading him. When Elis views the cavernous black entrance to the mine he feels a strong sense of dread, for this seems like a vision of hell. Indeed, the narrator even affirms this vision saying that this is the perspective which Dante might have used in portraying his Inferno.

Because of his sense of dread and horror while looking at the dark crater of the mine, Elis is on the verge of deciding to return to Göteborg. However, in the marketplace he encounters a festival celebrating the miners and their work and decides to stay. Moreover, Elis also sees Ulla Dahlsjö, a most beautiful young woman and the daughter of one of the prominent and respected miners and is truly captivated by her. In fact, Elis even thinks that Ulla was the young woman in his dream who had given him her hand to lead him into the wonders of the mine. Ulla's father encourages Elis to accept a position in the mine.

Initially, Elis finds the mining work difficult, for he is agitated by the hot fumes and by the dark vapors as he descends into the depths of the earth. However, when Elis descends into the mine, he thinks of Ulla, who represents for him an angel of light. The image of her in his mind enables him to forget about and overlook his dismal surroundings and proceed with the work. As Anselmus believes (and is encouraged by Lindhorst to believe) in "The Golden Pot" that his faith in the love of Serpentina and his diligent endeavors in the copying of manuscripts will ultimately allow him to achieve his goal of marrying Serpentina, so Elis in "The Mines at Falun" believes (and is encouraged by Ulla's father, Pehrson, to believe) that his industrious efforts as a miner and worker will be rewarded with the hand of Ulla, who seems to have developed an affection for him.

One day while he is working in the depths of the mine, Elis is astonished to see that the old miner whom he had first encountered in Göteborg is next to him. The miner admonishes Elis for not being truly devoted to his work and for not being dedicated to the service of the prince of metals, instead desiring the love of the mortal Ulla. When Elis mentions this incident to the head foreman of the mine, he is told that the individual whom he encountered was probably the spirit of old Torbern, a former miner who had shown a supreme devotion to his mining work, an uncanny capacity to find the richest veins of ore, and a profound love of the lovely stones and jewels which were taken from the earth. He even exhorted the other miners to develop a true love of these precious stones and not to be motivated by financial greed in their mining pursuits.

Elis soon discovers that Ulla is going to be married to a rich man from Göteborg and is terribly disheartened. In a state of emotional despair Elis returns to the mine crater in the night, when it seems to be a veritable hell, and summons old Torbern to assist him in his attempt to find a rich vein while also proclaiming that his only treasure lies beneath the surface among the glittering stones of the mine. As Elis descends into the mine and finds a rich vein of ore, he experiences a powerful and blinding light which filled the entire shaft while the walls became as clear as pure crystal. The dream which he had experienced before in Göteborg returns. Elis sees glorious metallic trees and shrubs displayed in fields of paradise, with fiery jewels hanging from them in colorful abundance. Elis also encounters the queen of the mines who draws him to her in a warm embrace. This is a sanctuary of illumination and warmth for Elis, disappointed by the vicissitudes of everyday mortality.

Later that evening Elis is found by Pehrson and the foreman with his face pressed against the wall of the shaft. In returning to the earthly domain Pehrson admits that Ulla, his daughter, loves Elis, and that he would like the two of them to be married. Even though Elis is happy, and even though the public believes that Elis could not have found a more beautiful and wonderful woman as his wife, there are moments when he seems to doubt his good fortune. A voice within Elis Fröbom suggests that marrying Ulla does not represent the highest earthly fortune, for he has already seen the countenance of the queen in the depths of the mines. Ulla notices that Elis seems distracted, but when he tries to reveal to her the intricacies of his glorious vision of the precious jewels and of his momentous experience of the queen in the mines, he is unable to express himself adequately.

After remaining away from the mines for several days and apparently restoring his awareness of his love for and appreciation of Ulla, Elis goes back down into the mines. He believes that he is blessed in always being able to find the richest veins in the mine. Yet, when the foreman and other miners explore these veins, they find only hollow rock and no precious metals at all. Despite this, Elis persists in claiming that only he knows how precious these veins really are and only he has the capacity to understand the mysterious inscriptions which the queen of the mines has carved on the rocks and stones. Ulla is afraid when she observes these conspicuous changes in her Elis, but her father asserts that everything will be fine after the wedding-day.

The devotion of Elis Fröbom to the queen of the mine and to her elusive and mysterious realm is similar in spirit to the experience of the figure in several paintings by Caspar David Friedrich. For example, in *Monk By the Sea, Traveller Looking Over a Sea of Fog,* and *Abbey in the Oak-Woods* the individuals in these paintings appear to have achieved an emotional and a spiritual communion with the surrounding natural environment comparable in intensity and in depth to the experience of Fröbom in the mine environment. The individuals in these paintings, as Elis Fröbom in the Hoffmann narrative, are isolated and lonely figures, separated from their contemporary society by a visionary capacity and an imaginative inclination.

On the wedding-day Elis, looking deathly pale, comes to the room of Ulla, his bride, and tells her that he has to go into the mine to procure her wedding present and to obtain the blessing of the queen of the mines for the wedding. Elis claims that on the previous evening it was revealed to him that in the mine there is a sparkling pink almandine gem on which is engraved the story of their lives. He says that is a truly beautiful object which, when they gaze into it, will allow them to perceive some of the inner mysteries of nature and of the universe. Ulla implores Elis not to descend into the mine, but he asserts that he will not be able to rest until he has brought this precious, gorgeous stone to the surface. Tragically, there is a disaster in the mine when Elis descends and he is never found. The sanctuary of light in the mine, nurtured and sustained by the precious stones, becomes a sanctuary of death for Elis.

Fifty years later, miners find the body of a young man in the mine preserved in a pool of vitriolic water. This was on St. John's Day, and Ulla, who returned on this one day every year since her sad wedding-day to view the mine crater, notices the body and proclaims that it is Elis, her departed bridegroom. Ulla, now an old woman, dies, clasping the body of her beloved Elis, which vanishes in her embrace. The ashes of Ulla and Elis are placed together in the nearby Koppaberg Church, where fifty years ago they were to have been married.

The protagonist of Hoffmann's "The Mines at Falun" is strikingly similar to the protagonist of Ludwig Tieck's "Der Runenberg" ("Rune Mountain") in inclination and motivation. Both characters are initially strangers in the society where they will ultimately prosper professionally. Both characters become devoted to a miraculous, beautiful, and otherworldly image which lures them from the world of everyday mortality into the world of dreams and visions; both characters are so enamored of the world of visions that they are not able to return to the world of mortality. One might even argue that both protagonists are so enraptured by the vision which captivates them that they have no interest in maintaining a constant or even an occasional contact with the mundane world of everyday reality. As artists of great commitment to their work, with whom these two protagonists share certain characteristics and qualities, such individuals become absolutely devoted to and even possessed (or obsessed) by their respective visions.

Another story by Hoffmann in which precious jewels play a vitally important role is "Mademoiselle de Scudery" (written in 1818 and published in 1819). As in "The Mines at Falun," precious stones are not always presented in a positive light, so in "Mademoiselle de Scudery" gorgeous jewels are sometimes associated with destructiveness, death, and evil. For example, at one point in the early part of the narrative Mademoiselle Scudery receives a casket of jewels. Even though the sun is shining radiantly through the window-blinds of red silk which makes the diamonds in the open box sparkle with a special gleam, this is not a positive gleam. For these diamonds are connected with the murderous spree occurring in Paris at the time.

Mademoiselle Scudery takes the jewels to the Marquise de Maintenon, who examines the stones carefully and proclaims that they are the work of the famous goldsmith Rene Cardillac. Cardillac is portrayed as a very talented and gifted goldsmith and craftsman who is devoted to his artistic endeavor. Each item which he creates is a masterpiece. However, after his long and arduous labor on each artistic work, Cardillac becomes hesitant and even unwilling to part with the gems. He invents various excuses so that he may retain the jewels for as long as possible before being compelled to bestow the artistic work on the individual who has paid for it.

Mademoiselle Scudery and Marquise de Maintenon decide to send for Cardillac to ask him who the owner is of the precious jewels which have ended up in the possession of the Mademoiselle. When Cardillac arrives he asserts that he had made these gorgeous jewels for himself and then asks Mademoiselle Scudery to accept them as a present from him, for he is an admirer of her character and her virtue.

Several months later Mademoiselle Scudery, in response to a note which she has received from a stranger imploring her to return the jewels which she has recently received to Cardillac, goes to see Cardillac. However, at his house is a crowd of people who are clamoring for the arrest of the apprentice of Cardillac, who is accused of having murdered the master. Mademoiselle Scudery sympathetically takes home with her Madelon, the distraught daughter of Cardillac who is engaged to Olivier Brusson, the apprentice, whose innocence and kindness she vigorously proclaims. Madelon tells the Mademoiselle the story of the recent events, which persuades her of Brusson's innocence. One of the leaders of the tribunal investigating the various crimes and murders occurring at this time in Paris (around 1680) allows Brusson to be brought before Mademoiselle Scudery to tell his story.

Mademoiselle Scudery is very astonished when Olivier Brusson appears before her to tell his story. He says that he is the son of a woman, Anne, whom the Mademoiselle had brought up with devotion in her own house. Olivier declares that he is innocent of the crime of murder with which he has been charged by the tribunal. Olivier, as Anselmus in "The Golden Pot" and Elis in "The Mines at Falun," is a stranger in the world in which he now lives. All three characters are brought up in an area, literally or symbolically, which is different from the domain in which they ultimately find a sense of success and happiness. All three protagonists also fall in love with the daughter of an individual who is a prominent figure in the realm of mortal activity to which they ultimately devote themselves. Olivier, who becomes an apprentice to the goldsmith Cardillac, falls hopelessly in love with Madelon, his daughter.

Olivier tells Mademoiselle Scudery of his discovery that Cardillac was responsible for various murders because he could not endure relinquishing his beautiful jewels to his patrons. Olivier also tells the story which Cardillac had narrated to him about his life and his motivations. It appears that Cardillac from a very young age was enchanted by beautiful objects, by gold and precious jewels. He became a goldsmith to satisfy this longing to have constant access to such lovely items. However, after he delivers the jewelry which he has made Cardillac feels oppressed and cannot stop thinking about the items, which he feels he must take back. Only when he has stolen or killed to gain the jewels again does he feel a sense of inner peace.

At one point Cardillac decides to send some jewels which had originally been made for a princess to the Mademoiselle Scudery as a testament of his admiration for her. When he heard this virtuous aristocrat's name, Oliver exclaims that it was as if a veil had been removed and as if the image of his happy childhood had emerged in bright colors. For Olivier, childhood represented a sanctuary of light, innocence, and hope which was revitalized in the presence of his beloved Madelon, but which has recently been undermined. Ultimately, through the extraordinary efforts of Mademoiselle Scudery, Olivier Brusson is freed upon the order of the King of France. After he and Madelon marry, they must leave Paris. They settle in Geneva for the rest of their congenial existence.

In the story "The Artushof" (written in 1815 and published in 1816), Hoffmann's concern with the power of the imagination, the importance of creativity, and the vitality of light is again apparent. The story begins with a discussion of the "Artushof," the court of King Arthur—in Danzig this is a commercial exchange during the day. When the twilight appears, it ushers in a magical atmosphere in which the figures and forms in the paintings of the halls seem to come alive. There is a marble statue of the king in the middle of the hall which assumes an awe-inspiring stature. There are beautiful women in exquisite and alluring gowns who seem to entice the viewer. A handsome youth in another picture entrances Herr Traugott, who is observing the procession of figures on the wall instead of listening carefully to Herr Roos and his business concerns. As Herr Traugott gazes at the figures in the Artushof he starts drawing.

Traugott, who seems to be more instinctively an artist than a businessman, also draws other figures in his vicinity. Traugott experiences an epiphanic moment in this episode which shows him more clearly than ever before what he had previously sensed. What is most important for Traugott is that a delightful world of fantasy and imagination had revealed itself to him in the Artushof. In this scenario Traugott begins to question his existence and his purpose in life. The image of light and vitality in nature inspires him to rethink his present condition. After observing that it is a beautifully radiant spring morning with the west wind infusing the bleak city streets with a breath of fresh air from the lovely open spaces of nature, Traugott begins to wish that he did not have to return to the confines of the business office of Herr Roos, where the only goal is the acquisition of increasingly more wealth. Traugott wishes to leave the city and enjoy the vernal beauty of a special natural space, a sanctuary of light, which can inspire his creativity.

After wondering to himself whether he could perhaps become a painter, Traugott looks through all of the sketches and paintings which he has done over the years. As he reviews this work, it seems even more interesting than it had before. However, the next morning when Traugott glances at the same work it seems mundane. Uncertain whether his artistic inclination is motivated by an external stimulus or a genuine inner calling and destiny, Traugott compels himself to go into the office of Herr Roos and work diligently, though he clearly now despises this daily ritual.

Some weeks later Traugott is in the Artushof looking at several of the painted figures, including those of the mayor and his page, and remarks upon the striking similarities between those two figures and the old man and his son who are near to him and with whom he has had a recent business dealing. The old man proclaims that he is the painter Berklinger and that he painted the two figures which Traugott so admires many, many years ago—he proceeds to declare that the mayor and his page were intended as a reflection of himself and his son. Traugott is amazed to hear this because that painting was produced a couple of centuries ago. The old man, Berklinger, declares that such a period represented a flourishing of artistic activity. Moreover, he claims that he created various works in the halls of the Artushof as a tribute to and in honor of King Arthur and his Round Table.

In the ensuing conversation Traugott asks if he might be permitted to see the old man's paintings. While showing some reserve, especially because Traugott's artistic apprenticeship is just beginning, as he says, the old painter Berklinger does say that he would be willing to show him his innermost sanctuary of artistic work. When Traugott visits the old man and his son on the next day in a distant street of the town, the old man shows him *Paradise Regained*, the painting on which he is currently working as a companion piece to his already completed *Paradise Lost*. The painter emphasizes that all of the features of *Paradise Regained*, the people, the animals, and the flowers, signify a lovely and harmonious whole of light and music. After the father intensively describes the painting and becomes exhausted, the son takes Traugott into another room to show him various paintings by the old man.

Traugott is very impressed by the quality of the paintings and feels that they have the aura of the Dutch masters. He is especially enraptured by one image, a beautiful girl in an old-fashioned German costume. Traugott is so entranced by this image that he even declares that she is his soul's beloved. The painter's son is moved and exclaims that this is a portrait of his sister Felizitas. Traugott is so impressed by the old man's paintings that he implores him to accept him as his pupil. Because of his devotion to art, Traugott neglects his work at the office of Herr Roos completely and his intended marriage to Roos' daughter, Christina, is postponed.

One day Traugott comes to the Berklinger household later than usual and finds a female figure who closely resembles the one he so admired in the portrait playing the lute. As he addresses her, the old man becomes enraged and throws Traugott out of the house. When Traugott next returns to this house he learns that the old man and his son have left with all of their possessions. Traugott is plunged into a state of emotional despair and even feels that his artistic inclination was merely a deception. He returns to work in the office of Herr Roos and once again agrees to marry his daughter.

On the eve of the wedding day Traugott happens to be in the Artushof staring at the painting which has consistently so entranced him, the portrait of the mayor and his page. In chatting with someone nearby Traugott learns that the youth whom the old man claimed was his son was actually his daughter. The old painter believed that he would die when his daughter would develop a love interest, so he reared her as a son. Traugott, who had instantly noticed the resemblance, is crushed that he did not express his love for Felizitas while she was so near him. Finding out that the pair are in Sorrento, Traugott plans immediately to liberate himself from his present existence, his business association with Roos, and the proposed marriage to Christina.

Traugott stops in Rome on his journey to Sorrento and is accepted by various artists there as a colleague and fellow painter. Traugott's philosophy of art is described as a supreme dedication and devotion to a higher, unearthly realm of eternally vital images and thoughts. There is a consistency in his portraits, for every female figure he creates is very similar to Felizitas, who represents his artistic ideal. It is noteworthy that Traugott devotes himself to his art vitally and does not for the time being attempt to travel to Sorrento to find Felizitas. He is content to paint her portrait over and over again. While working in Rome someone informs him that the woman whom he paints actually lives there. However, when he is taken to her Traugott realizes that it is not Felizitas, although she is physically very similar.

While initially disappointed that Dorina is not Felizitas, Traugott comes to develop an affection for the young Italian girl, whose father is a painter. Traugott's interest in finding Felizitas in person has lessened considerably. He appears content to have her in his life as an artistic ideal. Felizitas is present in his life forever in spirit—she inspires and motivates all of his female figures. After searching further for Felizitas and her father, Traugott is compelled to return to Danzig for business matters. Here he now discovers that the old man and his daughter had been living in Sorrento, the name of the villa of the guild chairman, for many years. The father had died, the daughter, Felizitas, had married and raised a family. Traugott is very dismayed to hear these facts about Felizitas, who had inspired a perpetual longing in him and who had been his artistic muse. As he reflects upon this dilemma, Traugott realizes that what was most important to him as an artist was the vision, the artistic vitality which the image of Felizitas inspired in him. He realizes that he has no interest in seeing the real Felizitas. It is only her image, her presentation as an ideal figure which interested him. After settling his business affairs, Traugott plans to return to Rome and marry Dorina, who is still hoping to marry him. The sanctuary of artistic inspiration and ideal vision within him will be matched by a sanctuary of earthly and mortal happiness which awaits him upon his return to Rome.

In his introduction to the *Tales of Hoffmann*, R. J. Hollingdale speaks of the schizophrenic nature of Hoffmann's personality and of his Jekyll and Hyde character (7-8). The attempt by E. T. A. Hoffmann to resolve and perhaps even harmonize the tension in his own existence between the artistic and the bourgeois, the miraculous and the mundane, is reflected in various of his literary protagonists. Anselmus in "The Golden Pot" and Elis Fröbom in "The Mines at Falun" exemplify such characters whose lives are permeated by the conflict between the artistic and the bourgeois, the supernatural and the everyday. Each of these protagonists is instinctively devoted to the artistic realm and the domain of the miraculous. Anselmus is fortunate that he enjoys the profound love of Serpentina and the generous assistance of the Archivist Lindhorst in his quest for a sanctuary of light and happiness. The blissful existence of Anselmus and Serpentina in Atlantis represents the ultimate sanctuary of light and serenity.

Elis Fröbom in "The Mines at Falun" reveals an experience and an approach to life which is strikingly similar to that of Anselmus. He is devoted in his work, is encouraged by his patron, and enjoys the love of Ulla, his patron's daughter. Yet, Elis does not achieve the happiness which Anselmus does, perhaps because he allows himself to be entranced and lured away from his love for Ulla and from his sense of responsibilities by the queen of the mines. One might say that Traugott in "The Artushof" is also enraptured by an aesthetically lovely image, that of Felizitas, but is ultimately compelled to realize that she exists only as an ideal. When Traugott understands that Felizitas will only represent an ideal for him, and that he should not think of her as a real dimension of his life, then he can reorient himself after his disappointment—he can make the decision to return to Rome and find happiness with Dorina.

The ultimate sanctuary of light and radiance in Hoffmann's stories is perhaps found in "Der goldene Topf" ("The Golden Pot") which celebrates the importance of luminescent spaces of creative vitality and serenity in everyday circumstances and in extraordinary scenarios, in Dresden and in Atlantis. The consecration to light and luminescent energy in "The Golden Pot" finds a comparably vital devotion to light and the expression of effulgence in Percy Shelley's "Hymn of Apollo." In the first two stanzas of this poem the persona, as the Archivist Lindhorst throughout Hoffmann's story, stresses his capacity for a diastolic spatiality for he can move freely not only through the air but also across the waves and the earth.

In saying at the beginning of stanza three that the "sunbeams are my shafts" (13) the persona of "Hymn of Apollo" asserts that he uses the power of his light not only to vanquish deceit and evil but also to inspire good minds and to stimulate positive actions, while at the same time realizing that the night will encroach upon his noble endeavors. The Archivist Lindhorst in "Der goldene Topf" uses the light in precisely the same manner. He represents a force for goodness and light who confronts and challenges the evil presence of the woman from the Black Gate.

The characteristics which the persona attributes to himself in stanza four of "Hymn of Apollo" are the same qualities which are of seminal importance to the Archivist Lindhorst in "Der goldene Topf": a capacity not only to color and influence the development of the clouds, the rainbows, the flowers, the moon, and the stars, but also to illuminate various aspects of the world. Apollo is a primary source of light and radiance in his extensive world as Lindhorst is in his domain. One might say that it is ultimately the capability to illuminate the world, to permeate the day and the night with a dynamic radiance, which the persona of the poem cherishes as his most significant quality. In proclaiming his ability to embrace in his spirit the light of Earth and of Heaven, Shelley's "I" argues for his potential to transcend mortality. The Archivist Lindhorst reveals a similar capacity in "Der goldene Topf" to shape his temporal environment and to transcend mortality.

In stanza five, Shelley's persona expresses an awareness that he participates in and shapes the daily cycle of temporality, of day and night, and that he represents an integral dimension of that eternal cyclicality. In Hoffmann's story, the Archivist Lindhorst is also aware of his power over the daily flux of time—for example, the different robes and colorful garments which Lindhorst wears could suggest a consistent affirmation of and awareness of certain times of day. In the last two lines of stanza five, Shelley's persona, praises his own smile, the radiance of his own powerful light, as being delightful and as having the capacity to soothe the afternoon and evening clouds and other aspects of nature which know intuitively and sadly that they must fade in the regular temporal cycle of the day.

In the final stanza, stanza six, of "Hymn of Apollo" the persona for the first time in the course of the poem not only implies his divinity but also refers to himself specifically as divine. The emphasis on the eye, on the power of the persona's eye, is significant because it counterbalances the image of the sleepless hours watching him as he slumbers "Curtained with star-inwoven tapestries / From the broad moonlight of the sky" (2–3). Stanza six encompasses the essential features and dimensions of Apollo as the god of light, of the sun, of poetry, of medicine, of prophesy, and of the arts. While the Archivist Lindhorst in "Der goldene Topf" is not presented as such a divine figure, he certainly signifies a quasi-divine aura with a capacity to influence and shape various dimensions of the world around him.

Both the Archivist Lindhorst in Hoffmann's "The Golden Pot" and the figure of Apollo in Shelley's "Hymn of Apollo" exemplify the strategy of the Immortals described in Hermann Hesse's *Steppenwolf* as well as the laughter of the Immortals which is so directly connected to their sense of eternity. Of the laughter of the Immortals Hesse writes:

> It was laughter without an object. It was simply light and lucidity. It was that which is left over when a true individual has passed through all the sufferings, vices, mistakes, passions, and misunderstandings of men and got through to eternity and the world of space. And eternity was nothing else than the redemption of time, its return to innocence, so to speak, and its transformation again into space. (176–77)

Both Apollo and Lindhorst approach life in such a spirit of light and lucidity; and both Apollo and Lindhorst appreciate that eternity represents a "redemption of time." One might even claim that Atlantis, the perpetual residence of Serpentina and Anselmus, in its representation of "innocence" and spatial expansiveness, signifies, nurtures, and sustains the qualities which Hesse attributes to eternity.

That the "I" in "Hymn of Apollo" sees himself in an image of reflection is also important because it implies his capacity to accept and to understand both a separation and a fusion of the "I" and the universe. Apollo presents himself not only as a profoundly divine individual in the last stanza, but also as one who is interested in creating and nurturing an atmosphere of harmony and affirmation. The positive tone which informs the end of the poem is reminiscent of and fulfills W. H. Auden's belief in the necessity of praise in poetry. Auden writes in *The Dyer's Hand* that "a poem must praise all it can for being as for happening" (51). Apollo, the persona in this poem, praises not only the creative self with its multidimensional capacities but also the universe which would promote the existence of such a vital self and which aspires to an ambience of holistic harmony. Such a strategy is precisely what the Archivist Lindhorst shows consistently throughout "Der goldene Topf" ("The Golden Pot") and especially at the end of the narrative as he promotes the eternal happiness of Serpentina and Anselmus in Atlantis. For without the vibrant radiance of Lindhorst's attentiveness and influence the love of Serpentina and Anselmus would not have been fulfilled and consummated in the luminescent sanctuary of Atlantis. Atlantis, the residence of Serpentina and Anselmus, is an earthly and a quasi-divine paradise which represents not only an exquisitely beautiful and colorful natural environment but also a sanctuary of perpetually vital, whether softly vital or more overtly dynamic, luminescence which guides, heals, and nurtures the heart and the soul of the individual beyond the limitations and vicissitudes of everyday mortality.

❋ Joseph von Eichendorff

Joseph von Eichendorff, one of the greatest and most lyrically vital poets in the history of German and of European literature, often describes and presents images of light and radiance in his poetry. Images of light play an important role not only in offering an aura of radiance or a sense of luminescence as a contrast or complement to images of darkness but also in suggesting the existence of a religious and a spiritual light which permeates the soul of the sensitive individual and creates an aura of transcendence beyond the challenges, hardships, and idiosyncrasies of everyday mortality. When images of light in Eichendorff's poetry are stressed within the context of the day, they are typically associated with goodness, hope, faith, happiness, longing, love, Wanderlust, or a spatial expansiveness. When images of light in the poetry of Eichendorff are revealed at night, they may be connected with the same qualities and dimensions as those of the day, but most especially with longing, Wanderlust, faith, and hope.

I would first like to examine a number of poems by Eichendorff which celebrate the importance of the light and which reveal sanctuaries of light, whether transient or permanent, quietly radiant or brilliantly effulgent. Eichendorff's "Abschied" ("Farewell") describes a profound sanctuary of light and spiritual comfort which will sustain the persona throughout his life, even when he has departed from this beautiful natural landscape.

In "Abschied" the persona achieves the continuity of the self which Wordsworth celebrates as being so important in his poetry. Eichendorff's persona achieves the continuity of the self by developing and sustaining the unity of the self established initially in the poem. In the first stanza the persona implores nature for a sense of protection and security against the outside world. In the second stanza the persona elaborates on the comfort which he receives from a close emotional affinity to nature. Stanza three introduces a moment of epiphany—the "I" claims that he has experienced a moment of inner revelation, which he then describes in more detail in the fourth and final stanza of the poem. In the fourth stanza, the "I" reveals that although he will inevitably leave the sanctuary of this beautiful natural environment, he will always be able to derive emotional, psychological, and spiritual inspiration and consolation from nature. The "I" asserts that wherever he may be in the future, nature will accompany him in spirit to give him solace.

The apostrophic richness of "Abschied" begins with an address of spatially significant features of nature, the valleys, the hills, and the beautiful forest. As in Clemens Brentano's "Nachklänge Beethovenscher Musik," Eichendorff's poem begins with a triple address. The first two objects of the apostrophe, the initial two aspects of nature described, are presented as unmodified generic nouns. Here, the "I" addresses two geographical extremes, the valleys and the heights. In the second line the "I" balances out these extremes by focusing his attention on the middle terrain, the forest. In modifying "Wald" (2) with the descriptive adjectives "schöner" (2) and "grüner" (2) the "I" gives the noun a more concrete presence in the text. By using these adjectives, the "I" expresses a personal relation to nature which he sustains throughout the poem. The spatial and orphic expansiveness of line one of the poem is tempered by the more hermetic approach of line two. While the persona mentions various aspects of nature which are meaningful to him, the focus of his address is the forest, which represents a special sanctuary of light and serenity.

Lines three and four of stanza one reinforce the notion that the aspect of nature which is the focus of the persona's attention and devotion is a personal locus amoenus. The use of the word "Andächt'ger" (4) to describe the type of "Aufenthalt" (4) which the persona experiences is especially important. The devotion which is implied here could refer to the emotional or the religious devotion which the "I" feels towards this special natural environment. The "Aufenthalt" (4) is presented as a private, not a public, haven of comfort which signifies the order and power of the natural and the divine worlds. Lines three and four of stanza one reinforce the inward-turning strategy of the persona.

The "I," the persona, establishes a clear distinction between the restful peace of nature and the clamorous disorder of the outside world. The outside world is "betrogen" (5) because it does not share an interest in the pure quiet of nature. Despite the strong semantic tension and contrast between this beautiful natural environment and the outside world, the world of everyday mortality, there is a conspicuous linguistic association between the two. The adjectives describing nature and society, respectively, that is "Andächt'ger" (4) and "geschäft'ge," (6) are similar in form. They share such structural features as the same number of syllables and the same stressed vowel. Such a formal relation suggests that nature and society do have a subtle, tacit bond and may not be as separated as the persona would like to believe. In fact, the "I" will himself represent this bond in the final stanza—he will be the link between nature and society when he leaves the comfort of this lovely natural space to wander through the world. In doing so, he fulfills the symbolic capacity of his own language in stanza one of the poem.

The nouns which these adjectives modify are also linguistically coupled. Both occur in line-final position and share the same consonant ending. This shared consonance binds together formally the two halves of the stanza. As in the relation of the adjectives, the "I" implies that although nature exists or may exist in its own splendid isolation, it is nevertheless at least theoretically, or even provisionally, bound to the outside world. The "outside world" refers to that part of the world of the persona, the poet, which does not offer the protective comfort and inspiration which nature so abundantly provides. While nature and the outside world may exist in a tentative harmony in the stanza, the persona clearly favors the world of nature for the positive qualities with which it can infuse his existence in contrast to the hectic clamor, superficiality, and deceitfulness which the outside world represents to him.

"Aufenthalt" (4) represents the formal and semantic focus or convergence of the first stanza. First, it balances the dialectical appearance of the nouns "Wald" (2) and "Welt" (6). "Wald" (2) suggests pure nature, unadulterated by "Welt" (6). "Welt" (6) implies an impure, somewhat artificial world, not profoundly affected by "Wald" (2). The notion of "Aufenthalt" (4) marks a middle ground, representing the most poignant moment of tension and simultaneously of harmony in the first stanza. There is the semantic pull towards "Wald" (2) and the formal inclination towards "Welt" (6). However, the aura of "Aufenthalt" (6) is one of serenity and quiet grandeur. The use of alliteration—"Andächt'ger"-"Aufenthalt"—reaffirms the strong sense of serenity here and even implies a capacity for timelessness or slowing down the flux of time.

Lines five and six of the first stanza, representing the outside world, contrast conspicuously with lines seven and eight, signifying the vernal vitality of nature. Yet, as mentioned before, the rhyme scheme in stanza one connects formally different aspects which are semantically clearly distinguished from one another. The imperative "Schlag" (7) is used not only to dissociate the persona from the outside world but also to separate lines 7 and 8 as a semantic unit as much as possible from lines 5 and 6. These semantic features cannot, however, be completely separated. Just as "Welt" (6) is associated with "Wald" (2), so it is also linked formally with "Zelt" (8). Once again the "I" in stanza one implies that nature and the outside world are more closely connected than he is willing to express candidly. Yet, the "I" wants to downplay or diminish this connection because he aims to proclaim the glorious beauty of a special natural space which is isolated and distinct from the chaotic outside world. The persona reinforces his assertion of the isolated vitality of this special natural place by modifying two central aspects of nature with the adjective "grün." The presence of such adjectives describing the forest and the canopy of comfort which the forest offers not only personalizes this moment for the persona but also distinguishes nature's capacity as a source of comfort for the persona from the outside world which is not infused with such positive attributes.

It is semantically and stylistically interesting that "Zelt" (8) is the culminating noun and concluding word of the first stanza. "Zelt" (8) simultaneously recuperates the semantic values of "Wald" (2) and "Welt" (6) while at the same time initiating a new semantic dimension with its all-encompassing vitality. The image of nature as a "Zelt" (8), as a lovely canopy of light and color, is central to the strategic strength of the "I". The "Zelt" (8) literally and symbolically protects the "I" not only from the dangers of the outside world but also from the emotional risks and psychological perils of exploring the connections between nature and the outside world. "Zelt" (8) appropriately culminates stanza one, for as a canopy it not only encompasses the richness of the beautiful aspects of nature but also embraces the disparate formal and semantic tensions of the stanza and fuses them into a unified whole.

In stanza two the persona delineates the elements of nature, and especially of the forest, which are so important and meaningful to him. Stanza two opens with the description of a new day. The persona, the earth, and the birds are energetic and flourishing—the dawn inspires the physical vitality of nature as well as the creative dynamism of the persona. The poet internalizes the beauty and vitality of nature to energize his own soul.

Because the persona is so inspired and soothed by various aspects he claims that he will be unaffected by the "Erdenleid," (14) the suffering present in the world of everyday mortality. The object of the address, the "du" (15), could be interpreted in different ways. One could claim that the "du" (15) which is addressed here is the spirit of nature which was so effusively praised and celebrated in stanza one. In the last two lines of stanza two the persona could be suggesting that the forest (the primary apostrophic object in stanza one) literally and the spirit of nature symbolically will be resurrected in luminescent glory.

The presence of the word "auferstehen" (15) is interesting because of the religious connotations inextricably linked with it. The word "auferstehen" (15) may suggest revitalization or even resurrection. The persona could be implying that the vitality of nature which occurs at the beginning of stanza two is so profound that it carries with it the aura of a resurrection of the spirit of the natural environment which inevitably impacts the persona of the poem. In suggesting the possibility that the spirit of nature is revitalized or resurrected at this moment of the poem, the "I" could also be implying that he, as an immediate observer of and participant in this scenario, shares in the glory of this revitalization and resurrection.

One could argue that the second stanza, unlike the other stanzas of the poem, does not participate directly in the temporal dimension of the poem by virtue of the presence of "auferstehen" (15). Such a word, such a concept, sweeps away any potential influence of "Erdenleid" (14). Ironically, the first stanza, which does not have any direct temporal reference in the world of nature, belongs to the main temporal sequence of the poem, while the second stanza, which does contain temporal references to the natural world, temporal references grounded in the imagery of the natural world, creates its own dimension of time in the context of the poem.

The first four lines of the second stanza are mutually reinforcing. Together they all reaffirm the vitality of nature. The relation, the rhyming, of "tagen" (9) and "schlagen" (11) is also significant because it implies the importance of temporality in the poem. The two verbs offer parallel temporal processes. While "tagen" (9) introduces the theme of periodicity (a process which occurs every day), "schlagen" (11) expresses singularity (a momentary event which can also become a daily and periodic ritual). Although "blinkt" (10) and "erklingt" (12) combine different senses, the most conspicuous sensory experience of the first four lines of stanza two is that of hearing.

The end of the second stanza, as the end of the first, reveals semantically divergent strategies in the rhyme scheme. As "verwehen" (13) clashes with "auferstehen" (15), so "Erdenleid" (14) is diametrically opposed to "Herrlichkeit" (16). It is noteworthy that the fifth and sixth lines of each of the first two stanzas signify the presence and qualities of the outside world and that the seventh and eighth lines of each of these stanzas represent a sense of sanctuary beyond the confines and vicissitudes of mortality. Even though these worlds are connected through the rhyme schemes, there is a difference in the nature of the association in the two stanzas. In stanza one there is a closer, more positive connection between these two pairs of lines because the most negative line-end word is "betrogen" (5) which rhymes with "Bogen" (7) and not with the culminating word of the stanza. In the second stanza, however, the most negative line-end word is "Erdenleid" (14) which rhymes with "Herrlichkeit" (16). Because of the sharp contrast between "Erdenleid" (14), mortal suffering, and "Herrlichkeit" (16), youthful glory and vitality, or even perhaps a divine youthfulness or vitality given the connotations of "auferstehen" (15), the relation between these last pairs of lines in stanza two is less congenial and more adversarial.

In the first stanza the "Wald"-"Wehen"-"Welt" consonance is semantically significant. In the second stanza the alliterative clusters of "Erde"-"erklingt"- "Erdenleid", "Vögel"-"vergehen"-"verwehen," and "Herz"-"Herrlichkeit" evoke new horizons and configurations of meaning in the poem. If we consider the first alliterative cluster we can say that "erklingt" (12) signifies a culminating gesture of positive energy in the stanza. It is syntactically bound to the "Herz" (12) of the persona. The noun "Erde" (10), the alliterative counterpart of "erklingt" (12) in this stanza, is, on the other hand, bound to nature, to a world literally external to the persona, yet intimately connected with him. The alliterative combination of "Erde" (10) and "erklingt" (12) demonstrates the symbolic unification or harmonization of the "I" and nature. If one includes "Erdenleid" (14) in this alliterative cluster, then the harmonization which is achieved by the association of the previous two words could be said to be challenged by its presence. Perhaps one could even argue that the final word of this alliterative arrangement is actually "auf-erstehen" (15) which triumphs over "Erdenleid" (14) and generates a positive and life-affirmative aura at the end of stanza two. Yet, in its context in the stanza, the "Erdenleid" (14) is depicted as a transient condition, so one could argue that this contributes to the sense of vernal vitality which is so effusively expressed in the following two lines.

There is also the semantic interrelation of "Vögel" (11), "vergehn" (13), and "verwehen" (13). The "Vögel" (11) represent the secure and congenial aspect of the world of nature, while the verbs "vergehn" (13) and "verwehen" (13) may suggest the passing or vanishing of a feeling, condition, or being. The typically negative connotation of "vergehn" and "verwehen" might perhaps be interpreted in a more positive light in this stanza because what is described as passing is actually a negative condition, namely, mortal suffering. The formal association of "Herz" (12) and "Herrlichkeit" (16) climaxes the alliterative energy of this stanza. These two words connect two important dimensions of the persona, the one which enjoys and revels in the daily emergence of the light and the cyclical awakening or reawakening of nature and the one which believes in a glorious resurrection of nature, a divine power which infuses the beautiful natural environment. Or, if one interprets "Herz" as focused on the emotional vitality of the persona and "Herrlichkeit" as relating to the divine power of nature, one could argue that this alliterative association reaffirms and reinforces the intimate connection between the persona and nature.

The image of the "Zelt" (8) is very important in the first stanza. One might view the notion of "Herrlichkeit" (16) at the end of the second stanza as reinforcing the canopy which covers and protects the features within its domain and radiance. The sense of the "Zelt" (8) is also affirmed in the arrangement of the verbs in the first four lines of stanza two. Two of the verbs with 'i' sounds, "beginnt" and "erklingt," bracket the other verbs, and especially those with 'a' sounds, "tagen" (9), "dampft" (10), and "schlagen" (11). Such a bracketing effect creates the atmosphere of a protective verbal canopy generated by "beginnt" and "erklingt."

The intensity of feeling inspired by the immediacy of nature which is implied by line 12—"Dass dir dein Herz erklingt:"—is similarly present in Eichendorff's poem "Der Abend":

Schweigt der Menschen laute Lust:
Rauscht die Erde wie in Träumen
Wunderbar mit allen Bäumen,
Was dem Herzen kaum bewusst,
Alte Zeiten, linde Trauer,
Und es schweifen leise Schauer
Wetterleuchtend durch die Brust.

While both poems share an emotional vitality, the persona in each poem experiences this vitality somewhat differently. In "Der Abend" the persona experiences some of his most profound feelings subtly and subconsciously from within. These feelings are motivated as much by inner turmoil as by external stimuli. In stanza two of "Abschied" the bliss and the emotional vitality of the persona are generated primarily from without, that is, by external stimuli from the world of nature.

The end of the second stanza anticipates the end of the poem and its message of hope and revitalization. In both contexts the "I" speaks of reenergizing and revitalizing himself emotionally, physically, and spiritually in a spirit of hope and confidence in the future.

In the third stanza the persona speaks of the "stilles, ernstes Wort" (18) which he experiences in the forest and which inspires him to have faith in genuinely vital work and love. In *Dichtung und Dichter bei Joseph von Eichendorff* H. Lüthi stresses that nature acts as a wise guide for the persona:

Die Natur kann dem Menschen ein Wegweiser sein, sie kann sein wie ein offenes Buch, dem treu Forschenden seine Hieroglyphenschrift lesbar werden lässt. Denn der Mensch ist nicht getrennt von der Natur . . . . Seine Seele besitzt das Organ, das die Möglichkeit hat, mit der Natur in Beziehung zu treten, und es kann sich in bestimmten Zeiten und in besonderen Stimmungen ereignen, dass ein völliger Einklang zwischen Natur und Seele entsteht. (190)

There are various examples in Eichendorff's poety of such a sense of communion and harmony between nature and the individual soul sensitively attuned to the beauty and sanctity of the natural environment. Eichendorff's "Abschied" is a perfect example of the presence of the "Hieroglyphenschrift" about which Lüthi speaks. The individual who can appreciate and understand the "Hieroglyphenschrift" of nature and its nuances may experience an epiphany and a sanctuary of light and hope in the natural environment, an epiphany and a sanctuary which will serve as a guide to the persona for the rest of his life.

The extraordinary discovery which the persona makes in the forest as described in stanza three prepares the way for and motivates the action of the fourth and final stanza of the poem. Stanza three of "Abschied" metaphorizes the persona's experience of nature in terms of language and linguistic vitality. In the sanctuary of the forest, the persona understands the essence of nature, of life, and realizes how he must approach his life in the future. In stanza three there is also the sense that the persona is one of the privileged ones who can truly appreciate and sensitively communicate with nature. One could claim that the "stilles, ernstes Wort" (18) to which the "I" refers is only perceptible in the "Zelt," in the forest sanctuary. Such a "stilles, ernstes Wort" (18) is only perceptible and comprehensible to a very select few who have the sensitivity to participate in the sanctuary in the forest and who have the capacity to appreciate the language of nature.

The nature-sensibility of the persona is further manifest in his ability not only to appreciate the language of nature but also to intuitively and fully comprehend the implications of nature's expression. The last several lines of stanza three also suggest a profound connectedness between the persona and nature. Only someone who has a deeply sensitive appreciation of nature, of its beauty, and of its vitality, could wish for and claim that his understanding of the words and of the signs of nature creates complete clarity in his mind and soul.

Eichendorff believes that the past may contain hieroglyphic indices of life. The hieroglyphic quality of language is strongly associated with the notion of the magic word. One might recall Eichendorff's famous quatrain:

Schläft ein Lied in allen Dingen,

Die da träumen fort und fort,

Und die Welt hebt an zu singen,

Triffst du nur das Zauberwort.

There are distinct similarities between this "Zauberwort" and the "stilles, ernstes Wort" (18) of "Abschied." It might seem outwardly as if both can be achieved by a passive reading of nature. However, one might claim that only an individual with a profound nature-sensibility who has achieved a vital sense of emotional and spiritual communion with nature can appreciate and understand the language of nature and its words and expressions of beauty, grace, harmony, and serenity. The persona in stanza three of "Abschied" makes it seem as if one could relatively easily "read" the words of nature; however, such ease is deceptive, for the persona is really an individual of great sensitivity for nature, as the entire poem demonstrates. Similarly, the "Zauberwort" is only attained by an individual who has an extraordinary capacity to appreciate and to value nature, who has the ability to unlock the mysteries and the magic of the song and reveal this to the world, which would presumably be comprised of those individuals who also have a vital appreciation of the natural environment.

Eichendorff's sense of the achievement of the "Zauberwort" is comparable in intensity and in scope to some of the statements which Percy Shelley makes about poetry in his essay "A Defence of Poetry." For example, Shelley states that a "poem is the very image of life expressed in its eternal truth." Shelley proceeds to say that poetry "lifts the veil from the hidden beauty of the world" and that poetry "enlarges the circumference of the imagination by replenishing it with thoughts of ever new delight." Shelley also asserts that a "great poem is a fountain for ever overflowing with the waters of wisdom and delight." The conceptual vitality, the perceptiveness, and the sensitivity of the poet enable him to discover the "Zauberwort" and manifest it in his poems which can nurture an awareness of beauty and an understanding of humanity in each new generation of readers. The poem which "is the very image of life expressed in its eternal truth" is the poem which embodies and exemplifies the "Zauberwort."

In both instances the "I" reads "the word" in the book of nature. The code of values, linguistic, emotional, and spiritual, is already present—the gifted "I" must simply read from it in nature and make it meaningful for the present context of his life and for those other individuals in society who share his abiding love for and reverence for nature. There is one key difference between these two passages with respect to the issue of making this moment meaningful beyond the context of the life of the persona. In the "Zauberwort" passage the goal appears to be not only to discover and reveal the "Zauberwort," but also to ensure that some portion of the world of everyday mortality will profit from this realization. In "Abschied" the aim is less orphic and more hermetic. While the understanding of the word of nature gives the persona insights into the world of humankind, the primary goal of this endeavor is to make this moment and the language of nature comprehensible to the persona, the nature-poet himself.

At the beginning of the third stanza there is a sense of static serenity. The "Wort" (18) has been written in the forest and is now properly established there. This quiet and serious "Wort" (18) is characterized by two fundamental qualities: it represents proper action and love and affirms a sense of sanctuary of sensitive souls away from the anguish and clamor of everyday mortality. The qualification of the "Wort" (18) as quiet, serene, and serious reaffirms the peaceful atmosphere which the persona has so far aimed to nurture in the poem.

In the third stanza the "I" expresses himself directly for the first time in the poem. That is, this is the first time the "I" appears as a subject pronoun in the poem. The "I" appears to gain confidence as he reads and reflects on the words in the forest and incorporates their wisdom into the process of his own life. In claiming that he has read the simple and true words faithfully, the persona enhances not only the world of nature as the source of such powerful expression and of his own vitality but also gives strength to his own existence as well. The persona proclaims an atmosphere of trust and faith in nature which contrasts conspicuously with the deceit and illusion which, according to the persona, often characterize the world of everyday mortality.

The third stanza of "Abschied," as the previous two stanzas, offers a rich display of stylistic associations which create and enhance the layers of meaning in the poem. The interplay of words with initial 'w' sounds gives insight into the meaning not only of this stanza but of the entire poem as well. The formal relation of "Wald" (17) and "Wort" (18) is significant. The "Wald" (17) designates the concretely idealized locus amoenus of nature; this is a special place of serenity and security which can offer solace away from the world of "Erdenleid." The "Wort" (18) is the verbal manifestation of this aesthetic and emotional sense of security and tranquility. It is interesting that "Hort" (20) appears as the last word of the first section of the third stanza because it seems to delineate the confluence of the form and meaning of "Wald" (17) and "Wort" (18). However, given the fact that "Wort" (18) bridges the gap between the world of nature and the world of humankind and harmonizes these two realms, one could say that "Wort" (18) is really the focal point of the interrelation of "Wald" (17) and "Hort" (20).

Unlike in the latter half of each of the previous two stanzas of the poem there is no semantic tension in the latter half of stanza three. In stanza three there are no such negative words as "betrogen" (5) or "Erdenleid" (14). The third stanza is permeated by a sense of cohesiveness and harmony centered around and generated by the "words" of nature. One example of this harmony is the "wahr" (22)-"klar" (24) relation which is of paramount importance because it unifies the world, the text, of nature, and the presence, the context, of the persona.

In the latter half of the third stanza the word, presented as ideal and abstract in the first half of the stanza, is concretized and pluralized. Through this concrete pluralization, the "Wort" (18) is revealed at the level of the "I" in the form of "Worte" (22). That the "I" asserts the veracity of the "Worte" (22) implies his attempt to underscore the significance of his own position in this moment of the poem. By emphasizing here the importance of the truthfulness of the "Worte" (22) the "I" anticipates his own claim at the end of the poem that the "Wort" (18), which along with the forest is transformed into the image of "des Ernsts Gewalt" (30), will always revitalize him and keep him young.

The "stilles, ernstes Wort" (18) is firmly established in the idealized world of nature, as is the noun phrase "die Worte" (22). It is interesting that "Wort" (18) and "Worte" (22) are bracketed by their qualifying adjectives, creating the sense of a linguistic sanctuary to reaffirm the sanctuary in the natural world. These attributes of the language of the forest reveal the aspects of nature which are most important for the persona: silence, seriousness, love, simplicity, truth, and devotion. Such features are intimately connected to the persona's awareness of the beauty of this sanctuary in the natural world.

While the last several lines of the third stanza describe the experience of the persona in the present context, they also have a future orientation because they anticipate the poetic argument of the fourth stanza. It is noteworthy that the line-final rhymes of these last several lines are mutually reinforcing. The noun "Wesen" (23) is connected not only formally through the consonance to words such as "Wald" (17), "Wort" (18), "Worte" (22), "wahr" (22) and "Ward's" (24) but also semantically to "Wald" (17) in particular because these two words represent the persona and the natural environment respectively as complementary dimensions of a coherent and unified whole. The "wahr" (22)–"klar" (24) rhyme at the end of the stanza is important because it affirms the capacity of the persona to interpret the language and being of nature sensitively. The final lines of the third stanza represent a moment of revelation by nature which is completely and insightfully understood by the persona in the ambience of the sanctuary of light and truth. H. Lüthi in *Dichtung und Dichter bei Joseph von Eichendorff* comments on the inspiration which nature offers the receptive individual who is attuned to its vitality: "Das sehnsüchtige Hinauslehnen in die Weite, der Aufbruch zur Wanderschaft sind Antworten der Seele auf den Ruf der Natur" (191). The persona in "Abschied" responds instinctively to the "Ruf der Natur," for nature will always make his life meaningful and worthwhile. Through his devotion to nature, the "I" in "Abschied" will avoid the possibility of "eine ästhetische Selbstvergötterung" which Lüthi describes as an existential danger for the persona in this context.

In stanza four the "I" acknowledges that he will soon have to leave the blissful sanctuary of nature for he will explore the "drama" of everyday mortality in its complexity and diversity. The fourth stanza affirms the personal connection which the persona feels towards nature, for he uses both personal pronoun and possessive adjective to address his beloved and inspirational apostrophic object. Uncertain of the future, the "I" will wander as a stranger into the unknown "Fremde" (26). Hermann Kunisch describes the "Fremde" as follows:

> Die Möglichkeit des Chaos im Herzen, in der Natur, in der Zeit und in der Kunst. Daher kann sie auch in den Gründen der Heimat beginnen; nichts, ausser dem zu Hause, ist eindeutig und dem Zwielicht entzogen. Nur wo Gott 'gewaltig' . . . die 'Konturen' durch die Fluren gezogen hat, ist Ordnung und damit Heimat. (144-45)

The "I" does experience a sense of uncertainty and anxiety because he knows that he will be a stranger in the world of everyday mortality. Yet, despite this uncertainty, the "I" knows that he can always turn to nature and to God in nature for the emotional, psychological, and spiritual supportiveness which he needs.

Only when the persona thinks of leaving the sanctuary of nature does he use a temporal expression. The poet anticipates and conceptualizes about the future still from the security of the natural sanctuary. In lines three and four of the last stanza the persona describes his anticipation of experiencing the intensity and vibrancy of everyday life. It is interesting that the negative words and tone which were present in the depiction of the world of everyday mortality in stanzas one and two have been diminished, sublimated, or even removed. The tone of "betrogen" (5) and "Erdenleid" (14) is no longer present; instead, the "I" anticipates the activity and dynamism of the "buntbewegten Gassen" (27) without any suggestion of negativity. Even though the "I" senses, as any "I" who has just been an integral part of such a blessed natural sanctuary, such a "chapel" of light and serenity, would inevitably do, that he will be a stranger in the world which he plans to visit and that he may never truly fit in, he is not daunted by the future. Rather, he welcomes it because he knows that whenever he feels isolated or lonely he can always reflect on the beauty and effulgence of the natural sanctuary which is so important to him and his heart and spirit will be soothed.

The use of the phrase "mitten in dem Leben" (29) suggests that the persona is aware that he can turn to his inspirational experience in the sanctuary at any time for guidance and support. The approach of the persona in Eichendorff's "Abschied" is similar to that of the "I" in Wordsworth's "I Wandered Lonely as a Cloud" and that of the "I" in Yeats' "The Lake Isle of Innisfree." In all three of these poems, the persona has enjoyed a delightful experience of beauty, peacefulness, and serenity in a special natural place. In departing from such a lovely space the persona feels that whenever he reflects upon its beauty and tranquility he will be comforted and soothed regardless of the difficulties and hardships which he may have to confront in the world of everyday mortality. Even though the persona may feel lonely or at odds with the everyday world, the power of nature's sincerity and the vitality of nature's emotional and spiritual comfort and guidance will always keep him youthful and emotionally and spiritually vibrant.

The rhyme scheme and formal connections of various words in the fourth stanza is as important as it was in the previous stanzas of the poem. The connections of the line-final words "verlassen" (25)~"Gassen" (27) and "gehn" (26)~"sehn" (28) emphasize the themes of departure, motion, and travel. The line-final words of the last four lines of the poem, by contrast, offer a sense of stasis and continuity in a world of change and dynamic motion. The "Leben" (29)~"erheben" (31) coupling, in particular, stresses the capacity of nature to uplift the soul and the spirit in the midst of the experience of everyday life.

The "Ernsts" (30)~"Einsamen" (31)~"erheben" (31) alliteration reaffirms the importance of the beauty and the language of nature which was emphasized in stanza three and the capacity of that beauty and language to nurture and sustain the heart and spirit of the persona wherever he may be in the world. The qualities of seriousness, loneliness or individuality, and elevation of the spirit are essential features of both stanza three and stanza four. The persona declares that his heart and spirit will remain perpetually vital and youthful as long as he can think about and glean a sense of comfort from the images and dimensions of the beautiful natural sanctuary which is epitomized by the lovely, green forest.

I would like now to examine some of Eichendorff's comments on poetry which are relevant for the discussion of his poem "Abschied." Eichendorff, as Shelley in his A *Defence of Poetry*, states that poetry should strive to represent the eternal and the beautiful: "Poesie geht auf nichts Geringeres, als auf das Ewige, das Unvergängliche, und absolute Schöne, was wir hienieden beständig ersehnen und nirgends erblicken" (Krabiel 91). Various passages of "Abschied" demonstrate this in the persona's attempt to represent the eternal significance of nature in images derived from everyday aspects of the natural environment.

The poet's song reveals the higher, eternal significance of earthly and mortal things. The poet must evolve this song from the objects, events, thoughts, and feelings of this world. The song remains bound initially to the worldly ambience, awaiting its liberation by the skillful poet. Through the song, the things of the world, animate and inanimate, regain their lost or diminished meaning. With his "Zauberwort" the nature-poet has the capacity to unlock and reveal the secrets and mysteries of nature. Eichendorff views nature to some extent as a hieroglyphic text of the divine which the poet decodes and interprets for humankind.

Krabiel discusses the significance of the symbolic dimension of poetry for Eichendorff:

> Die Forderung nach Darstellung der 'verhüllten geistigen Physiognomie' der Welt bedeutet für die Poesie das Zugleich von Wirklichkeit und Sinngebung im poetischen Bild. Dichtung, die das leistet, nennt Eichendorff 'symbolisch,' auch 'christlich' oder 'romantisch.' Sie ist die Poesie des Unendlichen im Gegensatz zur antik-heidnischen Verherrlichung des Endlichen und der sich selbst genügenden Sinnlichkeit. (92)

Eichendorff's message is presented or encoded in the "Zauberworte" of his poetic language. The poem "Abschied" exemplifies this type of poetry and this approach to poetry. Eichendorff's novel *Ahnung und Gegenwart* describes poetry similarly as the proclamation of God's eternal spirit through "rechte Worte und göttliche Erfindungen." The divine spirit is revealed through proper, correct words and divinely inspired creativity. One primary prerequisite for the individual who aspires to be a poet is a pure heart and spirit. Such a personal quality protects the poet from misusing the magic words and from becoming an "irrer Spielmann."

Richard Alewyn in his essay "Ein Wort über Eichendorff" describes the images in Eichendorff's poetry as signs which signify meaning, even if they do not present themselves as concepts and even if they are not translatable into any language:

> Sie sind so wenig bedeutungslos wie die Träume und die Mythen es sind. Sie sind nicht nur schöne, aber willkürliche Ornamente, sondern Symbole, die für ihre Wirkung auf eine Deutung zwar nicht angewiesen sind, die aber der Deutung darum nicht weniger zugänglich sind, solange der Interpret dessen bewusst ist, dass keine Deutung sie zu erschöpfen oder gar zu ersetzen vermag. (14)

Alewyn proceeds to say that Eichendorff takes his symbols from a collective language of symbols which is "as old as humankind" (15) and as familiar as the life and essence of the soul. The symbols of "Abschied" are the individual symbols of a personal confession of the "I" about the emotional and spiritual communion which he achieves with nature. The nouns function symbolically as icons—they represent distinctive features of the natural environment. Eichendorff uses these features to express a unique, personally vital conception and vision of nature.

Because of the prophecy, to some extent a self-motivated prophecy, of the "stilles, ernstes Wort," the "I" cannot remain for a prolonged period in the blissful atmosphere of the natural sanctuary. In trying to understand the charm and the challenge of the "Zauberwort," the "I" in "Abschied" expresses an implicit longing for the unknown and for as of yet unexplored spatial distances, which in the context of Eichendorff's work epitomizes and symbolizes a longing for the absolute and the eternal. Gerhard Möbus in his essay "Eichendorff und Novalis" describes Eichendorff's presentation of this longing in a passage in *Dichter und Gesellen* :

> Eichendorff gibt hier den Blick frei ins innerste Geheimnis seiner symbolischen Poesie; denn dem Sterbenden, der in die Heimat zurückgekehrt ist, die ihm einst so armselig erschien, enthüllt sich, dass sein Sehnen nach Italien und Rom, nach seinen Gärten und Palästen, in Wahrheit Sehnsucht nach dem Ewigen war. (179)

In Eichendorff's "Abschied" the persona expresses a sense of longing, implicitly and explicitly, for the beautiful and vital sanctuary of nature which inspired and soothed him.

In "Abschied" the persona's stance at the threshold between the inner world of nature and the outside world of everyday mortality is resolved by a longing for eternity and for a timeless spatiality. A similar threshold perspective is seen in Eichendorff's novel *Ahnung und Gegenwart* where the window is used to form the boundary and transitional marker between the hermetic space of the inner world of the subject and the space of the outer world of temporality and temporal finitude. There exist various similar images in Romantic paintings as well. For example, in Caspar David Friedrich's painting, *The Woman at the Window*, the figure looks out from the protective, hermetic space of the room into the unknown and indefinable space of the outside world, the domain of mortality. The distance, the "Ferne," can be presented as the unknown and the unknowable characterized by a sense of anxiety and uncertainty. However, the distance, the "Ferne," can also represent an affirmative vision of the unknown qualified by an atmosphere of infinity and magical possibilities.

Richard Alewyn, while suggesting that the landscapes of Eichendorff's poetry may have a magical quality, also states that such landscapes are often arranged in definite parts. Another view of the landscape in Eichendorff's poetry is expressed by Hermann Kunisch who stresses the infinite capacities in this natural environment: "Es geht immer über die fühlbare, als bewegt empfundene Landschaft hinaus ins Grenzenlose, in eine unendliche Weite, die das Nichts oder das Zuhause sein kann, das Gutsein der Kindheit, der alten schönen Zeit, der widerkommenden guten Zeit" (144). The landscape in Eichendorff, according to Kunisch, can signify a sense of endlessness and infinity or a sense of home, or even a special place of childhood, of a past congenial time, or a vision of a blissful future space.

Like the poetic persona in Friedrich Schiller's "Die Teilung der Erde," Eichendorff's "I" in "Abschied" feels a strong emotional and spiritual connection to the world of nature and to the world of the divine. The "I" in Schiller's poem, the poet, although arriving late on the scene when the material objects and possessions of everyday reality have been distributed, will finish his quest successfully because of his devotion to the divine. The image of eternity is present in the sense that the poet is always permitted by the divine to visit in heaven. The "I" in Eichendorff's poem, while assured within himself of his vital connection to the world of nature, does not have the same sense of divine intervention on his behalf. However, Eichendorff's persona believes profoundly in the vision of harmony and serenity which he has enjoyed in the sanctuary in the forest and which will sustain him as he wanders through the challenges of everyday mortality. By achieving and sustaining the continuity of the self, in the spirit of Wordsworth's "I" of the Immortality Ode, Eichendorff's "I" in "Abschied" will affirm his own emotional, psychological, and spiritual strength and show that he cherishes his perpetual appreciation of nature and his capacity to participate in the divine benevolence of the natural world and its luminescent sanctuary.

Eichendorff's "Der frohe Wandersmann" ("The Happy Wanderer"), which appears in his famous narrative "Aus dem Leben eines Taugenichts," celebrates the inspirational importance of the morning light most vitally. In the first stanza of the poem it is suggested that God sends the individual whom he favors out into the world to show him the wonders of the beautiful natural environment. Such an individual, whether he travels near or far, will experience the divine and extraordinary beauty of the mountains, forests, streams, and fields. The tone of the first stanza is conspicuously positive—this stanza implies that it is a distinct privilege to explore the "weite Welt" (2) to experience the breadth and the depth of the world's wonders.

Stanza two offers a contrast to the first stanza in thematic emphasis and in tone. In stanza two the persona describes "Die Trägen" (5), who stay at home in an attitude of lingering indifference to the world and who are focused intently on everyday concerns instead of developing a more open-minded approach to life and instead of trying to nurture a faith in and an appreciation of "das Morgenrot" (6). The lack of genuine appreciation of "das Morgenrot" (literally, the red of the morning sky, but more symbolically, the day, or even the light of faith) which these individuals exhibit is also directly connected to their lack of understanding and appreciation of the natural environment. The concerns of these individuals are domestic and do not typically expand beyond the confines of a limited environment.

In stanza three the beautiful aspects of nature which inspire the persona and those individuals who appreciate and who are motivated by "das Morgenrot" (6) are depicted in greater detail. There is a power and a vitality in the natural environment which energizes the persona. He admires the streams which spring from the mountains and which cascade dynamically down the mountainside; he also praises the birds whose delightful song inspires him to join in their harmonious melodies. Such a lovely natural environment represents a sanctuary of light and music for the persona, enraptured by the beauty around him.

In the fourth and concluding stanza of the poem the persona asserts his life-philosophy of an acceptance of God's desires and wishes founded on an implicit faith in the divine. The persona believes that God governs over the world and will aim to ensure that a sense of order and stability will be consistently preserved. The strong religious faith of the persona is reaffirmed in the last stanza. The end of "Der frohe Wandersmann" also proclaims that the persona feels himself to be a part not only of a divinely governed universe but also of a universe which is characterized by an orderly cyclicality and a rational coherence.

The "abab" rhyme scheme which appears throughout the poem reinforces the persona's belief in an orderly and a harmonious world. The prominent presence of the light, mentioned specifically in line two of stanza two, is strongly implied throughout the rest of the poem. The light of the morning, and by extension, the light of day, provides a haven for the persona, who has the sensitivity and the thoughtfulness to appreciate the beauty and the vitality of the divinely created and arranged natural world. The persona's faith in God represents a perpetual sanctuary of light which guides him and supports him as he makes his way through the world.

Two other poems by Eichendorff which emphasize the importance of the morning are "Morgengebet" ("Morning Prayer") and "Frühe" ("The Early Morning"). In "Morgengebet" the persona states that he feels revitalized by the morning light to strengthen his capacity to pursue his dedication to the divine and to strengthen his spiritual journey to God. "Morgengebet" represents a strongly religious morning prayer and a refuge of quiet devotion to the divine realm.

In "Frühe" a lark is sensitively described as the first being in the natural world to be aware of the appearance of the morning and of the morning light. In stanza one of "Frühe" there is an indication of the presence of "Nebel" (1), of fog and mist, which pervades the landscape. The gray in the east could be interpreted as a sign of the imminence of morning or of the gradual appearance of the morning as the darkness of the night diminishes. Yet, these are just the initial murmurings and rustlings of the morning, for in lines three and four of the first stanza "die Welt" (the world) is portrayed as still being asleep. For most animate beings the moment which is described in stanza one is still too early to sense or to perceive the first hints or indications of the day.

Stanza two of "Frühe" provides one notable example of an animate being who does appear to sense the imminence of the morning and of the morning light. This is a single lark, who alone has dreamed of or sensed the subtle presence of the light. Everything around the bird is silent and still encompassed by the reflections and imaginings of the night. The light is only barely perceptible along the horizon and in the heavens. The instinct of the lark is strong enough to feel that the light of day will be coming soon. The lark is enveloped in a sanctuary of early morning light and tranquility. One might even say that the lark, perhaps in some sense symbolic of the poet or creative artist, creates a sanctuary of imagined early morning light in its splendid isolation.

In "Frühlingsdämmerung" there is an abundance of light and vitality in nature which is emphasized in the first several lines:

In der stillen Pracht,

In allen frischen Büschen und Bäumen

Flüstert's wie Träumen

Die ganze Nacht. (1-4)

Although it is still nighttime, the landscape is suffused with a vibrant luminescence emanating from the moon. The silence of the night is permeated by a pleasant rustling in the bushes and trees—these are the dreams and visions of nature in anticipation of the spring. That the robes of the "schlanken Wolkenfrau'n" (7-8) can be clearly described as white reinforces the notion that the light of the moon spreads a powerful and penetrating radiance over the natural environment. In one of the following lines "die hellen Waldquellen" (11) rush downward from the rocky mountain heights to the depths of the valley, which would prefer to slumber and to maintain a semblance of quiet tranquility. Or perhaps one could say that the depths of the valley are merely awakening slowly from the stern serenity of winter to the effulgent vitality of spring and the vibrant energy of vernal growth.

In the next section of the poem the comprehensive power of the wind is described. As the light of the moon suffuses the entire landscape so the wind rustles vitally with a gentle and a persistent force through the blooming linden trees, over the grazing deer, and over and around various lakes. The wind affects all aspects of nature on the earth, in the sky, and on the waters. The presence of the wind over the lake is so profound that the water nymphs or naiads awake drowsily to inquire about the breath of air which touches them so sweetly.

The poem "Frühlingsdämmerung" depicts a sanctuary of light, tranquility, and inner harmony. The vitality of the natural scene is motivated by the potent light of the moon and by the clouds moving across the late night sky "wie geheime Gedanken" (8). The primary aspects of the natural environment in this poem are presented through personification. For example, in lines 2-4 the rustling in the bushes and trees is portrayed as the power of dreams. And in lines 5-8 the clouds are delineated not merely as "Wolken" but as "Wolkenfrau'n" who lithesomely float across the night sky like secret thoughts.

The notion of "Pracht" appears in the poems "Frühlingsdämmerung" and "Sehnsucht" in a similar thematic emphasis. "Pracht" suggests magnificence and splendor. The source or motivating force of this magnificence and splendor in both poems is the light. While this is not the bright light of day, the light in these two poems (the light which derives from the moon and the stars) is a powerful, profound, and effervescently lyrical radiance which illuminates and energizes not only its immediate environment but also the entire world of which it is an integral part.

In the poem "Jugendsehnen" Eichendorff reveals a profound faith in and an optimism about the future. At the beginning of the poem the persona stands on the verge of the "blauer Strom," which could suggest literally a stream or more symbolically the stream of life. The optimistic undertone of the beginning of the poem is reinforced by the fact that the persona addresses the "blauer Strom" in a personal and a congenial manner. When he says in stanza one that he is preparing his "Schifflein" in a spirit of pious longing, this could imply literally a boat or more symbolically that he is preparing his life for the future.

In stanza two of "Jugendsehnen" the persona says that the blue stream, the "blauer Strom," brings him greetings as well as unusual and pleasant sounds and melodies from distant mountains and faroff lands. In fact, the persona feels so comfortable in the presence of the "blauer Strom" that he states he is inspired to trust and to feel a sense of emotional and spiritual communion with the breezes of the spring.

In stanza three of "Jugendsehnen" the persona admits that he is not sure either of his destination or of his purpose or mission. Yet, he is encouraged and strengthened by the endless horizon of "Morgenrot," the red of the morning sky which fills his heart with a sense of virtue, power of devotion, and freedom. In stanza four of the poem the persona is so exhilarated by the beautiful morning light that he feels as if it shines for him. Inspired by this powerful light, which creates and nurtures a sanctuary of hope and faith, the persona declares that the sails of his boat are filled and that his life is ready to move towards the future. This poem ends optimistically with an emphasis on the presence of a spirit of eternal youth.

In "Ein Wunderland," which appears in Eichendorff's novel *Ahnung und Gegenwart*, the dominant image is a sanctuary of light. The "Wunderland," the wonderland, is characterized by golden streams of light and melodies which resound through the depths which want to share with the persona "ein hohes Wort." The phrase "ein hohes Wort" could suggest a sacred or pious word, phrase, or statement or even a word, phrase, or statement which represents a moment of wisdom.

Stanza two of "Ein Wunderland" is also pervaded by sound and musical resonances. In the last two lines of the stanza there is a fusion of music and longing. When there is such an abundance of tones or sounds that they fall like the rain in a spring shower, then "Sehnsucht" (longing) will be fulfilled and the persona will be transported to the desired place.

In stanza three of the poem the transported spirit would exist beyond the anxiety, sadness, and trivialities of everyday mortality. The persona would not have to look down and feel intimately connected with or influenced by the world of everyday mortality and its vicissitudes. Rather, he would be free to follow the lure of the love which continually elevates and soothes his spirit.

Stanza four of "Ein Wunderland" creates a culminating moment of beautiful music and holy melodies. Whoever is touched by and inspired by the holy and sacred melodies achieves an emotional and a spiritual communion with "die Musik der Sterne" (the music of the stars). Yet, this is not a static condition. Such an epiphanic moment of melodious light and radiant melody becomes an eternal movement into eternal distances. The ending of this poem is somewhat reminiscent of the ending of "Der frohe Wandersmann." In both poems the "Wunderland," the beautiful sanctuary, could be described as a luminescent state of mind inspired by a profound spiritual faith.

Even though Eichendorff's poem "Sehnsucht" ("Longing") describes an event at night, it is permeated with a strong sense of light. This potent light is manifest in the first line of the poem: "Es schienen so golden die Sterne" (1). This golden light infuses and pervades all three stanzas of the poem. In stanza one the persona describes himself as standing alone at the window and listening to the "Posthorn" (4) resounding in the quiet landscape. He thinks to himself how wonderful it would be if he would be able to travel along with such company in the splendid summer night. The stars spread a warm glow not only over the landscape described in the poem but also over the persona and over the poem itself. This warm luminescence inspires the persona to imagine creatively and to long for a more congenial experience.

Stanza two describes the nocturnal travelers as youthful and exuberant. There are two companions who are wandering on the mountain slope and singing as they proceed on their journey. In the spirit of the romantic atmosphere of this poem the distances are not specifically described. It is not clear how far the persona actually is from the Posthorn; nor is it clear how close the travelers who are singing are to the persona. Such an ambiguity, one might claim, helps to sustain the romantic atmosphere of the poem. One might even wonder whether the persona can hear or see the "junge Gesellen," the travelers, distinctly at all. Especially as the "Posthorn" (4) is described as sounding "aus weiter Ferne" (3), perhaps the scenario of this poem is more a tribute to the persona's imagination than a descriptive rendering of an event.

The song of the youthful travelers in stanza two is depicted as unrestrained, open, and vital—they are unafraid of expressing themselves dynamically in the nocturnal ambience of the wilderness, and their song fills the mountains and forest solitudes. Their melodies reaffirm the beauty and vitality of the natural environment, for they sing of the sublime aspects of nature, such as deep mountain ravines and streams which plunge from the cliffs into the dark night as well as of the more picturesque features, such as the gently rustling forests.

In stanza three of "Sehnsucht" the richly melodious song of the travelers concentrates more on the picturesque rather than the sublime:

Sie sangen von Marmorbildern,

Von Gärten, die überm Gestein

In dämmernden Lauben verwildern,

Palästen im Mondenschein,

Wo die Mädchen am Fenster lauschen,

Wann der Lauten Klang erwacht,

Und die Brunnen verschlafen rauschen

In der prächtigen Sommernacht. (17-24)

These individuals sing of lovely marble statues and images, of exquisite gardens which grow wild in twilight arbors and special nooks. The travelers also sing of women who listen at the window to beautiful melodies while fountains splash quietly and delicately in the lovely summer night. The senses of the persona and of the individuals within the ambience of the poem are very much alive in this luminescent night. Perhaps one reason for the vitality of the scenario and of the individuals within it is the aura of profound luminescence which is omnipresent.

While the "Marmorbildern" (17) could have a more negative connotation, as in Eichendorff's story, "Das Marmorbild," one could also view the "Marmorbildern" in this poem as creating an atmosphere of longing which lures the persona in a positive sense into its orbit. That "Marmorbildern" rhymes with "verwildern" suggests that the marble images are connected with an atmosphere of decay. However, the "Marmorbildern" are also an integral part of the dreamy aura at the end of the poem, which seems to uplift the spirit and lighten the heart of the persona. The palaces appear to come to life in the lovely light of the moon. Such palaces with their gently rustling fountains and delightful and melancholy melodies are sanctuaries of light which inspire the persona creatively and emotionally.

From the beginning of stanza two to the end of stanza three there is a thematic movement from the sublime to the picturesque. Conspicuously sublime features of the natural environment which predominate in stanza two become a more balanced array of the sublime and the picturesque in stanza three culminating ultimately in the picturesque notion of the young women listening at the window to the lovely melodies while the fountain rustles softly in the magnificence of the summer night. It is noteworthy that the poem concludes with the image of the young women at the window because this takes us back in a sense to the beginning of the poem. For the persona at the beginning of the poem portrays himself as standing at the window listening to the melodies of the splendid summer night. This arrangement of images gives the poem a sense of coherence and cohesiveness and also suggests a dimension of cyclicality in the experience of "Sehnsucht."

The poem "Sehnsucht" could also be interpreted as a hymn to the power of the imagination. For, as previously suggested, the persona only hears the "Posthorn" from a considerable distance. This would imply that he is unable to see clearly the travelers who are with the "Posthorn." Presumably then, the persona would be unable to see and perhaps even hear clearly the travelers who are described in stanza two. Given the sense of distance, it seems unlikely that the persona in stanza one would be able to hear so distinctly in stanza two that the travelers are singing of the ravines, the forests, and other features of nature. Moreover, the sublime landscape of which the travelers are singing appears rather inaccessible, which makes one wonder about the possible location of the persona in stanza one. At the time the poem was written, it is possible that there was a hostel or inn in the area which would have permitted the persona to have a special vantage-point to appreciate the presence of such nocturnal travelers. However, as this landscape seems rather inaccessible, one might also wonder whether stanzas two and three are more an imaginative creation of the persona than a realistic rendering of his direct experience. Moreover, if the "junge Gesellen" are wandering through the landscape, as is suggested in stanza two, they seem to be moving at a good pace as they traverse this scene, so one might wonder how it would be possible for the persona to hear from his relatively distant perspective the various topics about which the travelers are singing. Presumably, if they are moving through the landscape, only part of their song would have been audible.

Such questions about the location of the persona and the location of the travelers given the mountainous landscape which is described, might make one wonder whether the poem is not a tribute to the imagination and the creativity of the persona, the poet. The persona in stanza one might have a tremendous auditory capacity and be able to hear conversations, songs, and melodies from a considerable distance. However, one might also view the persona as having a fertile imagination which conjures up the scene of the travelers wandering through the landscape and sharing their lovely melodies with the surrounding natural environment. That the poem returns at the end to the image of individuals poised at the window and listening to the ethereal melodies which emerge from the surrounding ambience does reaffirm the importance of the intellectual and physical stance of the persona at the beginning. That the end of the poem returns to the locus of the beginning could be said to reinforce the significance of the persona as the focal point of the creative display of the poem.

Egon Schwartz writes in *Joseph von Eichendorff* that the images in the poem "Sehnsucht" are acoustic: "The horn is 'heard'; the young fellows announce their presence by 'singing'; the forests and wells 'rustle'; the lutes sound and the maidens listen" (96). Schwartz proceeds to speak of a "vagueness" in the poem which derives from "indefinite and haphazardly listed phenomena which first take on reality when joining together to form the overall atmospheric impression" (96). Schwartz elaborates on this point in his conclusion about the poem, saying that the "musical-acoustic character of Eichendorff's poem, the chaotic nature of the perceptions, the nocturnal indistinctness of this world, the loneliness . . . of the subject whose experiences these are . . . are a singularly pure expression of the Romantic inner turmoil" (98).

While I would agree that the musical-acoustic character and the loneliness of the lyrical "I" are prominent features of the poem, I view the presence of the golden light as so vital that it suffuses the entire landscape with its radiance. The perceptions, as diverse as they might seem, could be interpreted as being innately and inextricably linked through the verse itself. The rhyme scheme in each stanza unites the seemingly disparate images in a cohesive unity of expression. Line one of "Sehnsucht" is for me of paramount importance, for it establishes the tone and introduces the atmosphere of the poem. The golden light which emanates from the stars in line one illuminates the entire landscape of the rest of the poem as well as the creative vitality of the persona in his process of imaginative viewing and listening. Such a dynamic light as it fills the space of the poem could even be seen as the process of longing which manifests itself in different moments of this nocturnal experience. The golden light of line one of "Sehnsucht" is so powerful that it fills or touches, even if softly and subtly sometimes, the "Felsenschlüften," the "Wälder," the "Marmorbildern," and "die Brunnen."

Katja Löhr stresses the importance of "Sehnsucht" as a poetic principle or philosophical approach in Eichendorff's poetry in *Sehnsucht as poetologisches Prinzip bei Joseph von Eichendorff*: "Der Wunsch des Ich entspricht einem In-der-nacht-Reisen, das eher einem Zustand denn einem Prozess gleichkommt" (286).

Löhr proceeds to describe the nocturnal atmosphere in the poem in the following interesting manner: "Diese Nacht wird zweifach bestimmt; Von der Nacht im Sommer ist die Rede, und diese wird als 'prächtig' wahrgenommen, ja bewertet . . . . vielmehr wird diese von Lichtelementen durchleuchtete Nacht vom Ich als angenehm, wenn nicht gar verlockend empfunden" (286). The persona of "Sehnsucht" does view the bright night as congenial, for it illuminates and soothes his heart and soul.

There are several other poems by Eichendorff which focus on the description of the night and on a radiance or illumination within the darkness and the night. In "Frühlingsnacht" ("Spring Night"), for example, the power of the light of the moon is delineated as having the capacity to inspire miracles: "Alte Wunder wieder scheinen / Mit dem Mondesglanz herein." The spring night which is described so sensitively in "Frühlingsnacht" represents a nocturnal environment, a special sanctuary, of natural splendor, beautiful sounds, and divine light.

In "Abendlandschaft" ("Evening Landscape") the persona describes a scenario which suggests the dynamism and sensory vitality of nature before the end of the day. In stanza one of "Abendlandschaft" the sounds of the shepherd blowing his musical instrument, of a shot in the distance, and of the quietly rustling forests and quietly murmuring streams are prominent features of the natural landscape. In stanza two of "Abendlandschaft" the persona notices the shimmering glow of the evening sun behind a hill and wishes that he could have wings to fly towards such a beautiful natural spectacle. Such a golden evening radiance represents a sublime sanctuary of light which would comfort the spirit of the persona. Similarly, in "Die Stille," which focuses more on a longing for the morning and its radiance, the persona expresses a wish, as does the persona in "Abendlandschaft," to fly as "ein Vöglein" over the sea to heaven.

In "Nachts" ("At Night") the persona depicts a sanctuary of stillness and serenity as well as an atmosphere of ambiguity, melancholy, and uncertainty. The occasional and periodic appearance of the moon helps to create this soft and serene atmosphere, which is also characterized by the presence of music. In stanza one the nightingale awakens occasionally. Then everything is once again very quiet. In stanza two of "Nachts" the persona characterizes the

"Nachtgesang" (7) as wonderful, suggesting the presence of the miraculous. Perhaps because the light of the moon is not so conspicuous, the intensity of the darkness in the forest becomes rather overpowering. Ultimately, in a state of relative uncertainty the persona wonders whether his own meandering melodies are a call from the depths of his dreams or perhaps even a call from the depths of the dreams of the night.

In "Nachtlied" ("Song of the Night") the persona suggests that only the "liebe Nachtigall" is his true friend and companion. In a world characterized by falseness and deceit only one individual is loyal and true to the persona. Only the "liebe Nachtigall" shares the fears, the concerns, and the hopes of the persona. The persona concludes the poem by saying that together he and the nightingale will praise God until the bright morning appears. The "lichte Morgen" could be interpreted literally and symbolically. Literally, the "lichte Morgen" represents the morning of the new day which is bright and filled with light. Symbolically, the "lichte Morgen" signifies the light of eternity, the light of a divine moment which fills and illuminates the soul.

A number of poems by Joseph von Eichendorff are similar in spirit, theme, and tone to various paintings by his Romantic contemporary Caspar David Friedrich. Friedrich's *Monk by the Sea*, *The Solitary Tree*, and a *Traveller Looking Over a Sea of Fog* epitomize the situation and the stance of the individual creator and artist who is devoted to his work and who achieves an emotional and a spiritual communion with the beautiful natural world and with the divine. Friedrich's *Abbey in the Oak Woods* and *The Siebengebirge* suggest the reverence for nature and for the divine which is central to Eichendorff's poetic conception.

Another of Eichendorff's poems which describes the atmosphere of a night which is permeated by an inner light is "Mondnacht," which celebrates the beauty of the moon. In the first stanza of this poem there is a harmonious concordance and consanguinity between the heavens and the earth—this consanguinity is generated by an emotional and a physical closeness between the sky and the land. The earth is even presented as dreaming of the sky in a shimmer of blossoms.

Stanza two continues the portrait of the beautiful natural landscape. The air or wind moves softly through the fields, and the forests are gently rustling. Moreover, the night is described as being "sternklar" (8), which suggests not only the presence of an abundance of light emanating from the stars but also the dissemination of that light throughout the clarity and openness of the natural environment.

As in "Frühlingsdämmerung" and "Sehnsucht," so in "Mondnacht" the night is a time not of pervasive darkness, hardship, or suffering. Rather, in these poems, as well in various others by Eichendorff, the night is a time of serenity, of visionary and epiphanic moments of light, of sanctuaries of light which lighten the heart, illuminate and strengthen the spirit, and enliven the soul. In the third and final stanza of "Mondnacht" the persona is so inspired by the beauty and the vitality of the natural landscape delineated in the first two stanzas that his soul spreads its wings and "Flog durch die stillen Lande, / Als flöge sie nach Haus" (11-12). The persona feels such a strong sense of emotional and spiritual communion with the beautiful natural environment and with the luminescent night that he can achieve a radiant expansiveness of self in this picturesque ambience.

One might claim that multiple interpretations of the last line of the poem are possible. To what is the persona referring when he says that his spirit flew homeward? Does he mean that his spirit literally flew homeward? Or does the persona suggest such a wandering in a metaphorical sense? In the first two stanzas of "Mondnacht" there is no direct reference to an "I," to a persona. The persona, who is implicitly present as an observer, delineates the harmonious, tranquil, and luminescent atmosphere of the night in these stanzas. The connectedness and consanguinity of different features of nature is especially reinforced in the first two stanzas by the rhyme scheme. The "abab" rhyme scheme implies the vital interconnectedness of the various aspects of nature which are mentioned.

In the third stanza the persona instinctively and inevitably participates in this blissful interconnectedness. He feels so intimately a part of this beautiful and harmonious natural environment that his soul can wander freely in its spatial and temporal expansiveness. A literal interpretation of the last line of stanza three could suggest that the persona wanders homeward in a spirit of happiness and joy having been an integral part of the lovely harmony of nature. Because of his intimate connection to nature, the persona can return readily to this inspirational and lovely natural environment whenever he wishes. A metaphorical interpretation of the final line of stanza three would suggest that the soul of the persona, in the spirit of the congenial interplay of "Himmel" and "Erde" in stanza one, wanders into the heavens or to Heaven in travelling "nach Haus" (12). The soul of the persona feels perfectly at home not only in the congenial refuge of the beautiful natural environment but also in the sanctuary of the heavens which represents a vitally significant dimension of that environment.

Egon Schwartz interprets Eichendorff's "Mondnacht" as containing some of the poet's "favorite images and expressions" (100) while also representing "a night free of any torment" (100). The line "Es rauschten leis die Wälder" (7) is quintessential Eichendorff. Schwartz insightfully describes this poem as being "purged of all superfluities and immersed in a simplicity that is no longer of this earth" (100).

The title of "Sonette" relates to six sonnets by Eichendorff which focus on the theme of poets and creativity. In stanza one of "Sonette 1" the streams and waterfalls which plunge down from the mountains are described. Some are tempestuous whereas others have a softer tone, even communing melodiously with the nymphs who listen serenely in the lovely green landscape. Stanza two concentrates on the notion that all of the streams and rivulets ultimately flow into the larger "Strom" which rushes energetically through the beautiful countryside. In the first quatrain of this sonnet the "Strom" passes by isolated castles and between vineyards as it winds its way into the distance. In the second quatrain of the sonnet the stream finally flows into the sea: "Entwandelt er zum Meer, dem wundervollen, / Wo träumend sich die sel'gen Inseln spiegeln, / Und auf den Fluten ruhn die ew'gen Sterne."

Lawrence Radner describes these last few lines insightfully: "'Die sel'gen Inseln' are reflected on an ocean upon which the eternal stars rest; they do not simply shine upon the waves" (70). Radner proceeds to assert that this "suggests that the surface of the ocean and the firmament intersect at an 'infinite' distance, at the ultimate horizon, where time returns to eternity" (70). Radner concludes this point by saying that "here, as in a dream, man 'sees' the reflection of the blessed land" (70). Such a blessed land, permeated by the spirit of the "sel'gen Inseln," represents a sanctuary of blessed light beyond the vicissitudes of mortality.

In Eichendorff's novel *Ahnung und Gegenwart* there is an interesting conversation between Leontin, Friedrich, and Faber describing the innocence of Friedrich which is characterized by the aura of such a blessed light and sanctuary:

> Wenn wir von einer inneren Freudigkeit erfüllt sind, welche, wie die Morgensonne, die Welt überscheint, und alle Begebenheiten, Verhältnisse und Kreaturen zur eigentümlichen Bedeutung erhebt, so ist dieses freudige Licht vielmehr die wahre göttliche Gnade, in der allein alle Tugenden und grossen Gedanken gedeihen, und die Welt ist wirklich so bedeutsam, jung und schön, wie sie unser Gemüt in sich selber anschaut. (II, 41)

The innocence, the inner light, which is delineated here is that of divine grace. Radner describes this as "the world of the morning sun, God's love which illuminates, renders perceptible to our finite minds the true, unique significance of all that is" (72). Only in the luminescent warmth of this divine light do our minds and spirits perceive the nuances and subtleties of the everyday world as well as the genuine beauty of the natural environment and its precious sanctuaries of light.

One of Eichendorff's most important and effective poems is "Der Einsiedler" ("The Hermit"), representing the quintessentially romantic theme of an isolated individual who attains a sense of emotional and spiritual communion in the presence of nature. In "Der Einsiedler" the hermit addresses the night in a congenial manner as the "Trost der Welt." The night provides the existence of the hermit, the isolated individual, with a profound sense of comfort and consolation. As an individual who has a strong nature-sensibility, the hermit delineates the night and its essential features very sensitively and thoughtfully.

In stanza one of "Der Einsiedler" the persona says that the night rises softly from the mountains as the breezes and winds all sleep and rest. Perhaps as a parallel to the isolation of the persona in the forest the poem then offers the description of "ein Schiffer," weary and alone, chanting his evening song in the harbor to the glory of God. This sailor is a "kindred mutation" (to use Wordsworth's phrase) of the hermit, the persona of the poem. The sailor could also be viewed as a wanderer and as a manifestation of the relatively isolated hermetic existence which is emphasized in the focus.

In stanza two of "Der Einsiedler" the persona states in the opening lines that the passage of the years has left him alone and seemingly forgotten by the world. The rhyme scheme of the first two lines of this stanza, "gehn"– "stehen," is especially interesting because it might suggest a capacity on the part of the persona of the poem to establish a connectedness with time which he would not or would not likely have achieved if he had not lived in his existential isolation. For line one of stanza two, ending in "gehn," has to do with the passage of time. And line two, ending in "stehen," deals with the isolation of the persona. That these two lines share the line-ending rhyme suggests a semantic connection between the lines and reinforces the notion that the persona is more closely connected to time and its essence than other individuals in society. Line three, ending in "vergessen," focuses on society and the world. That this line does not rhyme with line one whose thematic emphasis is time, implies that the individuals who are of the world and who are intimately involved with society and everyday mortality do not necessarily have the intuitive capacity or sensibility to become intimately acquainted with time and with its visions of flux and of the future.

In lines four through six of stanza two the persona celebrates the beauty and grace of the night which came to comfort and to soothe him in his exceptional isolation. That the persona delineates his situation as being characterized by and permeated by "Waldesrauschen" suggests his intimate emotional and spiritual connection with the natural environment. This vital connectedness is further reinforced in stanza two by the overall rhyme scheme. The first three lines of stanza two, which portray the isolation and the loneliness of the persona, are joined to the final three lines of the stanza, lines four to six, by the rhyming of "vergessen" and "gesessen." One might claim that even though the persona seems isolated from the world, he really is more connected than he appears to be because of his emotional and spiritual closeness to the world of nature. That the persona in stanza two describes the appearance of the night as "wunderbar" is also significant because it suggests that there is something miraculous about this moment. The comforting emergence of the night to illuminate and assuage the soul of the persona is a miraculous occurrence.

That line one of stanza three repeats the first line of the poem reinforces the notion that the night is a supreme and revitalizing comfort for the hermit, the persona of the poem. The quiet and the tranquility of the night certainly contribute to its capacity to soothe the persona profoundly. Line two of stanza three introduces a note of personal weariness in the development of the poem. For the first time in the poem the persona openly admits that he is weary. Such weariness could derive from the physical weakness of increasing age or from an emotional-spiritual fatigue from confronting the hardships and vicissitudes of everyday mortality. In line three the persona states that the darkness is spreading over the expanse of the sea.

The presentation of the night in line three of stanza three seems to differ from the description of the night in line one of this stanza. In line one of stanza three, as in line one of stanza one, the night is portrayed as being a supremely positive and comforting force which has the ability to illuminate the persona's soul and to vanquish the anxieties caused by everyday mortality. However, in line three of stanza three a different dimension of the night is described. This aspect of the night is specifically associated with darkness and not with light. This dimension of the night suggests an ending to the day for it permeates the extent of the waters. The "stille Nacht," by contrast, is a softer, more serene, more luminescent, and more soothing aspect of the night.

In the last three lines of stanza three, the final lines of the poem, the persona anticipates eternity. Exhausted by the cares and sufferings of everyday mortality, the persona wants to rest. The persona awaits confidently the emergence of the "ew'ge Morgenrot," the light of eternity, shining through the serene forest. The use of the word "stillen" in the last line of the poem is as affirmative as the presence of "stille" in the first lines of the first and third stanzas. This word infuses the poem and the life of the persona with an aura of profound stillness and ethereal tranquility. The night of "stille Nacht" is made a little more luminescent by its formal connection with the quiet of the "stillen Wald" at the end which exudes an atmosphere of eternity. And the "stillen Wald" is made more profoundly serene by its formal association with the "stille Nacht" which displays a soothing peacefulness which can remove and wash away the pains and sufferings of everyday mortality.

Eichendorff's poetry, as the poetry of Wordsworth and other similar poets and artists, reveals the importance of childhood and familiar places, places of perpetual relevance and significance for the creative artist who has been inspired by them. A statement by Eichendorff reinforces the importance of such places: "Wer einen Dichter recht verstehen will, muss seine Heimat kennen, auf ihre stillen Plätze ist der Grundton gebannt, der dann durch all seine Bücher wie ein unaussprechliches Heimweh fortklingt." Eichendorff asserts that it is important to become familiar with the home area, the inspirational places, of a poet to be able to truly understand the spirit and the nuances of the poet's work.

In his book *Joseph von Eichendorff* H. Ohff stresses not only the importance of understanding the places of the poet's childhood and youth to appreciate the spirit of his poetry but also emphasizes the imaginative foundation of Eichendorff's writing. One example which Ohff gives of Eichendorff's visionary capacity is that despite the vital emphasis on music and musicality in the poet's writings, at home in his daily life music was not at all of the essence.

H. Ohff proceeds to describe Joseph von Eichendorff as "ein ausgesprochener Pechvogel" (12) who was not very "successful" professionally or materialistically. That Eichendorff transcended this undervaluation and devaluation by his contemporaries is effectively asserted by Ohff in the following statement: "Es lässt sich nichts dagegen sagen. Eichendorff selbst im realen Leben ist das beste Beispiel dafür. Ihm gelang so gut wie nichts, dem Pechvogel unter den deutschen Romantikern, nur das eine, nämlich unsterblich zu werden" (13). Yet, Eichendorff, despite such undervaluation or perhaps because he was not truly appreciated by the society in which he lived, has achieved creative eternity with his poems, stories, and novels.

In Eichendorff's story "Aus dem Leben eines Taugenichts" ("The Memoirs of a Good-for-Nothing," 1826) the protagonist is a similar kind of character, an individual who is undervalued and devalued by various individuals throughout his life, yet who ultimately triumphs at the end of the narrative to find a mortal bliss. "Aus dem Leben eines Taugenichts" contains an abundance of references to luminescent spaces and to sanctuaries of light, whether transient or more permanent. In Section One, for example, the estate in Vienna where the protagonist works as a gardener represents a sanctuary of light and tranquility, especially in the morning. The park of the estate is particularly beautiful; various features of this natural landscape have a golden hue in the morning sunlight. The aesthetic vitality and sanctuary-like atmosphere of this scene is reinforced in the delineation of the silent and solemn atmosphere of the avenues of tall beeches.

The importance of the light for the protagonist is evident from the very beginning of the story when he is sitting in the sunshine and is criticized by his father for being lazy and negligent. The Taugenichts is a child of light, of luminescent spaces.

In Section Two the protagonist of the narrative becomes the new tollkeeper. He savors the relatively minimal responsibilities of the new position as well as the beautiful landscape of the estate where he works. Moreover, he develops his creativity and establishes a flower garden from which he takes various bouquets to the young lady at the palace. The natural beauty of this environment is poignantly described in the following passage about the vitality of the evening light on the estate: "The sun was just setting, covering the countryside with a carpet of glowing color, and the Danube, like a ribbon of fiery gold, meandered off into the distance" (German Romantic Stories 199). This is the evening of a hunt in the forests around the palace—in the course of this event the protagonist encounters the lady whom he admires and notices that she is wearing one of the small bouquets which he had prepared. Inspired by the moment and by the presence of the lady, the protagonist says that he would do anything for her. The sudden emergence of voices of some participants in the hunt compels her to resume the hunt without responding to the protagonist.

Later in Section Two of the narrative the protagonist is asked by the chambermaid of the lady whom he admires to pick some pleasant flowers for her mistress who needs them as part of her dress for a ball which she will be attending. In the process of picking the flowers for the woman he reveres the protagonist portrays the scene as a sanctuary of beauty and light: not only is it a tranquil and lovely evening but the softly soothing and pleasant murmuring of the Danube can be heard in the distance. One could claim that the love which the protagonist feels for the young lady strongly influences his perception of the surrounding natural environment. And yet, there is an essential natural loveliness to the estate and park encompassing the palace which would be delightful even if the protagonist were not describing the scene through the eyes of an admirer or a lover. A further passage which offers the aura of a sanctuary is presented as the protagonist carries his basket with the lovely flowers into the park. In the moonlight he walks across white bridges beneath which swans were sleeping, and continues further past gorgeous arbors.

The palace and immediately surrounding parkland where the festivities are taking place are so brilliantly illuminated that the garden is suffused by a radiantly golden aura of exceptional vitality. Such a powerful golden light at this narrative moment epitomizes the vital light of a special sanctuary which is beyond the vicissitudes of everyday mortality. That this vibrant scene represents a sanctuary of light and that it has the atmosphere of a luminescent space is further reinforced by the fact that the surrounding environment is depicted as being dark and quiet.

At the end of Section Two, on the morning after the ebullient party, the protagonist, after awakening to the brilliant morning light in the park, decides to travel once more, admitting that he cannot resist the feeling of melancholy and Wanderlust which suddenly permeate his soul. He is also saddened by the fact that the lady whom he admires seems to be in a relationship with an officer. Moreover, the protagonist's garden near his house is overgrown and would need considerable effort to revitalize. Taking his violin with him on his journey to Italy, the protagonist is enveloped in a setting of verdant growth and natural vitality which seems to suggest that he has made the right decision to leave and to travel. Despite the beautiful sanctuary of light which he experiences in Vienna, in the estate in Vienna, the protagonist is especially inspired to travel when he looks into the distance and sees the spatial expansiveness of the natural landscape. There is a sense of expectation and hope which the sight of this expansiveness of natural space seems to offer.

In Section Three of "Aus dem Leben eines Taugenichts" the protagonist is travelling southwards to Italy. On the convoluted journey he experiences various moments of luminescent and aesthetic vitality. One such moment is when he observes a beautiful orchard. The morning sun is shining so brilliantly through the branches of the trees that the grass seems to have a golden carpet draped upon it. Lying down under one of the apple-trees in the orchard, the protagonist has a special vantage-point to view the surrounding countryside—this is a moment of sensory expansiveness. Not only does he hear the church bells pealing over the fields but he also sees the local people going to church. The singing of the birds in the tree above him is so mellifluous that he falls asleep and reflects upon the lady whom he admires and his past. Unfortunately, this vision and dream is interrupted and undermined by a local farmer who questions the protagonist's motives in wandering through this area.

As the adventurer wanders onward he spends an entire day walking through a forest. In the evening he encounters a distinctive sanctuary of light and serenity which is generated by the rays of the sun shining brightly through the trees. The Taugenichts finds a beautiful valley in the twilight surrounded by mountains and containing an abundance of red and blue flowers as well as many lovely butterflies. The narrative further elaborates this depiction of the solitary landscape by saying that the outside world seemed to be many, many miles away.

As lovely as this quiet sanctuary is, it seems to some extent less inspirational than such a sanctuary typically would be for the protagonist, perhaps because he is searching for culinary sustenance and is eagerly looking for the nearest village. As any wanderer who appears to be destined to find his way, or, at least, not to experience evil influences on the journey, the protagonist, the Taugenichts, does manage to locate a village in the dusk. He starts playing his violin at a local inn—the music which he creates encourages various people to dance merrily. The Taugenichts does not remain in this locale, despite the temptation to do so.

In continuing his journey the protagonist encounters two painters, Leonhard and Guido, who take him along with them towards Italy. Guido sings a song which impresses the Taugenichts greatly. This is an enchanting melody celebrating the beauty of the morning light which peacefully embraces and envelops various individuals in an aura of happiness and radiant joyfulness. The protagonist is weary from the journey and falls asleep, feeling himself unable to listen further to the song, as lovely as it seems to be. One might also say that the vitality of the light contributes to this condition. As before in the narrative, the presence of the light is so strong that, along with other influences, the protagonist falls asleep and dreams. When the protagonist awakes, he feels the intensity of the morning light shining into his eyes—he truly appreciates the sparkling light of the morning which greets him. One might describe this as a sanctuary of light, for the light which permeates the spirit of the individual is powerful and pervasive. This is a light which can fill the soul with hope and radiance and can also inspire the wanderer to persevere on his journey.

As the protagonist journeys forth in the company of the two painters they descend into a valley. This landscape is so beautiful and so filled with manifold delightful sounds and sights of nature, as well as with an abundance of brilliant light, that the protagonist feels as if his soul could fly from the mountainside into the valley below.

In Section Four of "Aus dem Leben eines Taugenichts" the protagonist and the two painters arrive at a country inn which has a disorderly atmosphere, both with respect to the setting and the people who inhabit the place. Here the two painters abruptly leave the Taugenichts behind; yet, they do provide him with some money for the continuation of his journey. Disappointed that the painters left without a word of explanation, the protagonist nevertheless catches the Post-coach to proceed with his adventure.

In Section Five of the narrative the protagonist is being driven by the dynamic coach in a hectic manner through the countryside towards an unknown destination. The protagonist feels anxious and harried because the coach continues consistently onwards day and night, leaving him very little time to rest and to collect his thoughts. The coach proceeds through a landscape which becomes increasingly more desolate and isolated. Eventually, after a consistently hasty, occasionally pleasant, and sometimes frightening journey through various natural environments the coach arrives at an ancient, isolated castle in the mountains. The potent moonlight spreads its radiance over the profound silence of this landscape.

When he enters the castle property the protagonist senses that this is an unusual place, but his concerns are temporarily assuaged when he is given a lovely and splendid chamber in which to stay. The ceiling of this chamber is decorated in gold and the walls are hung with exquisite tapestries. After a sumptuous meal in this splendid chamber the protagonist falls asleep in a tranquil and complacent mood.

In the morning (at the beginning of Section Six) the protagonist awakens in a state of relative confusion, for he is not precisely sure where he is. To some extent he feels as if he were still riding in the coach and had dreamt about the castle and the unusual figures in it. Yet, with a renewed sense of hope and vigor, in part inspired by the song of a forest-bird, the protagonist picks up his violin and wanders for a while through the dark and somber castle and its grounds. Despite his initially favorable impression, the more the protagonist sees and senses in this ancient castle, the more troubled and concerned he becomes. For the morning atmosphere of the castle is characterized by a deathly silence. And when the protagonist walks around he notices broken statues, overgrown paths, and a generally disorderly aura throughout the property. Later in the morning the protagonist plays his violin skillfully—the other few inhabitants of the castle seem to be impressed by his musical ability.

Wolfgang Paulsen describes the importance of the violin of the Taugenichts as follows:

> Wenn die Geige also so etwas wie ein symbolisches Attribut für das potentielle Kunstlertum des Taugenichts ist, so erfüllt sie diese Aufgabe doch nicht mit gewünschter Eindeutigkeit, denn sie dient ihrem Besitzer nur dazu, ein höchst beschränktes Repertoire von Volksliedern—oder solchen, die es werden wollen—daherzuspielen, wenn ihn dazu die Stimmung überkommt, und ausserdem höchstens noch zum Aufspielen beim Tanz. (17-18).

Paulsen elaborates on this point effectively by distinguishing between Eichendorff's protagonist and Grillparzer's "Spielmann" and their approach to music. Paulsen proceeds to say that the violin symbolizes for the Taugenichts his Austrian love for music, yet does not necessarily indicate his possession of an artistic consciousness (17-18). Paulsen makes the interesting point that only once on his adventures is the Taugenichts viewed as an artist: "Nur ein einziges Mal wird der Taugenichts auf seiner Reise von einer zufälligen Bekanntschaft für einen Künstler gehalten—dann aber nicht für einen Musiker, sondern ganz einfach . . . für ein 'vazierendes Genie'" (18). One might describe the Taugenichts more as a musical dilettante who enjoys music but does not have the devotion and dedication to his art which one would expect of a musician.

As Section Six continues the protagonist admits that he feels as if he were an enchanted prince in this isolated castle, for he is given all of the food and drink which he desires while enjoying a very leisurely and carefree lifestyle. Yet, the enchantment is relative because the protagonist is uneasy about various features of this environment—for example, he notices that none of the inhabitants ever leave the castle or ever seem to want to leave. One day as he is looking out from his mountain retreat into the valley below, he hears the sound of the coach's horn approaching the castle. The sound reminds him of an old song which mentions the persona thinking about the happy moments when he went to the home of his beloved; the song ends with a sense of hope and optimism motivated by the glow of the morning light.

When the protagonist returns to the castle, he is given a letter which was just received from Aurelie, the lady whom he admired in Vienna—she says that life has been dreary without his presence and she encourages him to return. The positive effect of the letter on the protagonist is reinforced and animated by the powerful light of the sun. The sun's rays are depicted as glistening brilliantly through the branches of the trees and onto the words, making the letters appear as gold and green blossoms. The protagonist is blissful in response to this news and says that his heart and spirit feel much more radiant than the valleys which are shimmering in an abundance of evening light.

Although the protagonist is very happy as he reflects upon the positive letter, this happiness is not sustained, for the day ends on a sinister note. The old caretaker and the old housekeeper appear to have diabolical plans and lock the protagonist in his room. Sensing a sinister plot against him, the protagonist climbs out of the window and with the help of the lanky student escapes into the nearby forest. Hearing voices coming after him, the protagonist liberates himself from his pursuers by rushing deeper into the forest.

The beginning of Section Seven gives the reader a special insight into the depiction of space in this narrative. In the first sentence of this section the protagonist declares that he hurried night and day to escape his dangerous pursuers. Then in the second sentence of this section the protagonist encounters someone who tells him that he is only a few miles from Rome, which is his destination. In the spirit of a Romantic adventure, spatial distances are presented as being relative. The protagonist can traverse extensive spaces in a short period of time, in a few hours, or in a day, while requiring significant time to wander through other places. He may even linger over other spaces and in other places for as long as he wishes, without any sense of the real passage of time. As in other narratives of Romanticism, time and space are not only relative but also subject to the imagination and the vision of the creative individual.

The protagonist's initial experience of Rome is at night. As in various poems by Eichendorff, the night is depicted not as dark and bleak but rather as filled with light, for the moon is shining brightly as the protagonist leaves the forest. From a hilltop the protagonist gains a very positive initial impression of Rome, which is reinforced by the glistening sea in the distance and the twinkling stars in the sky. After passing a graveyard where Venus is presumably buried, the protagonist has a clear and glorious vision of Rome. The fortresses, the gates, and the golden domes are delineated as shimmering in the radiant moonshine as though angels in resplendent robes really were animating the scene. The light of the moon is very potent, for the protagonist even says that everything looked as bright as during the daytime. Such an observation might make one wonder whether this is dream or reality or a combination or fusion of the two. Does the protagonist really wander away from Vienna and experience this entire series of adventures? Or does he leave Vienna and fall asleep a short distance from the city and dream imaginatively the remainder of the journey? Or does the protagonist actually experience all of the adventures which are described in the narrative?

The presence of Venus in the context of the Christian heritage of Rome in this story is reminiscent of the conflict and interplay of the forces of Christianity and paganism in Eichendorff's story "Das Marmorbild" (1819). The protagonist in "Das Marmorbild," a young poet of considerable sensitivity and innocence who resembles the Taugenichts in various respects, almost yields to the seductive allure of the Venus figure, but is ultimately saved by the strength of his Christian upbringing. When he resists the temptations of the Venus figure, the splendid palace in which the encounter takes place vanishes. Only fragments of the building remain. The heroic figure is rewarded with the love of a young woman who has admired him for a while. The physical attractiveness and allure of the Venus figure which had motivated his infatuation for her had clouded his feelings for the other woman who truly loved him.

In "Das Marmorbild" Florio, the young poet of considerable sensitivity, is entranced by a statue of Venus which he sees at night. A woman whom he meets seems to be the physical embodiment of the statue, or perhaps one might say that she seems to be the statue come to life. Schwartz describes the seemingly positive aura of this moment: "He felt indescribably well. The beautiful marble statue had come to life and descended from its pedestal, the quiet pond was suddenly transformed into a vast landscape, the stars therein into flowers, and the entire spring into the image of the lovely one" (123). This natural space only has the appearance of a sanctuary. Such a place is really only a part of the lure to capture the soul of the protagonist. Florio, the young poet, is warned by Fortunato to be aware of heathen temptations. Fortunato's singing along with Florio's recollection of a pious song from his childhood helps to break the spell of the Venus figure.

The Taugenichts, as the protagonist in "Das Marmorbild," encounters various temptations and challenging situations, the danger and the seriousness of some of which he only seems subconsciously aware. As the protagonist of "Aus dem Leben eines Taugenichts" strolls through moonlit Rome, he believes that he hears the voice of the lovely lady from Vienna whom he admires. However, when he approaches this figure, she runs away. When the protagonist hears the sound of a guitar he thinks that this must be the mad student playing, the one who had helped him escape from the ancient castle. The protagonist falls asleep on the stone outside of the house into which the female figure, whom he thought was familiar, ran the night before. When the protagonist awakens the next morning, he observes the city and the world around him as a spacious sanctuary of light. The painting which the protagonist is shown at the end of Section Seven appears to be that of the lovely lady from Vienna. As he gazes at the portrait, the entire landscape in which she is portrayed seems to resemble the palace and the estate in Vienna with the Danube and the blue mountains in the distance. At the end of this section the protagonist is informed by an acquaintance that the lovely lady, whom he views as a countess, is looking for two painters and a young musician with a fiddle. Presumably, the protagonist is the musician and the painters are his two previous travelling companions.

In Section Eight of "Aus dem Leben eines Taugenichts" the protagonist, having seen the portrait of the lovely lady at the end of Section Seven, feels energized and hurries towards the house where he thought he heard her singing on the previous evening. Initially, he loses his way and says that everything seems bewitched, as if his most recent adventures, including the experiences in Rome, had been a dream. Soon thereafter the protagonist falls asleep in the afternoon heat in front of a large house and does dream of a landscape near his village. The most salient aspect of the dream is that the raindrops are transformed into flowers which are covering him. When he awakes, it is interesting that he is surrounded by radiant flowers which are bountifully present around the large house. After various incidents, which include the revelation that the woman whom the protagonist thought was his lovely lady is actually someone else, he is told by the chambermaid that the lady whom he admires, "the countess," has returned to Vienna and is waiting for him.

In Section Nine of the story the Taugenichts has travelled out of Italy and is standing on a mountain peak and looking down on his beloved Austrian landscape below. Various individuals are talking about an imminent wedding celebration at the palace estate in Vienna where the protagonist used to work and live. He believes that they are talking about his marriage to "the countess." At the end of this section the protagonist is especially inspired to musical expression because he observes his old tollhouse and the palace nearby.

In Section Ten of the narrative the protagonist is very excited to be on the palace grounds again. He stops briefly in the tollhouse before proceeding to the garden. Here the protagonist is in an ebullient state of mind and even feels that the golden trees, the trees suffused with a golden light, are inclining their branches towards him in a gesture of welcome. Shortly thereafter the protagonist finally sees his lovely lady, the lady whom he esteems, near the lake imbued with the golden rays of the evening sun. The protagonist also encounters once again the two painters, Leonhard and Guido, whom he met on his travels. To his astonishment the protagonist learns that Leonhard is really a wealthy nobleman and that "Guido" is his bride (and the daughter of the countess who owns the palace). Her name is Flora and she had to disguise herself as the painter Guido to prevent treacherous individuals from interfering with her relationship to Leonhard.

The final important revelation of the story comes from the lovely lady whom the protagonist admires and whom he will marry. After saying that the count has given her and the protagonist a pleasant nearby villa with vineyards to live in, she explains that she is not a countess at all. Rather, she is an orphan child who was brought to the palace by her uncle, the footman, and has been brought up by the countess. The last paragraph of the narrative reinforces the lovely atmosphere of the moment. The sound of congenial music and the flares lighting up the night sky mingle gently with the nearby murmurs of the Danube to create an experience of luminescent harmony and serenity. Many of the moments or descriptions of light in the narrative are connected with the night and with the moonlight—there is an inner radiance within the darkness or a light which is generated and strengthened by the lovely moonlight which permeates the natural landscape and the soul of the protagonist and of any similar individual with a comparably sensitive nature-sensibility.

Egon Schwartz describes the significance of the ending of "Aus dem Leben eines Taugenichts" as follows: "The ending brings for the Taugenichts the inevitable consequences of his decision to forgo the urge to lose himself in nature and to wander. He has been tamed; love has harmonized the two worlds in his soul" (148). Schwartz asserts that a steadfastness (motivated considerably by his faith and trust in God) is "the only virtue required in Eichendorff's world in order to attain heavenly and earthly bliss" (148).

In *Eichendorff: The Spiritual Geometer* Lawrence Radner asserts that Eichendorff views the development of the Taugenichts in "Aus dem Leben eines Taugenichts" as spiritual. In the world of the palace in Vienna, for example, Radner writes that "the 'Taugenichts' is becoming immersed in a way of life which disregards man's high calling, to love God above else . . . . He is 'im Brote,' but the bread is not spiritual" (293). The Taugenichts needs to learn to focus less on material things and more on spiritual concerns. One of the characteristics of the Taugenichts which enhances this process of spiritual development is that, as Radner stresses, he thinks and is self-reflective (294). Radner suggests that the protagonist in "Aus dem Leben eines Taugenichts" has to "undergo the painful process of rejecting his own notion of self" (294) before he can truly love Christ.

In the poem "Denk' ich dein, muss bald verwehen" the persona suggests that "whenever he thinks of her, the Queen of Heaven, all despondency is gone and the world is like a garden filled with ancient songs and angels" (299). Radner proceeds to argue that such a garden, represented by "die Pracht," is a "vision of the soul's eternal home toward which the entire panorama of human existence sails" (299). Such a garden of angelic light and music signifies a lovely sanctuary of light and serenity for the persona who is sensitive enough to appreciate it.

There is in various works of Eichendorff the spirit of fairy-tales, perhaps not surprisingly as he is such a quintessentially Romantic writer. The importance of the light at the end of "Aus dem Leben eines Taugenichts" is similar to the significance of the light at the end of Madame de Beaumont's "Beauty and the Beast." At the end of both narratives there is the presence of light (moonlight and the light derived from man-made activities) and music to signal and to reinforce the celebratory mood of the moment. The essential difference in the presentation of the light in these two narratives is that in the Eichendorff story the moonlight already spreads its lovely radiance across the landscape as the "countess" and the Taugenichts are pleasantly conversing, while in the de Beaumont narrative the castle becomes "radiant with light" (Tatar 41) when Beauty agrees to marry the "beast." There is also a personal transformation at the ending of the narratives.

As the "beast" in "Beauty and the Beast" is transformed into a prince, so the "countess" in "Aus dem Leben eines Taugenichts" reveals to the protagonist that she was an orphan child who was generously reared by the countess. Both narratives also stress the importance of virtue, for both the Taugenichts and Beauty succeed in their respective situations because of the beauty, integrity, and virtue exemplified by their characters. The Taugenichts also reveals qualities of a Cinderella-like figure for despite his goodness and virtue, he is often undervalued by his contemporary society until the end of the narrative when he achieves a personal triumph.

The poetry and the prose of Joseph von Eichendorff reveal numerous sanctuaries of light which comfort, inspire, and strengthen the mind, heart, and soul of the individual reflectively and sensitively wandering through the world of everyday reality and confronting the manifold demands and tribulations of such a world. The beautiful light, the extraordinary luminescence, in these sanctuaries, whether present during the day or at night, is conspicuously similar to the light of intellectual beauty in Percy Shelley's

"Hymn to Intellectual Beauty" and to its healing potential and rejuvenating power:

Thy light alone—like mist o'er mountains driven,
  Or music by the night-wind sent
  Through strings of some still instrument,
  Or moonlight on a midnight stream,
Gives grace and truth to life's unquiet dream. (III. 32–36)

The radiant light of a beautiful sanctuary is exemplified in Eichendorff's work in poems about the morning such as "Der frohe Wandersmann," "Morgengebet," and "Frühe," as well as in poems about the evening and night such as "Frühlingsdämmerung," "Sehnsucht," "Nachts," "Mondnacht," and "Der Einsiedler." The profound effulgence which is created and sustained in the ambience of this lovely sanctuary can be the light of present vitality in the natural environment (generated and disseminated by the sun or the moon), the radiance of a profound nature-sensibility and a creative artistic expression motivated by such a sensibility, the light of the visionary imagination, the light of the divine, the symbolic radiance of an extraordinary space which has the aura of a cathedral or chapel, or the light of eternity which encourages, inspires, heals, and soothes the heart, mind, and soul of the individual confronting and thoughtfully responding to the challenges and the vicissitudes of everyday mortality.

✳ *Charlotte Brontë*

Images of light and luminescence abound in Charlotte Brontë's *Jane Eyre*. The light may have a powerful radiance which soothes the heart and soul of a character in the novel or the light may have an effulgence which inspires the creativity of the individual. The light may be localized in a special natural space or in a particular room or it may permeate the surrounding landscape. In this essay I will examine images of light and luminescence in Charlotte Brontë's work which suggest directly the aura of a sanctuary or which are implicitly related to the notion of a sanctuary.

The idea of and experience of a sanctuary is important to Jane from the beginning of Charlotte Brontë's *Jane Eyre*, for she is treated as an outsider and needs to have a place where she can recover from the mistreatment which she receives in the world of everyday mortality. The suffering which Jane endures in her early youth encourages her to a considerable extent to develop and to strengthen a sense of imaginative vitality to compensate for and to transcend the anguish of her emotionally painful environment. The capacity for imaginative vitality is present at the beginning of the novel, as W. A. Craik argues in *The Brontë Novels*: "At the beginning of *Jane Eyre* what Jane thinks is not fact, but an imaginative heightening and distortion" (77).

In Chapter 1 of *Jane Eyre* Jane finds a temporary sense of sanctuary in the small breakfast-room adjoining the drawing-room of Gateshead, where the Reed family members are located. Jane is not only somewhat physically isolated and secluded here by the "folds of scarlet drapery" (10) and by the panes of glass which protect her from the dreary chill of the November day; she is also intellectually separated from the world around her because she explores a book, Bewick's *History of British Birds*, which takes her away from the anguish of her present existence. Each of the individual images on which Jane focuses in her reading further represents a sanctuary which allows her to remove herself from feeling that she is in the presence of the Reed family members who abuse and mistreat her. The images which Jane notices and thinks about, "the rock standing up alone in a sea of billow and spray" (10), "the broken boat stranded on a desolate coast" (10), the chill moon, or the solitary and desolate churchyard, are interesting not only for their consistent emphasis on loneliness and isolation, reflecting Jane's own state of mind, but also for their similarity to Jane's future artistic creations.

Jane's dispassionate consideration of these images of isolation and bleakness represents a prelude to and preparation for her future stance as an artist who stands back to observe the world around her. By saying in this scenario that the "words . . . connected themselves with the succeeding vignettes" (10) and gave significance to the images Jane implies the important interconnection of image and word, of visual construct and language, which will be at the heart of her own aesthetic endeavor. Not only do the images of the rock standing up alone, the broken and strained boat, and the ghastly moon help to develop and stimulate Jane's imagination but they reinforce her claim that each picture told a profoundly interesting story, a strategy which she will aspire to fulfill in her later artistic activity.

The happy seclusion of this moment of physical and intellectual sanctuary behind the curtain is soon disturbed by John Reed, who abuses Jane verbally and physically. Even though John is the aggressor and hurts Jane, she is blamed for the altercation and compelled to spend time in the red room as a punishment for her actions. The intensity of Jane's sufferings in the Reed household can be seen in the fact that she says to John that he is like a murderer and a slave-driver, or even like one of the more brutal Roman emperors.

At the beginning of Chapter 2 Jane, while resisting, is thrust into the red room, which is a spare room and rarely used by the Reed family. Theoretically, the red room is a kind of sanctuary characterized by opulent furnishings. The red room is, in fact, one of the most lavish and exuberantly decorated rooms in the house, but it has a chill atmosphere. This silent and dismal chamber was the place where Mr. Reed had died. Jane's feeling of being imprisoned in this room reinforces her sense of being mistreated at Gateshead.

One interesting moment in the red-room experience for Jane is her observation of herself in the looking-glass: " . . .the strange little figure there gazing at me, with a white face and arms specking the gloom, and glittering eyes of fear moving where all else was still, had the effect of a real spirit" (16). As Jane looks at herself, she is reminded of the fairy-like creatures who emerge abruptly from the lonely dells and other isolated natural environments. Such an elfish quality and strong nature-sensibility which Jane appears to observe in herself will also be apparent at Lowood and at Thornfield, where Rochester will make a similar observation about Jane.

As Jane continues in her red room imprisonment she is noticeably upset about her situation. Jane feels a painful sense of despair regarding the abusive and unjust treatment which she has received from Mrs. Reed and her children. In describing herself as "a discord in Gateshead Hall" (17) who does not share any interests or sympathies with the members of the Reed family, Jane reaffirms her sense of isolation and distance from her immediate environment.

In the waning daylight, as the twilight arrives, Jane is given to more speculative reflections about her dilemma, mortality, and Mr. Reed. For example, Jane says that she senses that Mr. Reed, her mother's brother, had he been alive, would certainly have treated her more kindly than Mrs. Reed had done. Jane even thinks about the possibility of Mr. Reed's ghost arising in the bedchamber. In the midst of this frightening thought Jane observes the sudden appearance of a gleam of light in the room and wonders whether this could be a ray of moonlight. Even though Jane later acknowledges that the source of the light was probably a lantern being carried across the lawn, at the time she is terrified by the sudden appearance of this light in the dark room. Jane even imagines that the light might be a sign of an otherworldly vision or spirit. She feels so oppressed emotionally and physically at this moment of anxiety that she rushes to the door, shakes the handle, and tries to escape. Mrs. Reed is very unsympathetic to Jane and her cries and compels her to return to the red room for a while longer.

Even though this is not a congenial experience for Jane, the red room could be said to represent "a sanctuary" of light and the visionary imagination. Although Jane wishes to free herself from the dismal atmosphere of the red room, this is actually a place of safety and security for her, for here she is isolated from the tyranny and abuse of the various Reed family members. This is not to diminish Jane's emotional and psychological anguish in the red room, which is very real. However, while Jane may not be safe from the reflections and visions of her own imagination in the red room, she is safe there from the direct mistreatment by the Reed family.

One might even view the light in the red room as a manifestation of Jane's own fertile imagination. For Jane shows a strong visionary capacity as the novel develops. The red room, although offering seclusion, does not offer a profoundly positive sense of sanctuary because of the problematic circumstances of Jane's presence there. Yet, even though this is not an emotional haven, the red room does offer Jane a "sanctuary" for her aesthetic sensibilities. The red room does inspire Jane's imagination—and Jane, as an artistic and creative individual, does savor, whether consciously or subconsciously, such moments of aesthetic stimulation.

At the beginning of Chapter 3 Jane awakes in a nightmarish state of mind and sees a potent red glare, which she soon realizes is the nursery fire in her own room. Jane only slowly recovers from the mental and physical anguish of the red room experience. On the next day Jane, who still feels rather wretched, affirms how terrible her life at Gateshead really is. Jane says that even though the Reed family members are away for the day and even though Bessie was occasionally kind to her, a state of affairs which should normally have represented a "paradise of peace" (22), Jane is in such emotional anguish from her recent debilitating experience that she cannot feel a sense of serenity. It is noteworthy that Jane is in this chapter no longer as entranced by *Gulliver's Travels* as she used to be. One might say that Jane knows intuitively and feels strongly that she needs a new place to nurture her imagination—Gateshead has become too painful and severe for her.

In treating Jane for her condition and in talking with her, Mr. Lloyd, the apothecary, hears her strident lament about her mistreatment and sense of alienation at Gateshead. Not only does Mr. Lloyd ask Jane if she would like to go to school, a prospect which she finds pleasing, but he also speaks to Mrs. Reed and suggests this idea to her. Jane's sense of alienation increases dramatically in Chapter 4 for the abusive treatment of her by Mrs. Reed intensifies in one particular episode; moreover, Jane is deliberately excluded from all of the family parties and festivities of the holiday season.

During these festive occasions Jane, who admits that she has no desire to be in the company of the Reeds, retreats to the quiet nursery. This is a kind of sanctuary for her, for there is no atmosphere of torment here. She is left alone and occasionally exchanges kind words with Bessie, who seems to have developed a more pleasant attitude towards Jane when she noticed how harshly she was treated. In her solitary sanctuary Jane develops her imaginative vitality and shows her need for affection. Jane speaks of the pleasure she receives from loving her doll, "half-fancying it alive and capable of sensation" (31). Jane's need for affection and for a complementary other to cherish her is fulfilled in her affection for the doll. Through her emotional devotion to the doll Jane strengthens her imagination which enables her to counteract the anguish of this period of her life.

Jane's desire for escape from the constraining, debilitating circumstances of the Reed family and her potential for imaginative conceptions are exemplified in Chapter 4 by the image of her breathing on the frost-flowers of the window so that she might look out upon the grounds, though they were still affected by a strong frost. Although Jane observes only realistic details (or perhaps one should say that Jane observes details realistically) this incident symbolizes Jane's inclination to develop an imaginative vision which transcends the contours of her present existential context.

In the conversation between Jane, Mrs. Reed, and Mr. Brocklehurst there is the implication that Mrs. Reed blocks so consistently Jane's attempt to nurture a sense of hope that she has to develop an imaginative capacity as a survival strategy. This conversation demonstrates not only the mean-spirited cruelty of Mrs. Reed towards Jane but also the emotional sterility of Mr. Brocklehurst. Perhaps the only glimmer of hope for Jane in this situation is that she learns that she will be spending her vacations at Lowood, and thus away from the mistreatment of the Reed family. After Mr. Brocklehurst, informed by Mrs. Reed that Jane is deceitful, has left, Jane accuses Mrs. Reed of being an insensitive, hard-hearted person; what is important about this episode is that Jane feels that in expressing herself in such a way she has achieved not only an expansiveness of soul but also a sense of freedom from the fetters of her emotional and psychological "imprisonment" in the Reed household. Jane, exhilarated and dismayed by her harsh reaction to Mrs. Reed, is soothed later by Bessie, especially by her stories and her songs which to some extent inspire Jane's imaginative development.

In Chapter 5 Jane's arrival at Lowood is somewhat similar to her discovery of the Rivers' house later in the novel. Both of these moments are experiences of despair and struggle for Jane which are made more bearable by the presence of the light. Even though Jane in Chapter 5 is beginning a new life by leaving Gateshead and travelling to Lowood, the journey is very difficult and prolonged. When Jane arrives at Lowood on this bleak and cold night, she sees a house with lights. In Chapter 28 when Jane in considerable despair and dismay sees the light of the Rivers' house in the distance, the light of hope in the wilderness, a glimmer of anticipation and positive faith emerges in her spirit.

When Jane arrives at Lowood on that bleak night she is ushered into a room with a fire. As she warms her chilled fingers, she observes the "uncertain light from the hearth" (45) permeating the room and revealing various objects within it. The first night Jane spends at Lowood is a turbulent one characterized by strong wind gusts and torrential rain. During her first couple of days at the school Jane sees that Lowood is a well-ordered school with a generous-hearted and noble-spirited superintendent, Maria Temple. In talking with Helen Burns, her new friend, Jane receives confirmation that Miss Temple is an exceptional individual and an inspirational mentor for the girls at Lowood.

In Chapter 6 Helen reveals to Jane her Christian outlook on life and stresses that the Bible encourages people to return good for evil. Helen also suggests to Jane how important her imagination is in her daily life. At the end of the previous chapter Jane senses this capacity in Helen. While Helen is being punished Jane notices that her friend "looks as if she were thinking of something beyond her punishment—beyond her situation" (54). In Chapter 6 Helen explains this to Jane by saying that she sometimes daydreams very effectively. For example, instead of listening to one of her teachers, Helen says that she imagines that she is in a beautiful landscape, that she is in Northumberland enjoying the lovely natural setting. Helen has the capacity to create in her mind a sanctuary of light and beauty which transcends her anguish and suffering in the world of everyday mortality.

The theme of light appears especially at the end of Chapter 6 when Helen shares with Jane her views about the eternity of the soul. One of the essential aspects of eternity which Helen describes is its radiance. Helen says that ultimately only "the spark of the spirit will remain" (61) at the end of one's life. She also states that this "spark of the spirit" will perhaps "pass through gradations of glory, from the pale human soul to brighten to the seraph" (61). Helen culminates her discussion by asserting that eternity represents a vision of home, a sanctuary of light and serenity beyond the anguish and sufferings of everyday mortality.

In the first part of Chapter 7 Jane describes the physical challenges and stresses of her first quarter at Lowood which was not especially pleasant because of the cold and poor living conditions. Jane is not blissful at this stage of her Lowood experience, though she is certainly very grateful for the acquaintance of such inspirational individuals as Helen Burns and Miss Temple. At the end of Chapter 7 Jane is humiliated by the hypocritical Mr. Brocklehurst who condemns her unfairly as being an interloper and an alien and exhorts the other girls to shun her company because of her deceitful tendencies.

Although very downcast by such mistreatment, which is motivated by the negative and false statements which Mrs. Reed had made to Mr. Brocklehurst about Jane, Jane is encouraged by the very congenial response of Helen. Helen passes Jane twice on her painful pedestal and her lovely smile sheds a radiance on Jane in her moment of despair. The light of Helen's eyes which touches Jane represents a sanctuary of light which Helen shares with Jane and which connects both of their spirits. Jane depicts Helen's smile in the following glowing terms: "What a smile! I remember it now, and I know that it was the effluence of fine intellect, of true courage; it lit up her marked lineaments, her thin face, her sunken grey eye, like a reflection from the aspect of an angel" (70). The presence of Helen enables Jane to transform what would have been a very wretched experience to one which is bearable and reveals her capacity for heroism as well as a sustained glimmer of light through the influence of Helen's radiant smile.

In Chapter 8 Helen elaborates on her Christian perspective more fully, suggesting that beyond the world of everyday reality and mortality is "an invisible world and a kingdom of spirits" (72) which is omnipresent. Helen encourages Jane to believe in and to appreciate the importance of this kingdom of spirits who watch over and guard us in preparation for eternity. Jane seems to believe in a world beyond the vicissitudes of everyday reality as well, in a world of the visionary imagination, though for her its motivation and vitality are less religious than aesthetic and spiritual.

At the end of Chapter 8 Miss Temple invites Helen and Jane to share a meal with her. This meal is characterized by an abundance of light. Not only "the brilliant fire" (75) in the room but also the generosity and kindness of Miss Temple and the delightful meal help to create a sanctuary of glorious light. Jane says that she feasted "as on nectar and ambrosia" (75). The luminescent vitality of the scenario is reflected in and reinforced by the glow of vitality within Helen, whom Jane describes with admiration. Jane says that the powers within Helen "glowed in the bright tint of her cheek . . . then they shone in the liquid luster of her eyes, which had suddenly acquired a beauty more singular than that of Miss Temple's—a beauty . . . of meaning, of movement, of radiance" (75).

Jane is inspired that evening by the wondrously clever and thoughtful conversation of Miss Temple and Helen to be a more diligent and accomplished student. Their discussion enhances and nurtures Jane's imaginative potential and her instinctive belief in the importance of imaginative vitality. One might even claim that the fascinating conversation between Miss Temple and Helen represents an intellectual and an aesthetic challenge to Jane, which she responds to in the course of the novel. In speaking of past cultures and civilizations, of distant countries, and of various books Miss Temple and Helen inspire Jane to develop a spatial, temporal, and intellectual expansiveness of soul.

At the end of the chapter Jane, who has just begun to draw, "feasted . . . on the spectacle of ideal drawings" (77) which would signify her own creativity and sense of accomplishment. Jane conceives various images which she would like to draw and explore artistically. She imagines "freely penciled houses and trees, picturesque rocks and ruins, Cuyp-like groups of cattle, sweet paintings of butterflies" (77) in addition to other images of the natural environment. The mention of Cuyp is noteworthy because his paintings of natural harmony and stability suffused with a golden light contrast so conspicuously with some of Jane's darker and more tempestuous present and future conceptions. The luminescent moment of sanctuary which Jane shares with Miss Temple and Helen is extremely important for it inspires Jane to greater creativity and imaginative vitality. This congenial meal also signifies a turning point for Jane at Lowood as it is a prelude to the announcement (several days later) by Miss Temple in front of the whole school that Jane has been cleared of the negative charges which had been made against her.

In Chapter 9 Jane says that the hardships at Lowood seemed to decrease with the coming of the spring. Jane enjoys not only the colorful displays of flowers, but also the pleasure of a sense of spatial expansiveness, especially represented by the "prospect of noble summits girdling a great hill-hollow, rich in verdure and shadow" (78). The presence of a bright stream and an abundance of light contribute to the seemingly pleasant setting. In saying that she enjoys observing the noble summits beyond the garden walls, Jane implies the need to experience an expansiveness of soul which will take her beyond the confines of her everyday existence.

Tragically, the forest-dell in which Lowood is located becomes the site of fog-bred pestilence so that the school is forced to exist in a diminished capacity as disease and death become rampant. Jane shows a remarkable resilience and is one of the fortunate ones to survive the spread of typhus. In this episode Jane is portrayed as a kind of nature-priestess or prophetess who is able to appreciate and to understand the sensibility and the subtlety of nature and who is untouched by the sufferings of the everyday world of mortality. In the midst of all of the anguish and death at Lowood Jane is able to find a congenial and comfortable haven in the natural world. She describes her favorite place as "a smooth and broad stone, rising white and dry from the very middle of the beck, and only to be got at by wading through the water" (80). The sense of kinship which Jane feels for nature is implied earlier in the novel in Chapter 6 when she describes her affinity for the tempestuous aura of nature. On a stormy and snowy day when many individuals would have wished for calm, Jane says that she wants the wind to howl more fiercely and the gloom to become darker and more profound. Only an individual with a vibrant nature-sensibility would have reacted in such a manner to such a tempest.

At the end of Chapter 9 Jane visits Helen, who is very ill. After reaffirming her strong Christian faith and her belief in eternity, Helen dies in Jane's arms.

The very end of the chapter suggests that Jane is gradually influenced by Helen's Christian outlook on life. For Jane is the one who years later places a marble tablet with Helen's name and the word "Resurgam" on the grave. The presence of the word "Resurgam" (Latin for "I am resurrected") suggests not only that Jane respects Helen and her faith but also that Jane herself has been directly influenced and motivated by this faith.

Jane's yearning for liberation, articulated in Chapter 10 after the marriage of Miss Temple, is epitomized in her profound longing for the blue peaks at the horizon, which she says she wishes to surmount. Miss Temple is described by Jane as having created a sanctuary in Jane's life, a "serene atmosphere" (87), by her very physical, emotional, and intellectual presence. Miss Temple's departure from Lowood makes Jane realize that she must also leave Lowood, which can no longer inspire her, and explore the outside world. Jane expresses a profound desire for liberty of spirit, for an emotional and a spiritual liberation from the limits of Lowood.

Chapter 11 marks the beginning of a new phase in Jane's life. As the new governess at Thornfield Hall, Jane is pleased with the kindness of Mrs. Fairfax and enchanted by the material beauty of her surroundings. Jane appears to feel very much at home in Thornfield Hall and in its aura of spatial expansiveness, which is an appropriate location for her to develop her imaginative capacity. When Jane awakens in her own room on the morning after her arrival, the sun is shining brightly into the room. Jane also appreciates the abundance of light and sunshine over the groves and fields around the mansion. This is an ambience which has the potential to reveal sanctuaries of light both within the mansion and in the surrounding environment. There is even a congenial drawing-room in the mansion which seems to Jane like "a fairy-place" with its rich furniture, carpets, mirrors, and luminescent atmosphere.

Speaking of the third story of Thornfield Hall, Jane admits that she liked the quiet and the gloom of this area during the day. That Jane's aesthetic and emotional sensibilities seem to have found a congenial and a suitable home here is exemplified in her statement that she was pleased with the various bright and tranquil features of the natural environment surrounding the mansion. Yet even though there are aspects of Thornfield and its environs which seem to be serene sanctuaries of light, Jane also notices the excessive darkness of the attic which seems to offer a notable contrast to other parts of the house in its atmosphere. Jane's imaginative vitality is presented here not in negative terms as a capacity to overcome pain but in a positive spirit as a strategy to expand her appreciation and understanding not only of her inner world, exemplified in the aura of Thornfield, but also of the outside world of everyday mortality.

In Chapter 12 Jane reinforces a concern which she expressed prior to coming to Thornfield, namely, that she yearns for a power of vision which might transcend her immediate physical environment. In aspiring to know more about the outside world, about regions she has heard of but never seen, Jane reveals an inner restlessness and a quietly dynamic nature. Moreover, to complement this physical expansiveness of self, Jane wishes to achieve an emotional expansiveness of spirit—she says that she admires what was good in Mrs. Fairfax and Adele but she also believes in the existence of other and more vivid kinds of goodness.

Jane's initial encounter with Rochester occurs in the twilight when he passes her on his way home to Thornfield after a considerable absence and his horse falls on the ice. There are still some traces of daylight and the moon is beginning to make its appearance. Sandra Gilbert and Susan Gubar emphasize in *The Madwoman in the Attic: The Woman Writer and the Nineteenth-Century Literary Imagination* the fairy-tale elements of Jane's first meeting with Rochester: "Charlotte Brontë deliberately stresses mythic elements: an icy twilight setting out of Coleridge or Fuseli, a rising moon, a great 'lion-like' dog gliding through the shadows like a 'North-of-England' spirit, . . . followed by 'a tall steed and on its back a rider'" (Modern Critical Interpretations 77). In the ensuing discussion Gilbert and Gubar make the very interesting point that "though in one sense Jane and Rochester begin their relationship as master and servant, prince and Cinderella, in another they begin as spiritual equals" (Modern Critical Interpretations 77).

After Jane's brief encounter with Rochester when his horse falls on the ice Jane asserts that she did not like reentering Thornfield because she felt that to pass its threshold was to return to stagnation. She suggests that it would have been better for her to endure a tempestuous and an uncertain existence (similar to, though perhaps more restrained than, her longing in Chapter 6 for the wind to howl more wildly and for the gloom to deepen) so that she would be more appreciative of the serenity which Thornfield offered. As before in the novel, when Jane feels constrained or confined she looks towards a geographical summit or expansive space, typically either the horizon or the sky.

The expansiveness of the sky symbolizes the potential expansiveness of her imagination. At the end of Chapter 12 Jane's vision and spirit are drawn away from the melancholy limits of the house to the sky that expanded before her. That Jane describes the sky as a "blue sea absolved from taint of cloud" (119) is important because it suggests her longing for an infinity of visionary power.

Her longing is embodied in and symbolized by the image of the moon, which "aspired to the zenith, midnight-dark in its fathomless depth and measureless distance" (120). Jane is instinctively and sincerely interested in such profound depths and extensive distances. Her imaginative vitality is developed as she expresses her sense of unity with the moon and the stars. Jane's affinity for infinity, for an aesthetic, emotional, and spiritual expansiveness, is complemented by the objects which receive her devotion. In saying of these lovely objects of the natural environment that her heart trembled and her veins glowed when she viewed them Jane reveals not only a sympathetic responsiveness to and connectedness with nature but also an imaginative capacity of burgeoning vitality.

In Chapter 13 Jane articulates an imaginative linguistic vitality as well. She reveals not only a narrative vitality but also a clever thoughtfulness and versatile wit in her response to Rochester's questions. Rochester's statement that Jane has an otherworldly look about her reaffirms the earlier image of Jane as a nature prophetess or priestess who effectively and thoughtfully answers the questions placed before her. Perhaps one could even describe Jane as an intuitively wise, oracular character. This point is suggested when Rochester implies that Jane is a semblance of a forest sprite, a figure of mythological vitality, which complements her role as a nature priestess or prophetess.

In describing Jane's pictures as "elfish," Rochester is offering a subtle praise of her work. Jane's watercolors are of considerable significance not only because of the interesting array of images comprising them but also because of the artistic devotion Jane reveals as an integral part of her creative process. In her works Jane appears to create a surrealistic dream-world. Maggie Berg suggests in *Jane Eyre–A Portrait of a Life* that all three pictures "have a solitary and isolated figure that seems formed out of the natural elements: they represent the three fundamental states of sinking, rising, and stasis" (56). One might perhaps argue that such a figure signifies a manifestation of Jane's own quest for an emotional and a spiritual unity and totality of self.

Berg argues that the first picture "symbolizes Jane's inability to discover a solid ground of belief in herself" (57) while the second "represents a birth or a victorious resurrection, perhaps the birth of Jane's self at Lowood concurrently with the triumphant discovery of her creativity" (57). Berg suggests that the third picture "epitomizes the masculine, seeming to be a combination of Rochester and St. John" (57). Rochester, Berg states, represents "the as yet unexplored region of Jane's mental territory, her unfathomed imagination, which arouses her desire to penetrate further inwards" (61). The power of

Jane's imaginative vision is shown not only in the creative depth of these images but also in her capacity to bring the elemental forces of these pictures into an apparent aesthetic and emotional unity by the end of the novel.

One might claim that the first two pictures refer to events of the past, the first signifying Jane's experience of the death of Helen Burns (the aura of death infused with the light of inspiration or resurrection) and the second representing the birth of Jane's self at Lowood. Yet, the second picture might also foreshadow Jane's experience at Thornfield, implying an aesthetic and emotional revitalization of self undermined by anguish and travail resolving itself ultimately in a vision of hope (provisionally embodied in the presence of the evening star). The third picture seems to project a vision of Rochester's physiognomy. That the second and third pictures are linked by a shared capacity to overcome despair by the power of an inner illumination or radiance, as pale as it may seem outwardly, might suggest the ultimate reconciliation of Jane and Rochester.

One might also argue that all three pictures, and especially the second and the third, anticipate the future in the spirit of the notion of "invisible pictures" expressed in Siegfried Lenz's *The German Lesson*. One primary protagonist of the novel, the painter Max Nansen, whose life is a fictionalized biography of the artist Emil Nolde, responds to the ban of the Nazi authorities by creating "invisible pictures," which are described as follows: "You must realize that these pictures are not entirely invisible. They are small hints, pointers, allusions–like arrow-heads–that's something one can see, of course. But what is most important, the things that matter, that's invisible. Some day . . . it will all be visible" (247). Although Jane Eyre might not agree completely with Max Nansen in his assertion that the invisible paintings contained all he had to say about the age in which he lived, representing a confession including everything he had experienced in his life, she would affirm the anticipatory, projective, and prospective nature of such images. For she, like Nansen, has internalized such images and preserves in her indomitable inner spirit a vision of a more congenial, nurturing, and dynamically pleasant future.

The pictures of both Jane Eyre and Max Nansen not only articulate a vision of the present, partially influenced by an awareness of the past, but also create a vision of the future. The difference between the two artistic conceptions appears to be more one of degree than of kind. While the aesthetic intensity of Nansen is incomparably vital, both Jane Eyre and the expressionist painter believe in their pictures as symbols, as the aesthetic signs of the future, as the seeds of future aesthetic, emotional, and spiritual development.

Jane's initial conversation with Rochester in Chapter 13 is presented in the ambience of an enclosed place or sanctuary of light. When Jane enters the room to meet Mr. Rochester there are two lighted wax candles on the table and two on the mantelpiece—and there was a brilliant fire in the fireplace. This conversation represents a sanctuary of radiance, aesthetic, physical, and intellectual. The primary features of this sanctuary of light and conversational vitality are repeated in Chapter 14. On another occasion, several days after the initial conversation, Mr. Rochester and Jane are talking in the dining-room, which is permeated with an abundance of light not only from the lustre which spread "a festal breadth of light" (133) around the room, but also from a large fire in the fireplace. The conversation which Jane and Rochester have on this occasion is as interesting and as vital as the previous conversation. Jane shows an intellectual and a linguistic capacity to converse with Rochester as an equal. As the conversation in Chapter 14 develops, there is also the sense that an emotional and intellectual connectedness between Jane and Rochester is being nurtured. Jane's imaginative vitality is developed further and more intensively in her conversations with Rochester, whom she enjoys challenging intellectually. Rochester stresses his awareness of Jane's potential for provocative and challenging conversation after she tries to soften her initially seemingly negative reaction to his question whether she thinks him handsome. In her conversational exchanges with Rochester Jane sometimes does not offer affirmational or assuaging responses when she senses that Rochester desires her to respond in such a way—instead, she challenges herself, her own linguistic awareness, and Rochester in such dialogue.

Jane's linguistic self-assertiveness is exemplified in her response to Rochester's claim that he has the right to be somewhat masterful by virtue of his experience. Jane answers him by declaring that he does not have the right to command her to do something because he is older or because he has seen more of the world than she has but only because of the superior use which he has made of his time and experience. The integrity of Jane's linguistic vitality and intellectual presence is further reinforced by the narrative position which she occupies as a first-person narrator. Kathleen Tillotson stresses the power of Jane's role in the narrative: "For the peculiar unity of *Jane Eyre* the use of the heroine as narrator is mainly responsible. All is seen from the vantage-ground of the single experience of the central character, with which experience the author has imaginatively identified herself" (258).

The versatility of Jane's linguistic vitality is intimately linked to the complexity of Brontë's narrative technique. Cynthia Linder suggests that Charlotte Brontë may have derived a sense of her complex narrative technique from a study of a similarly complex technique in Joseph Turner's paintings. Linder argues that the diversity of objective correlatives used for Jane's thoughts and feelings does not suggest an irrationality of character nor an uncertainty of authorial style but may be appreciated in the spirit of the following statement which was made about Turner's paintings: "In spite of the bewildering variety, there is an underlying uniformity of procedure which is what we should expect of a highly professional artist for whom style was always subservient to the compelling demands of creative imagination" (35).

In Chapter 14 Rochester tells Jane that he envies her peace of mind, her clean conscience, and her memory. Of course, at the time Rochester does not know about the intense suffering which Jane experienced in her childhood and early youth which makes her memory less congenial than he thinks it is. Rochester continues by making the insightful point to Jane that because of her great capacity as a sensitive listener she will often find herself to be the confidante of the secret feelings and thoughts of various individuals. One might conclude that Rochester views Jane and her presence as a sanctuary of hope and light which can vanquish some of the darkness in his soul. If Rochester is speaking subtly of Jane when he mentions a figure who "has put on the robes of an angel of light" (140) and to whom he must give entrance to his heart, this is further evidence that Jane by her very presence represents a sanctuary of light and hope for an individual who has been compelled to suffer in difficult circumstances. It is also noteworthy that Jane can be as comforting as she is challenging in her verbal exchanges. For example, Jane advises Rochester at one point that if he would focus from the present moment on correcting his thoughts and actions he would have developed in the course of a few years a new store of positive recollections which might give him pleasure.

In Chapter 15 Jane notices that Rochester shows an increasingly more congenial manner towards her. Jane is so pleased by Rochester's cordial and friendly treatment of her that she says that she felt occasionally as if he were her relative and not her employer. Jane admits at one point that she feels that Rochester's "presence in a room was more cheering than the brightest fire" (149). Just as Rochester had viewed Jane as having an aura of sanctuary about her, so Jane thinks of Rochester as a source of personal and comforting luminescence.

In saying that she was saddened by Rochester's grief about his past life and in asserting that she wished she could comfort him, Jane initiates her role as Rochester's guardian spirit and protector. Jane's emotional sensitivity and imaginative vitality will save Rochester not only in the immediate present but also later in the novel when she hears his voice calling from the vaporous depths of her own soul and returns to illuminate his existence and to complete her own unfulfilled past. After Jane saves Rochester from the fire in his room, he affirms the redeeming, genial capacity of Jane by saying that he saw in her eyes that she would be extremely helpful and important to him someday. In calling Jane his "cherished preserver" (154) Rochester affirms his sense of attachment to her and appreciation of her presence in his life. In this episode Jane shows not only an imaginative power but also a mythological vitality, an Athena-like, Apollo-like presence in a world which needs her wisdom, her visionary imagination, and the capacity of her emotional and intellectual illumination.

In Chapter 17 when Rochester returns with a party of wealthy friends, Jane feels isolated and uncomfortable in such a situation. As Jane observes him, she confesses that her love and admiration for him have increased. She says that when Rochester smiles his eye became brilliant and "its ray both searching and sweet" (171). Rochester's presence provides Jane with a sense of sanctuary in her life. Jane's observation of Rochester continues more intensively in Chapter 18 where she shows an increasing interest in appreciating and understanding the depths of Rochester's mind and soul. At the end of Chapter 19 Jane demonstrates again her interest in being Rochester's "cherished preserver," for she says to him, as he reels after hearing the news of Mason's arrival, that she would give her life to serve him.

Charlotte Brontë once wrote of the Bells' (the Brontë sisters') unbowed determination to write as they saw fit: "The first duty of an author is, I conceive, a faithful allegiance to Truth and Nature; his second, such a conscientious study of Art as shall enable him to interpret eloquently and effectively the oracles delivered by these two great deities" (309). Jane shows a devotion to truth and nature when she renews her imaginative vitality in the scenario of her return to the Reed family when the aunt is very ill. That Jane sits near the window apart from the others in the family circle on several occasions during this visit is important not only as a reminder of her past position in the family but also because it suggests her differentiation as an artist from society as well as her sense of an openness of self which is fulfilled in her claim that she represents any scene "that happened momentarily to shape itself in the evershifting kaleidoscope of imagination" (235). In this transitory "enchanted" moment of artistic vitality, Jane creates images of a mythological spirit in a threshold environment.

One might claim that they are images of Jane's own emotional and spiritual selves, especially in the present and future. For example, a "glimpse of sea between two rocks" (235) could symbolize the painful dilemma for an individual in choosing between two existential possibilities. Or it could signify Jane's less consciously articulated problem of choosing to develop her aesthetic vitality directly through her creative work or indirectly through her assistance and support of Rochester. Or perhaps such an image implies the tension between reason and feeling which infuses and motivates her character. As Pauline Nestor writes in *Charlotte Brontë*, "Jane's survival depends on her ability to mediate between the potentially destructive extremes of her own character—between the poles of Reason and Feeling, 'absolute submission and determined revolt'" (50).

The image of "an elf sitting in a hedge-sparrow's nest, under a wreath of hawthorn-bloom" (235) could represent Jane's attempt to portray Rochester's vision of her as an elf or a sprite. Perhaps she is trying to fulfill the visual image which Rochester initiated and established. The "naiad's head, crowned with lotus-flowers" (235) might symbolize Jane's own sense of herself as a nature-priestess which has manifested itself at Lowood and even to some extent at Thornfield. In shaping these images and the sketch of Rochester, Jane aspires to create an expansiveness of the soul which leads her beyond the frailties and vicissitudes of everyday mortality. The versatility of the images which Jane creates affirms the vitality of her aesthetic imagination.

That Jane produces a portrait of Rochester during this visit to her dying aunt is also important not only because it implies her emotional affinity for him but also because it demonstrates the power of her aesthetic vision. In describing specifically the features of Rochester's physiognomy, Jane affirms her capacity to represent and interpret the human condition insightfully and perceptively. This creation is also significant because Jane is so absorbed and content with the work, as if she exists in her own world, in her own self-determined artistic and emotional sanctuary. Another reason why Jane is so absorbed is because she is smiling at a likeness of the face which she loves. It is interesting that Jane describes this work as a "speaking likeness" (236), implying that she has the capacity to bring the likeness to life, to endow it with an existential vitality. One might consider Jane as a Pygmalion-like artist in this creative endeavor, bringing to life an image for which she has a great affection. It is noteworthy that Jane does not wish to reveal the identity of the portrait to Eliza and Georgiana because this creative work signifies a private artistic sanctuary which is not accessible to public evaluation.

In the spirit of the intensity of Jane's creative images, David Lodge argues in "Fire and Eyre: Charlotte Brontë's War of Earthly Elements" that various aspects of Jane's character are presented through images of fire: "She feeds her vague, romantic longings on 'a tale my imagination created, and narrated continuously; quickened with all of incident, life, fire, feeling, that I desired and had not in my actual existence'" (126). Lodge asserts further "that the visionary grows very naturally out of the literal in Jane Eyre because the objective correlatives for the heroine's emotional life are susceptible of very varied treatment" (132). It is through the richness of her visionary imagination that Jane establishes herself as an artist of aesthetic vitality.

Margaret Blom writes in *Charlotte Brontë* that "intensifying these descriptions of physical separation is Jane's oppressive knowledge of a deep and terrifying spiritual loneliness which she reveals . . . in her hallucinatory paintings of drowning strugglers overwhelmed amid vast seas" (90). Blom also writes persuasively that Jane reveals this spiritual loneliness "in her sudden realization, when she learns of the gravity of Helen Burns' condition, that the individual soul is trapped in a meaningless and turbulent universe rushing toward ruin" (90). After Jane's departure from Thornfield later in the novel, she experiences directly a sense of the loneliness and turbulence of the universe which she is able to overcome to some extent by finding emotional and spiritual solace in nature.

Cynthia Linder discusses in *Romantic Imagery in the Novels of Charlotte Brontë* the issue of Jane's seeking her own world as a lonely child at Gateshead. Linder states that Jane focuses on those pictures which are similar to her own dismal emotional state (36). Linder claims further that "Jane's relief in being accepted as a worthy member of the community at Lowood, and her sense of belonging to it, is reflected in the subject matter she chooses for her imaginary drawings" (39). Linder's point is effective in suggesting Jane's instinctive and intuitive capacity for vital aesthetic expression and for representing her feelings with appropriate images.

Of the three pictures that Jane shows Rochester, Linder writes that they all symbolize feelings of death. The first painting could even represent Jane's feelings of constraint and restriction at Lowood after the departure of Miss Temple (40). Linder proceeds to say: "The quotation from Milton's *Paradise Lost* gives the reader a clue as to the meaning of the third picture: it is that of the figure of Death, in Book II" (40). These images are certainly powerful representations of Jane's present existence and distinctive foreshadowings of Jane's future.

An important image of a sanctuary appears at the end of Chapter 20. This scenario signifies a contrast between Rochester's unpleasant memories of the past, made all the more immediate by the presence of Richard Mason, and his being attacked by Bertha, and the beautiful garden, characterized by a lovely, luminescent freshness. The radiance of the sun nurtures a calm and soothing atmosphere—despite the turmoil in his soul caused by the arrival of Mason and his being attacked, Rochester cannot conceal his feelings for Jane and offers her a half-blown rose. In this delightful setting Rochester tells Jane his personal story in general terms. At various points of the narrative, Rochester implies how important Jane is to him. For example, at one point Rochester says that he has found the instrument for his cure in ⁓, but does not complete the sentence. It is clear that Rochester would like to reveal his feelings to Jane, but hesitates to do so.

In Chapter 22 when Jane returns to Thornfield after visiting her dying aunt, she encounters Rochester outside in the evening. In the ensuing conversation it seems as if Jane feels a sense of sanctuary in the presence of Rochester, for she says that wherever he is, is her only home. Rochester is also very pleased to have Jane back again even though he once again playfully calls her an elf and a figure who comes from another world. Literally, this is true for Jane returns from the world of the dead, from visiting her aunt, who recently died. Symbolically, Jane has always had an otherworldly aura about her—even in the mirror in Chapter 2, Jane seems to herself to have the features of a spirit. That Jane and Rochester are kindred spirits and that each feels a sense of sanctuary in the presence of the other is reinforced by the fact that they both are able on occasion to read each other's thoughts. For example, near the end of Chapter 22 Jane thinks to herself that Rochester's "sternness has a power beyond beauty" (247). Rochester's subsequent smile was "the real sunshine of feeling" (248), suggesting the power of light in a space of sanctuary to soothe and revitalize the heart and soul.

In Chapter 23 Jane reveals her interest in and appreciation of the beauty of a self-enclosed, gorgeous space (comparable to her earlier appreciation of the lovely interior spaces of Thornfield), which fulfills the aesthetic aspirations and desires of her imaginative vitality. In wandering into the orchard, Jane describes it as "sheltered" (250) and "Eden-like" (250), a delightful place of blossoming exuberance protected and sheltered from the outside world. Jane chooses to walk alone in this place of sacred and blooming tranquility so that she can wander with carefree ease and so that she may strengthen an inner expansiveness of soul which revels in such a sheltered, lovely space.

As Chapter 23 develops, Jane and Rochester declare their love for one another in a sanctuary setting. The sunset—moonrise meeting is symbolic of the connection between Rochester and Jane. When Rochester teases Jane about the prospect of having to depart from Thornfield, she responds with considerable sadness that she would be very sorry to leave because she has enjoyed her life here so much. Finally, Rochester admits his love for Jane and desires her to accept his marriage proposal. The aura of sanctuary which Rochester and Jane experience in each other's presence is reinforced by the fact that Rochester proclaims that Jane is his equal. The sense of an emotional and intellectual equality existing between Rochester and Jane sustains and strengthens the atmosphere of a sanctuary which they feel when they are together. Jane accepts Rochester's proposal gladly when he affirms that he truly loves her and that he will take an oath to that effect. This statement by Rochester is directly connected to one which he makes several paragraphs later, saying that he does not care about the world's judgement and that he defies popular opinion. That Rochester would make such a statement, which exemplifies the individualistic strain in Romanticism, shows that he has a strong capacity to appreciate the importance of a sanctuary away from the world of everyday mortality.

The theme of a sanctuary away from the world of everyday reality is connected to the importance of dreams and the domain of the supernatural. In *The Art of Charlotte Brontë*, Earl Knies asserts that "Jane's belief in dreams and the supernatural provides a setting in which the call from Rochester can take place" (112). Such a world of dreams and the supernatural is established from the beginning of the novel. For example, when Jane is compelled to stay in the red room at Gateshead, the apparent gleam from a lantern seems to be "a herald of some coming vision from another world" (19). Moreover, Rochester occasionally describes Jane as an otherworldly figure, as an elf or a sprite. For example, when Jane returns from visiting her dying aunt, Rochester says that Jane comes from another world, from the realm of the dead.

Knies asserts that the world of *Jane Eyre* is "one in which dreams come true" (114). Knies proceeds to argue that Jane tries "to dispense with time completely, and in exciting or particularly memorable moments it does disappear" (114). Knies and other critics discuss the interaction of past and present in the novel: "Rochester and Jane begin to talk and soon the tense changes inconspicuously to past again. The device is used at least six more times in the novel, bringing key moments into brilliant focus and suggesting that past and present are very nearly one in this intense life of Jane's" (115). Two of Jane's dreams which do come true are those revealed in Chapter 25.

In Chapter 25 there are three images or visions in particular which foreshadow future events. At the beginning of the chapter Jane returns to the shelter of the orchard where she finds the symbolically interesting image of the cloven halves of the chestnut tree not broken from each other, perhaps foreshadowing the break in the relationship of Jane and Rochester and the potential for their ultimate reunion. Jane's visionary capacity is also revealed in her dreams of the future. Jane describes her first dream in which she was following the windings of an unknown road, burdened with the responsibility of a little child, and trying to catch up with Rochester, who appeared to be ahead of her on the road—but she only felt that he withdrew more from her at every moment. This dream represents a vision of the development of her own relation with Rochester, of their possible separation, and of the provisional fragility of such a relation.

In another dream Jane's imaginative vitality anticipates the demise of Thornfield Hall. Jane dreams that Thornfield becomes a ruin, that only a shell-like wall remains of the stately front. On a moonlight night Jane, still carrying the unknown child, encounters the marble hearth and another fragment of the interior on the enclosure overgrown with grass. As in the previous dream Jane tries to reach out to Rochester, but with no success. When she gains the summit of a fragile wall with great difficulty, Jane sees the image of Rochester, or the person whom she believes is Rochester, disappearing further into the distance. Suddenly the wall crumbles and Jane falls and awakens.

These two dreams are especially interesting because they suggest Jane's yearning for the distance, for a perspective of distance, whether the object of yearning is the horizon or a more immediate animate being or inanimate object. Jane's imaginative vision and dream culminates in an awareness of reality, in the sight of a savage face in her proximity. In overcoming the barrier between herself and Rochester which she senses in dream Jane will ultimately also revitalize her creative vitality.

Jane also relates to Rochester her experience of a strange figure reminiscent of a vampire which came into her room, examined Jane closely, and tore the wedding veil. Jane declares that whereas her other visionary moments were actually dreams, the experience of the dangerous and frightening figure who tore the wedding veil was actually reality. While such a moment does not represent any sense of sanctuary, the daylight does play an important role here. For Jane admits that looking at each object in her room in the daylight provided a sense of comfort in contrast to the sight of the torn veil. Rochester, of course knowing the truth of the matter, tries to assuage Jane and tells her that the intruder must have been Grace Poole. Moreover, he promises to explain to Jane a year and a day after their marriage the reasons for keeping such a strange character in the household.

At the end of the following chapter, after the cataclysmic wedding day, Jane is sitting alone in her room. This quiet place which used to signify a sanctuary for her has been transformed into a mausoleum of broken dreams and disappointed hopes. Jane is emotionally desolate and describes herself as "a cold, solitary girl again" (298). The light in Jane's life has been suddenly extinguished. Jane feels as if the darkness overcomes her and as if the floods of despair overwhelm her soul. The only faint glimmer of hope for Jane is a recollection of God. In muttering a brief prayer to be delivered from this extreme despair and wretchedness, Jane still feels a sense of life in her spirit.

In Chapter 27 as Jane prepares to leave Thornfield, Rochester tries to explain his painful past and tries to assure her that she is the one whom he has been seeking all of his life. Rochester says to Jane: "You are my sympathy—my better self—my good angel—I am bound to you with a strong attachment" (317). He speaks of the profound love, the deep passion which he feels for Jane and that it culminates in a pure and powerful flame which should fuse their two lives and spirits. However, even though Jane forgives Rochester and says that she loves him more than ever, she is determined to leave for the sake of her self-respect, her integrity, and the vitality of her soul.

W. A. Craik makes the following interesting point about the fragility of Thornfield: "Thornfield is precious because Jane has 'lived in it a full and delightful life'; but it is insubstantial and doomed to perish, representing the falsity that must be burned away by suffering before Jane and Rochester can come together" (10).

At the end of Chapter 27, the end of her life at Thornfield, Jane has a dream of childhood which becomes a dream of the light of the moon which is in turn transformed into a vision of a white human form, the spirit of her mother, who gazes upon Jane and whispers into her heart the idea that she should flee temptation. Of Jane's dream of childhood, the dream of the red room at Gateshead, Helene Moglen writes: "At the moment of her decision, Jane returns to the critical scene of her childhood. She is alone in her room as she was alone then—powerless before external circumstances and internal pressures. The limits of the rational world are lost in the boundless universe of imagination" (Modern Critical Interpretations 47).

In departing from Thornfield and from the desolate Rochester, Jane has to compel and to persuade herself to think only about the present because contemplation of the past or the future would be too wretchedly painful. Jane's spirit finds some sense of solace during this prolonged feeling of despair by a rememberance of God and of the importance of the divine being in her life. Jane even says that in her state of emotional oppression and unutterable sadness God must have guided her, for she had no strength to motivate herself to go on. Jane is so emotionally distraught as she wanders through the landscape after leaving Thornfield that she does not even notice the lovely features of the summer morning.

At the beginning of Chapter 28 Jane is left by the coach at Whitcross, a stone pillar at the juncture of several roads. Jane experiences extreme despair in her isolation, for not only is she alone but she is also destitute, having forgotten her parcel in the coach. When Jane leaves the coach at Whitcross she epitomizes the lonely individual wandering hopelessly through an unknown landscape. Surrounded by great moors and mountains Jane experiences the primordial tension of the universe, as if she were the thematic and formal focus of John Martin's painting of the last bard or of Joseph Turner's painting *Shade and Darkness–the Evening of the Deluge.*

Jane frees herself from the imminence of the abyss which her arrival at Whitcross represents and gains emotional sustenance from the natural environment. In moving upon the heath Jane experiences the universal mother, Nature, intimately in her dynamically silent, tranquil spatiality. Jane is able to overcome the feelings of anguish and despair which had threatened to overwhelm her by this profound connection to nature and by the belief that nature loves her even as an outcast from society. It is the enclosed space of the evening heath with its calming silences, not a space of human construction, which comforts Jane.

When Jane seems to be at the emotional and physical nadir of her existence, when she appears to be crushed by fate, she revitalizes herself through her profound emotional and spiritual sensitivity for nature and through the power of her aesthetic, imaginative vitality. As Jane reveals that she is tormented by melancholy, bittersweet thoughts of Rochester she asserts that she is comforted not only by nature but also by God. Jane is especially soothed by the sense of infinite space which the conception of the divine offers, symbolized by the "unclouded night-sky, where His worlds wheel their silent course" (326). In observing the Milky Way and reflecting on its diastolic spatiality Jane says that she assuages and soothes her sadness by feeling the might and the strength of God. Jane concludes this soliloquy by declaring her conviction in the capacity of the divine to save his creation and to watch over Rochester and assure his safety.

Jane's longing for the infinitude of the horizon in Chapter 12, which finds a visual analogue in a Romantic painting such as Caspar David Friedrich's *Monk by the Seashore,* which articulates a similar yearning for the eternity of the horizon, culminates in Chapter 28 in her appreciation of God's infinity and omnipresence in the unclouded night-sky. The appeasing, consoling powers of nature and the divine fuse in this chapter to sustain Jane and to give her a sense of meaningfulness in the midst of the emotional chaos which threatens her at the edge of the abyss. By the end of the novel Jane has reinforced her earlier stature as a quasi-divine figure, a nature-prophetess, by becoming as important to herself as to Rochester and as powerful as the "soft trace of light" (327) sweeping the space of the Milky Way. Harold Bloom addresses this issue of Jane's mythological vitality in his introduction to *Modern Critical Interpretations: Charlotte Brontë's Jane Eyre* when he makes interesting connections between the Brontës and Byron: "Between them, the Brontës can be said to have invented a relatively new genre, a kind of northern romance, deeply influenced both by Byron's poetry and by his myth and personality . . . ." (1). Jane exemplifies the heroic and mythologically vital character of this "northern romance," who not only expresses an intensity of profound feeling but who also has a generosity of heart and a nobility of character which gives her an exemplary stature.

Perhaps Jane's experience of a sense of continuity and a sense of totality with nature is enhanced and strengthened by the fact that there are several features of the natural environment which are consistently used to describe and to portray her. For example, as Robert B. Heilman argues in "Charlotte Brontë, Reason, and the Moon" in the life of Jane Eyre "every crucial event has its special lunar display" (42).

As Jane wanders helplessly through the hot summer landscape, she is almost overcome by fatigue and starvation when she hears a church bell and turns in the direction of the chime. Jane's experience in the village and at the church is humiliating, for she receives no viable assistance and is shown no genuine caring for her desperate situation. The concern which people show for Jane is symbolized by the incident in which she receives the cold porridge from a mother and daughter because the pig does not want it. After this emotionally debilitating experience Jane searches for a hollow where she can rest and suffer her physical demise away from the frequented haunts of humanity.

At this ultimate moment of despair, Jane's vision is drawn towards a light in the distant twilight. For Jane this light represents a symbolic horizon which leads her onward to find temporary salvation in the Rivers' household. That Jane is inspired by the dim light to keep striving despite her abundant misery is significant because later in the novel she will represent the source of illumination for Rochester as he overcomes his blindness. In *The Appropriate Form: An Essay on the Novel* Barbara Hardy writes that in "*Jane Eyre* Providence is still very much alive" (Modern Critical Interpretations 21). Hardy states that "Jane finds that prayer always meets a practical response, and the relationship of prayer and answer is an important thread in the action" (Modern Critical Interpretations 22). One prominent example of the importance of Providence in the novel is Jane's observation of the light in her cousin's house at a moment of considerable despair.

The light of Moor House which guides Jane out of the wilderness is a light of hermetic vitality. At a moment of profound despair Jane is taken in by the family at Moor House. From the very beginning of her relation with Jane, Diana feels a desire to help and benefit "the poor little soul" (341). Jane is from the very beginning of their connection impressed by Diana's charming countenance, lovely eyes and voice. The friendship which Jane develops with Diana and Mary Rivers is very important to her and to her emotional and aesthetic development. Helene Moglen writes that through Jane's friendship with Diana and Mary Rivers she becomes stronger and more confident (Modern Critical Interpretations 50). Moglen proceeds to argue effectively: "She shares with them their love of nature. She admires and respects their superior learning, their fine minds. She listens to them talk as she had once listened to Miss Temple and Helen Burns, as Charlotte had listened to Emily and Anne" (Modern Critical Interpretations 50). Jane and Diana and Mary appear to be kindred spirits. Not only do they share various interests but they also have similar characters and motivations in life.

Through her imaginative vitality and emotional and spiritual affection for nature, Jane affirms the beauty of the Moor House landscape. Moor House represents a sanctuary of serenity and natural beauty which Diana and Mary Rivers and Jane all appreciate. Jane says that she felt "the consecration of its loneliness" (352) and that the various interesting features of the landscape were "so many pure and sweet sources of pleasure" (352) and as significant to her as they were to Diana and Mary Rivers. Jane's nature-sensibility appreciates diverse spatial and temporal aspects of this natural sanctuary and says that she felt enraptured by its spell.

Diana and Mary Rivers will soon have to leave Moor House for their positions as governesses in a large city in the south of England. Jane suggests that they are treated as secondary beings and as dependents in these positions and not valued for their superiority of mind and heart. Such mistreatment is very reminiscent of the devaluation of Jane at Gateshead. There exists a noteworthy duality in Diana and Mary Rivers, as in Jane. All of these characters have a romantic appreciation of nature and a profound emotional sensitivity as well as a rational understanding of the necessities of life.

Terry Eagleton addresses this issue in *Myths of Power: A Marxist Study of the Brontës* in describing Charlotte Brontë's protagonists as "an extraordinarily contradictory amalgam of smouldering rebelliousness and prim conventionalism, gushing Romantic fantasy and canny hard-headedness, quivering sensitivity and blunt rationality" (Modern Critical Interpretations 30). In saying that this contradiction is related to the role of the governess, Eagleton describes the nature of such a protagonist further: "The governess is a servant, trapped within the rigid social function which demands industriousness, subservience, and self-sacrifice; but she is also an 'upper' servant, and so furnished with an imaginative awareness and cultivated sensibility which is precisely her stock-in-trade as a teacher" (Modern Critical Interpretations 30).

Through her emotional and spiritual closeness to nature, Jane's soul expands to participate in the spatially and temporally expansive aura of the natural environment around her. This expansiveness of soul which Jane cherishes and nurtures is enhanced by the fact that Jane describes her association with nature as encompassing conspicuously antithetical features. By claiming that she is entranced both by strong winds and soft breezes, by tempestuous days and tranquil days, by sunrise and sunset, by moonlight and cloudy nights Jane implies the diastolic vitality of her soul, which can encompass not only the heart but also the contours and the horizon of the spatial and temporal versatility of nature.

The sense of sanctuary which Moor House offers is suspended at the end of Chapter 30, for Mr. Rivers goes to the parsonage, Diana and Mary Rivers proceed to their positions as governesses, and Jane accepts the position of schoolmistress in Morton which St. John had offered her. As Jane observes the simplicity of her life and the austerity of her material surroundings in her new cottage, she thinks about Rochester. While admitting to herself that no one will ever love her as Rochester did, Jane also proclaims that she made the right decision according to moral and legal principle—she is grateful to God for having guided her in this important decision.

In Chapter 32 Jane continues her diligent work as the schoolmistress, has consistently vital dreams of Rochester, and develops a friendship with Rosamond Oliver. Rosamond has an affection for St. John Rivers, who appears to be too devoted to his missionary endeavors to notice her feelings (although there are indications that he suppresses his feelings for her because he thinks they will interfere with his calling in life). Rosamond and her father are very pleased with Jane's portrait of Rosamond. St. John, too, is impressed with Jane's portrait of Rosamond as being a correct likeness. Jane's painting has become more realistic and less romantic since the earlier parts of the novel, for she is more interested in "accurate" depiction than in creating romantic or provocative imagery. Linder suggests that this realistic tendency culminates in Jane's Ferndean experience where "the talent which she formerly used to express her thoughts and feelings is now diverted to an altruistic end, in making Rochester's world meaningful" (43).

Linder agrees with W. Gerin's assertion in *Charlotte Brontë: The Evolution of Genius* that Charlotte Brontë thought of art as a profession for herself from an early age and spent much time copying various works until her eyesight became affected, that she attended art classes and was especially influenced by the works of John Martin, whose mythological conceptions show similarities to Jane's own artistic images. Linder proceeds to argue "that Charlotte Brontë obtained her technique of multiple perspectives from a study of Turner's works, who we know was one of her favorite artists" (62). Furthermore, we know that when Charlotte Brontë met Mrs. Gaskell in 1850 she expressed an appreciation of Ruskin's *Modern Painters*, which praises Turner so vitally and thoughtfully.

In Chapter 32 Jane's dreams of Rochester reflect a need for an expansive sense of self. These tempestuous, romantic, emotionally charged, dynamic dreams in which Jane meets Rochester consistently and thinks about spending her life with him reaffirm Jane's quest for an emotional expansiveness of self. As much as Jane enjoys teaching at the village school, this is a confined environment which does not fulfill the depth of her need for an emotionally vital and aesthetically enriching existence.

Jane's desire for an emotional expansiveness of self, for a life which will allow her to express her emotional vitality and the inclinations of her visionary imagination, is enhanced in Chapter 33 by the news, which she receives from St. John Rivers, that she is an heiress. When Jane learns that she has received a legacy which assures her financial independence she says that her heart swelled. The emotional expansiveness of soul which Jane experiences, coupled with the love for the distant Rochester and the elation of attaining a sense of financial independence, finds a further manifestation in Jane's sharing of her wealth with Diana, Mary, and St. John, who she learns are her cousins. Blessed with her own good fortune, Jane, who has a great generosity of heart and spirit, wants to provide a sense of comfort and support to Diana, Mary, and St. John, who have been so kind and helpful to her.

One of Jane's culminating statements about the capacity of the heart to open and reveal itself is at the beginning of Chapter 34: "Good fortune opens the hand as well as the heart wonderfully; and to give somewhat when we have largely received, is but to afford a vent to the unusual ebullition of the sensations" (391).

In asserting the potential of the individual to whom fate has been kind to proclaim an emotional expansiveness of soul, Jane also anticipates and foreshadows her imminent change of heart with respect to Rochester. However, when Jane is unable to receive information about Rochester, her spirit is diminished to such an extent that she could not enjoy the fine spring weather. A melancholy sadness pervades Jane's spirit in Chapter 35 until she hears a distant cry, the voice of her former beloved. Only an individual with Jane's emotional sensitivity, spiritual sensibility, and generosity of heart could have heard such a cry.

Jane had already refused St. John's marriage proposal, saying that she could go with him to India as a fellow-missionary but not as his wife, for she knows that he does not love her as Rochester loves her. Even after Jane's harsh words to St. John in Chapter 35, saying that he would gradually destroy her spirit, he persists and almost manages to sway and persuade her with his gentleness. Yet, at the moment when Jane seems almost on the verge of accepting St. John, she hears the distant and familiar voice of Rochester which was in pain and urgent. One might describe this voice as being as much a part of Jane as it is of Rochester. Ernst Knies describes this voice effectively: "The mysterious call from Rochester—the voice which seems to Jane to be in her, not in the external world—comes just in time" (134).

The ambience of this moment is one of abundant light, for the room in which Jane and St. John are conversing is described as being "full of moonlight" (422). This atmosphere is reminiscent of the nocturnal aura in Eichendorff's "Sehnsucht." In both contexts the individual expresses a sense of longing and yearning for a distant being. In both situations there is a stream of moonlight which permeates the scene. The primary difference between the two contexts is that whereas Eichendorff's persona is inspired to follow the magical possibilities of longing imaginatively, Jane is motivated to leave her new home and seek Rochester directly and in person.

Jane's physical reaction is to break down the barriers which restrain her from seeking and returning to Rochester. Because Jane does not receive an external affirmation of Rochester's existence, although she thinks about him consistently, she searches within her soul which is where the answer was all along. Jane's capacity for an imaginative expansiveness of soul is revitalized in her prayer that night, which leads her to the aura of a Mighty Spirit—that she is able to elevate her soul to such an extent implies an emotional and a spiritual expansiveness of renewed intensity and vitality.

Early the next morning Jane prepares to leave Diana and Mary for several days so that she can search for Rochester and try to fulfill her uncompleted past. Although shocked and dismayed to see Thornfield in ruins and to hear about the current condition of Rochester as a blind cripple, Jane is determined to go to Ferndean to see him. Jane, as Gulliver in one of her formerly favorite readings, has been accustomed to being a "desolate wanderer" and has always been fascinated by "forlorn regions of dreary space." When Jane returns to this scene she is no longer the desolate wanderer she was when she said farewell after the disrupted marriage, for she now has a strong inner hope to fulfill what was undermined before.

Ferndean represents a relative sanctuary of tranquility, although when Jane arrives it does not signify a space of light. Jane's initial impression of Ferndean is that it is a place of isolated seclusion, but not a sanctuary. The decaying walls of the house give this building the appearance of being a part of the surrounding nature. The grounds in front of the house are not described as picturesque, for there are no flowers and no garden-beds. There is an aura of enclosure and limitation here which will challenge Jane's imaginative vitality.

As Jane is wondering whether there is life in this desolate spot, she notices a figure emerging from the house in the twilight, a figure symbolizing sadness and melancholy. When Jane takes the tray in to Rochester it is noteworthy that it contains candles, as requested by him even though he cannot see them in his blindness. In Jane's presence the candles suggest that she is restoring the light to his life. The episode in which Rochester and Jane meet again in the gloomy parlor of Ferndean is one of the most moving, poignant, and emotionally vital scenes imaginable. Jane assures Rochester that she has come back to him and will never leave him.

Helene Moglen makes an interesting parallel between Jane Eyre and Little Brier Rose, suggesting that Jane's seeking Rochester at Ferndean is reminiscent "of the Prince who comes to awaken the sleeping Beauty with a kiss" (Modern Critical Interpretations 58). Moglen argues effectively that this scenario offers a role reversal in the novel. In the past Jane had reminded Rochester of a small and rather helpless bird and now when she observes him emerge from Ferndean he seems to resemble "some wronged and fettered wild-beast or bird" (Modern Critical Interpretations 58).

The gloom of Rochester's life at Ferndean is immediately transformed with the arrival of Jane into an aura of enchantment. Rochester says that the return of his beloved is for him a dream. Rochester calls Jane his "fairy" (440) when he declares that he is so grateful to hear and feel her. He even proclaims that there is "enchantment" (440) in the hour which he is now spending with her. The next morning Rochester emphasizes the importance of Jane's return to him, saying that all the melody on earth is generated by the presence of Jane's voice and that all of the light and sunshine which he can feel and sense is in her being near him.

Jane's imaginative vitality culminates in and with her love for Rochester—each is an emanation, a manifestation of the other. One of the greatest challenges for Jane's imaginative capacity is to signify and become Rochester's eyes, to illuminate the world for him in his blindness. Patricia H. Wheat in *Adytum of the Heart* claims that "if ever a novelist existed who created eyes as windows to the soul, that novelist was Charlotte Brontë" (67). Wheat argues that the eyes of Brontë's characters are related intimately to internal states, especially in the relationship of Jane and Rochester but also in the presentation of minor characters (71). The importance of the eyes is reinforced, for example, not only in Jane's portrait of Rochester in Chapter 21 where she says that she saved the eyes for last because they required the most careful work but also at the end of the novel in Jane's role as a profound source of illumination and revelation for the blind Rochester.

Perhaps one reason for Jane's strength of imagination is that she is the central character and the most important thematic force in the narrative. This strength of imagination is reinforced by the fact that Jane is such a reliable narrator. Earl Knies asserts that one of the reasons for Jane's being such a reliable narrator is "her frankness with her readers and with other characters in the novel" (175). In his discussion of Jane Eyre's reliability as a narrator Knies makes some interesting contrasts between Jane Eyre and Lucy Snowe in *Villette*. Knies suggests that Lucy Snowe is not as dependable a narrator as Jane because "Lucy withdraws periodically and reports what other characters are doing . . . . The focus frequently shifts from Lucy as it never does from Jane" (175).

A notable difference between Jane in *Jane Eyre* and Lucy in *Villette* is that Jane is dependent on her imagination from the very beginning of her difficult life at Gateshead to enable her to survive, whereas Lucy proclaims initially that she is free from the curse of a discursive imagination.

Robert Colby in *"Villette* and the Life of the Mind" makes an interesting distinction between Jane in *Jane Eyre* and Lucy in *Villette*: "Where Lucy's impulse is to take up the pen, Jane's is to reach for the crayon. Jane feels that she has 'pinned down' a character when she managed to sketch his lineaments at the drawing board. Lucy, on the other hand, is every minute the writer" (43).

Charlotte Brontë felt that her creative vitality, her imagination, by differentiating her from the external, social world might eventually undermine her existence. This fear is revealed in her letters to Robert Southey. As Andrew Hook points out in "Charlotte Brontë, the Imagination, and *Villette*" one letter especially "seems unquestionably to suggest the characteristic self-doubt of the nineteenth-century artist: a distrust of the imagination itself expressed in a sense of the latent opposition between the imaginative world of dream on the one hand, and the world and responsibility on the other" (137).

Hook proceeds to argue that Brontë strives to resolve the opposition between these two worlds not in choosing between them "but in working the problem itself into the texture of her writing. Rather than trying to solve her problems, Charlotte now chooses to articulate them. In that articulation lies the true realism of her art" (142). In *Villette* it is the power of the imagination that lures Lucy away from the "glimmering gloom, the narrow limits of the dormitory" towards "dew, coolness, and glory." Hook asserts that Jane Eyre rationalizes the imagination. As Jane develops and nurtures her emotional imagination, she restrains her aesthetic imagination.

Of the setting of Ferndean, Gilbert and Gubar write: "As a dramatic setting, Ferndean is notably . . . asocial, so that the physical isolation of the lovers suggests their spiritual isolation in a world where such egalitarian marriages as theirs are unlikely, if not impossible" (Modern Critical Interpretations 93). Gilbert and Gubar conclude this discussion effectively by saying that true minds and spirits such as Jane and Rochester "must withdraw into a remote forest in order to circumvent the strictures of a hierarchal society" (Modern Critical Interpretations 93-94).

Jane is not only a lovely, generous-hearted woman, but also a fairy, a sprite, and a figure of mythological vitality who can be a nature-priestess or nature-prophetess when she chooses. In becoming Rochester's eyes and vision as she describes to him various aspects of the beautiful natural environment around them, in loving Rochester deeply and in encouraging him in his debilitated state to feel "green and vigorous" (447), and in rejuvenating his forlorn spirit, Jane transforms her mythological vitality into a stream of present-focussed energies. Carol T. Christ writes of the conclusion of *Jane Eyre*: "The narrative ultimately satisfies both the claims of desire and the claims of control by giving a more powerful Jane a subdued and disciplined Rochester" (65). Christ continues to argue that the novel "takes its energy and its coherence from Brontë's ability to express and in some manner resolve her aesthetic conflict through Jane's struggles for self-definition" (65).

Through Jane's love and affection, Ferndean is transformed from a lonely place to a sanctuary of light and serenity for herself and Rochester. What guides and motivates Jane and Rochester is their love for one another. The depth and the intensity of their love is as great as the love which Elizabeth Barrett Browning depicts in "How Do I Love Thee." For Rochester there is no need to have "fine clothes and jewels" (449) on their wedding-day. Rochester has learned to love Jane for the beautiful person and soul she is—the material objects connected with her are secondary. The aura of a sanctuary at Ferndean for Jane and Rochester is perhaps reinforced by the fact they both have a faith in the divine realm and in a divine being. The sense of sanctuary which Rochester and Jane feel is so vital that they do not need any material surroundings to reaffirm or protect it. One might say that the most vital dimension of this sense of sanctuary is that Jane and Rochester feel a sense of spiritual connectedness. The aura of a sanctuary is created and nurtured by the intimate association of their souls. All of the other aspects of the sanctuary which they enjoy develop from this spiritual connection. One indication of the profound spiritual relation of Jane and Rochester is the moment when Rochester in his despair called out to Jane and she, although many miles away, heard the voice and felt that she needed to be with him.

Although Jane is content and happy with Rochester at the end of the novel she does seem to have given up to some extent her quest for an imaginative vitality generating an expansiveness of soul. Unlike Lily Briscoe in Virginia Woolf's *To the Lighthouse*, Jane cannot seem to find a satisfying independence of mind and spirit in her artistic work. Or perhaps Brontë is suggesting that the most important expansiveness of soul which Jane experiences is an inner expansiveness which culminates ultimately in her profound love for Rochester. Perhaps Jane's expansiveness of soul is really a burgeoning capacity for love and affection. For she says in Chapter 37: ". . . for with him I was at perfect ease, because I knew I suited him: all I said or did seemed either to console or revive him. Delightful consciousness! It brought to life and light my whole nature" (440).

Helene Moglen writes in *Charlotte Brontë–The Self-Conceived* that "Jane, like Charlotte Brontë herself, must be loved in order to know herself lovable and she cannot accept love without imagining its cost, without expecting, even embracing the necessity of sacrifice" (115). Moglen goes on to say that Jane feels and knows the world "through her emotions" (115). Perhaps for this reason Jane must motivate her aesthetic vitality in the direction of love and romance, in the development and the preservation of a profoundly romantic emotional vitality.

The last chapter of the novel affirms the perpetual bliss of Jane and Rochester. Their shared life is a sanctuary of light, love, and mutual appreciation and understanding. The image of light is as important at the end as it has been throughout the rest of the novel. Diana Rivers responds to Jane's announcement of her marriage that she will come to visit her as soon as the honeymoon is over. Rochester's verbal reaction to this plan is that if she waits that long, "she will be too late, for our honeymoon will shine our life-long" (453). The luminescence of the love which Rochester and Jane have for one another will last throughout their mortal lives.

Jane, unlike Lucy Snow in *Villette*, or Esther Summerson in Dickens' *Bleak House*, does not need multiple mirrors to understand the self—she only needs a unique, complementary "mirror" who represents her kindred spirit. In the love that Jane gives to and shares with Rochester, one might argue that she does not abandon her creative vitality—instead she reinforces it by devoting herself to the dynamism and the magnanimity of her love. Friedrich Schlegel wrote that only the individual who has a sense of eternity and a religion of his own can be a significant artist. Jane has developed such a religion and a sense of the infinite in her profound devotion to love, in her consecration of her emotional and aesthetic strength to the development, nurturing, and preservation of a dynamically sensitive and vitally unconditional love.

Jane ultimately reveals herself to be a character of Promethean vitality, for she creates harmony, serenity, and love out of disorder and misery in the spirit of Demogorgon's monologue at the end of Percy Shelley's *Prometheus Unbound*. Jane signifies the mortal embodiment and immortal emblem of the love of which Demogorgon speaks at the end of Act 4:

> Love from its awful throne of patient power
> In the wise heart, from the last giddy hour
> Of dread endurance, from the slippery, steep,
> And narrow verge of crag-like Agony, springs
> And folds over the world its healing wings. (IV. 557-61)

Jane, having emerged from the "last giddy hour of dread endurance," has saved herself from the abyss to heal Rochester's life and make her own whole and delightful as well. Jane has suffered "woes which Hope thinks infinite" (IV. 570) and yet she has still, through her indomitable spirit, creative vision, imaginative vitality, and noble heart, sought "To love, and bear; to hope, till Hope creates / From its own wreck the thing it contemplates" (IV. 573-74).

✳ Conclusion

In this book I have discussed numerous sanctuaries of light and serenity in nineteenth-century European literature. In examining diverse works of William Wordsworth, E. T. A. Hoffmann, Joseph von Eichendorff, and Charlotte Brontë I have shown that the personae in the poems and the protagonists in the prose works are often able to attain or create a sanctuary of light and blissful serenity which comforts and heals the heart and soul. In some scenarios, as in Wordsworth's "I Wandered Lonely as a Cloud" or Eichendorff's "Sehnsucht" this is not a daunting task but rather a thoroughly pleasurable experience. In other works such as Hoffmann's "The Mines at Falun" or Charlotte Brontë's *Jane Eyre* the creation of and the participation in a sanctuary of light and peace is the result of a very challenging and difficult developmental process which involves emotional peril and physical danger for the protagonist. The quest for a sanctuary of light and serenity in the works of Wordsworth, Hoffmann, Eichendorff, and C. Brontë may have different characteristics and motivations and may be developed in very distinctive environments, but there is ultimately in most of these works a sense of success, a sense of the effective participation by the personae or the protagonists in the creation of a sanctuary of light and tranquility which is comforting, healing, and inspiring. In these works if the personae or the protagonists do not themselves create a sanctuary they show a sensitive appreciation for and understanding of an existing luminescent and peaceful sanctuary beyond the vicissitudes of the world of mortality.

In various poems of William Wordsworth the persona attains a sanctuary of light and tranquility in a beautiful natural environment of relative seclusion. Wordsworth's persona may achieve a sanctuary which is motivated by the past as in the Immortality Ode, which stresses the "first affections" (148), which can function as "the fountain-light of all our day" (151). The persona in "I Wandered Lonely as a Cloud" experiences an epiphany of luminescence, suggesting that wherever he is in the world as long as he reflects on the beautiful past vision of the daffodils, his soul will be comforted. Wordsworth's persona may also achieve a sense of sanctuary in the present, for example, in "Nuns Fret Not at Their Convent's Narrow Room." In Wordsworth's poetry a sanctuary of luminescence and tranquility may also be achieved in the spirit of a future-directed vision. For example, Book 14 of *The Prelude* emphasizes the importance of the majestic intellect, "the emblem of a mind / That feeds upon infinity" (14.70-71) which has the capacity to communicate not only with the spiritual world but also with past, present, and future generations of humanity "till Time shall be no more (14.111). Wordsworth's persona typically attains a sense of sanctuary in a beautiful natural environment which may be characterized by a powerful radiance during the day or even by a more subtle light at night. The experience of a sanctuary often generates an epiphanic moment for the persona in the poem which may guide and inspire his future life.

In the literary works of E. T. A. Hoffmann, the sense of a luminescent sanctuary is more often consistently achieved in a domestic interior, and especially in a distinctive architectural interior, rather than in the context of the natural environment. In "Ritter Gluck," for example, the sense of sanctuary exists in the private room of Ritter Gluck, which contains all of his precious manuscripts. In "Der goldene Topf" Anselmus feels an aura of sanctuary in one or more of the gorgeous rooms in the house of the Archivist Lindhorst. At the end of this narrative Anselmus and Serpentina experience a shared feeling of sanctuary in the lovely environment of Atlantis, which could be an extension of one of the beautiful interiors in the architectural wonder signified by Lindhorst's house, or an inspirational landscape of the mind, or a delightful setting which is by its very nature as isolated and separate from the world of everyday mortality as Shangri-La in Hilton's *Lost Horizon*. In "The Nutcracker" the sense of sanctuary could be said to be in the delightful imagination of Marie Stahlbaum which has been so carefully nurtured by various individuals around her; yet, this sense of sanctuary, as most others in Hoffmann's works, is generated in an interior space, in the domain of her own house.

In the poems and narratives of Joseph von Eichendorff, the sense of sanctuary which is created is characterized by a beautiful and effulgent natural environment, which may be graced by the lovely daylight or by the delightful moonlight. In "Frühe" a lonely lark, having dreamt of the light, awakens early in a misty landscape permeated by a profound silence. In "Sehnsucht" the natural environment and the landscape of the poem are pervaded by a golden light which streams from the stars over the nocturnal ambience. The persona has a longing to wander and follow the travelers through the landscape. The song which he hears them singing of various sublime aspects of nature, of marble statues, and of decaying palaces in moonlight gives his spirit a sense of expansiveness and makes him feel as if he were a part of this effulgent landscape. In "Aus dem Leben eines Taugenichts" the protagonist does wander extensively through various areas in the spirit of "Der frohe Wandersmann" and ultimately returns to the palace in Vienna where he had initially experienced a blissful sense of sanctuary and love. In Eichendorff's work a faith in God and a belief in the divine play an important role. For example, in "Der Einsiedler" the persona, weary of the tribulations of the world of mortality, longs for the sanctuary of the night and for the "Morgenrot," the light of eternity which will ultimately comfort and soothe his heart and soul.

In Charlotte Brontë's *Jane Eyre* the protagonist experiences a sense of sanctuary at various points of the novel and at diverse episodes of her life. At Gateshead Jane creates an ambience of sanctuary to protect her from the abusive treatment of the Reed family members. At Lowood Jane experiences different moments of sanctuary, including one in the natural environment and most especially the important and inspirational meal with Miss Temple and Helen Burns. At Thornfield Jane has a feeling of a sanctuary of light and peace occasionally in some of the aesthetically interesting rooms, either alone or in the presence of Rochester. Jane also experiences a sense of sanctuary outside the house in the beautiful natural environment. After the cataclysmic wedding day experience and the anguish of Jane's arrival at Whitcross, Jane does find an atmosphere of sanctuary at Moor House in the presence of Diana and Mary Rivers. Finally, at Ferndean Jane and Rochester enjoy a shared sense of sanctuary, a blissful repose of contented seclusion away from the ravages and sufferings of everyday mortality. As Serpentina and Anselmus in Hoffmann's "The Golden Pot," Jane and Rochester create their own Atlantis in the isolated ambience and quietly effulgent sanctuary of Ferndean, while still maintaining contact with several dear and supportive friends.

The experience of a sanctuary of light and serenity is perhaps most viable and vital in the Romantic period and in works which have a Romantic motivation or sensibility. In the first half of the nineteenth century there are various important works of European literature which exhibit a sense of sanctuary or an ambience which has a semblance of a sanctuary. In the second half of the nineteenth century, when a realistic life-philosophy and a realistic aesthetics are more conspicuously present and in the ascendancy, the sense and spirit of sanctuary appears less important and prominent in European literature. Yet, there are attempts in the works of several writers in the second half of the nineteenth century and at the beginning of the twentieth century to create an aura or a spirit of sanctuary. I would like now to examine the quest for a sanctuary, for a transcendent space, in the works of several post-

Romantic writers who encompass in their works various important and essential contemporary issues and themes. I will first discuss the quest for a sanctuary of light and peace in two dramatic works of Henrik Ibsen.

In Ibsen's *The Master Builder*, Solness tries to create a sacred architectural space, an architectural space which either in its own right or in conjunction with the surrounding natural environment can represent a sanctuary. In this drama the quest for a sense of sanctuary is intimately connected to the theme of creative vitality. The notion of absolute commitment to his work is crucial to Solness as the master builder. Solness speaks in Act 3 of the development of his creativity and commitment to his artistic work. Initially, Solness, reared in an atmosphere which respected the divine and religious faith, believed that building churches was the worthiest goal he could have as an architect. He explains to Hilde that he built various churches with such genuine "sincerity and devotion" (348) that he thought God would have been pleased with him. Instead, Solness claims that God made him suffer so he could develop and refine his art. Solness blames God not only for letting loose the troll within him "to rampage almost as it will" (348), but also for letting the previous family home burn down.

In trying to understand God's motivation for making him and those around him suffer, Solness claims that God wanted to encourage him to become a thorough and an exemplary master of his profession. Solness further interprets the loss of his children as a sign from God that he should devote himself completely and unreservedly to his work. There should be no personal life which might distract Solness from his work—here Solness is symbolic of many creative artists (painters, architects, sculptors, writers, etc.) through the centuries who have dedicated themselves completely to their work and have not allowed a "personal" life to interfere with such dedication. R. M. Rilke speaks similarly of the devotion which an artist should show—this devotion should be absolute, allowing for minimal personal interference or intervention from the world of everyday mortality.

The statement which Solness makes about the absolute commitment of the artist to his work is also similar to a comparable assertion made by Thomas Mann in his story "Tonio Kröger." Tonio Kröger, a capable, sensitive, and thoughtful writer, devotes himself to the power which seems to him the greatest on the earth and to which he feels instinctively drawn, the power of the intellect and of language. Mann describes the commitment which Tonio develops towards his work as follows: "He worked, not like a man who works that he may live; but as one who is bent on doing nothing but work: having no regard for himself as a human being but only as a creator" (93).

A turning point in Solness's career occurred when he climbed the tower of the completed building in Hilde's home town to hang a wreath on the weathercock and signify the successful completion of the project. Before that Solness had always been afraid of heights, but on that day he seemed to be impelled by an inner force to climb the tower. Solness asserts that when he reached the top he spoke to God and proclaimed his artistic freedom as a master builder. One could describe this scenario as Solness's declaration of independence from his career of building churches. Solness tells God that from now on he will only build homes for the people, sanctuaries of domesticity. This passage is also interesting because Solness creates an analogy between himself and the divine, claiming to God that he is a "master builder free in his own field, as you are in yours" (349). Solness tries to create a sanctuary of intellectual and spiritual independence here, a sanctuary which celebrates his own integrity as an artist.

Solness's sense of absolute commitment to his work evolves into his quest for transcendence. Once he has achieved what he aimed to accomplish in the sphere of everyday reality, then he aspires to something greater. Errol Durbach describes this aspiration of Solness as follows: "He commits himself, in soul-camradeship with Hilde Wangel, to that most Romantic of impulses: the lure of the impossible, the temptation to transcend not only his own physical infirmity in high places but the mortal and temporal limitations of mankind" (127).

As the conversation between Solness and Hilde progresses Solness admits that his ambition of building homes for the people did not come to fruition as he wished because he observed that such architectural creations did not ensure the happiness of the people in those homes. Solness is very self-critical in this passage in Act 3, even proclaiming that until now he has not really built anything. This is an extraordinary statement for the master builder to make, for he appears to be doubting the value and questioning the validity of his entire architectural career. Solness concludes this point by suggesting to Hilde that he will now embark upon a new architectural philosophy, an innovative and grand strategy of creation—Solness declares that he will devote himself from now on to the construction of the only buildings which can contain human happiness, castles in the air. Such castles in the air are sanctuaries of freedom, liberation, and openness beyond the constraints and limitations of everyday mortality.

Happiness is an important issue for Solness as the master builder. In Act 2, for example, Solness argues that everything he has achieved has had to be paid for in human happiness, not only his own, but especially in the happiness of others.

Solness even suggests that he succeeded as a master builder through the anguish and the suffering of his wife, Aline. Her capacity for "building children's souls" (316) had to be crushed for his talent as a builder to develop and to thrive. Moreover, the burning of Aline's family home helped to promote the career of Solness, although he says that he was not directly responsible for the conflagration.

That Solness, who has spent his professional life building "real" and solid structures with "real" and concrete foundations, would claim suddenly that the only constructions that really matter are "castles in the air" represents not only profound self-criticism but also an ironic and deeply critical commentary on society. Ibsen appears to imply in this passage that there is little genuine happiness in the world of everyday reality—the only source of true happiness is the ideal and the world of the imagination and of dreams.

For Ibsen, as for some of his European literary predecessors, and especially for those of Romantic inclination and motivation, this world of dream and of the ideal is subtly and sometimes even more directly connected to the realm of death and eternity. In several poems of Novalis and Clemens Brentano, for example, there is a "Sehnsucht nach dem Tode," a longing for death to liberate the spirit from the hardships and the suffering of everyday reality. Death is viewed by various Romantic writers and artists as a pleasant, interesting, and congenial realm which can offer healing and solace for the soul overwhelmed by the frailties, inadequacies, and vicissitudes of mortal existence. The realm of death is even viewed by some creators as a sanctuary of peace, harmony, and light beyond the ravages of mortality.

One could argue that Solness demonstrates such a "Sehnsucht nach dem Tode" as well. At the end of *The Master Builder* Solness feels that he has reached the pinnacle of worldly success for he has attained the position of the master builder and has enjoyed a long and distinguished building career. Yet, Solness seems very dissatisfied with his career and with his creativity. One indication of such dissatisfaction, which is simultaneously a symptom of self-doubt, is that Solness believes that his position as the master builder is threatened by youth and by more innovative architects such as Ragnar.

The "castle in the air" which Solness aspires ultimately to achieve could represent the notion of the ideal, in the sense of an ideal of architectural creation or in the sense of a Platonic ideal of creative endeavor. Such a "castle in the air" could also signify a longing for death, for the "süsser Tod" (the sweet death) in Clemens Brentano's "Schwanenlied" which transforms all sufferings to pleasures. Although Hilde appears to be manipulating Solness in Act 3 and urging him softly and irrevocably to his demise (for she is certainly aware that his attempt to climb to the top of the most recently completed structure would be very dangerous), perhaps Solness is using Hilde as well. Solness, imbued with a sense that his career has reached a climax and an impasse, might consider this climb to the top of the structure as potentially his final ascent—he knows intuitively that there will be no viable descent and that such a situation would represent an honorable death.

One might claim that Solness, as Gustave von Aschenbach in Thomas Mann's "Death in Venice," senses that his death is imminent and to some extent even longs for it. Aschenbach, like Solness, is tired, if not exhausted, by his work and needs a dramatic change in his life, perhaps even sensing that his future professional career will no longer approximate the vitality which he has enjoyed in the past and for which he has been celebrated in the past.

James McFarlane suggests that "potency" is a central concern of *The Master Builder*: "The possession, the lack, the loss of it, the search for it, the submission to it, the stimulation of it, the wonder at it—all contribute to the composition of the play" (293). McFarlane argues that there are three kinds of potency in the play: "artistic potency; sexual potency; and what one might variously call personal potency, volitional potency, or charisma" (293). McFarlane stresses the decline in the creative power which is manifest in the work of Solness: "The grand designs, the churches and towering spires of the past have yielded to humble domestic buildings; and the desire to do even this seems to be on the point of drying up altogether" (294). Related to Solness' awareness of the decline of his artistic vitality is his sense that he has exploited others in the development of his career: "He is conscious of draining the energies of others and applying them to his own purposes; he is secretly filled with a sense of his own inadequacy" (294). McFarlane asserts insightfully that although the artistic and the creative potency of Solness has decreased, "his personal potency, magnetism, the potency of his will, seem undiminished" (295).

The two narratives, Ibsen's *The Master Builder* and Mann's "Death in Venice" reveal other similarities as well. Solness has claimed prior to climbing the tower at the end that he will speak to God at the top, that he will converse with the divine and tell him that from now on he will build only one kind of structure, the loveliest architectural creation in the world, his castle in the air, with Hilde. Aschenbach, at the end of Mann's narrative, is sitting near the ocean gazing at Tadzio along the shore "while his whole face took on the relaxed and brooding expression of deep slumber" (73). Solness ascends to the threshold of earth and sky to die, whereas Aschenbach journeys to Venice, to the threshold of earth and sea, to end his life.

Tadzio appears to lead and to lure Aschenbach towards another world, a new domain of existence: "It seemed to him the pale and lovely Summoner out there smiled at him and beckoned; as though, with the hand he lifted from his hip, he pointed outward as he hovered on before into an immensity of richest expectation" (73). Tadzio, as the Summoner, symbolizes a quasi-divine figure comparable to the divine character with whom Solness anticipates holding a conversation at the top of the tower.

One could also make an interesting parallel between Hilde and Tadzio. Hilde could be interpreted as the troll in Solness, the outward manifestation of the troll in the master builder. That is, Hilde is in some sense a creation of the fantasy of Solness which he is perhaps trying to deny. For example, in Act 1 Solness tries to deny Hilde's claims of their past intimate contact. Tadzio could be viewed as Aschenbach's creation. Aschenbach names Tadzio, symbolically giving him life. It is moreover noteworthy that Tadzio, described as a "living figure, virginally pure and austere" (33) is a vital manifestation of the primary character-type which permeates Aschenbach's literary work. This character-type, this novel kind of hero which Aschenbach wrote about consistently, is analyzed by a critic as exemplifying "an intellectual and virginal manliness, which clenches its teeth and stands in modest defiance of the swords and spears that pierce its side" (11). Such a description applies especially to Tadzio who, Aschenbach senses, has physical frailties and problems which will prevent him from achieving a long life.

Hilde and Tadzio are also similar because they lead or guide Solness and Aschenbach respectively to their deaths. Hilde encourages Solness to climb to the pinnacle of the structure as he did so impressively ten years before in her home town. In the very last statement of the drama Hilde affirms the death of Solness as well as the fact that he seemed to attain his goal, for she says that she heard "harps in the air" (355). Of course, this is Hilde's perspective and could merely reflect what Hilde wanted to glean from this tragic episode. One might say that Hilde wanted, for her own selfish purposes, to hear the harps in the air which she felt such an episode would provide her, without any genuine interest in or regard for the feelings or perspectives of others. Tadzio is the individual whose presence in Venice keeps Aschenbach from leaving for the sake of his physical health. Unlike Hilde in her association with Solness, Tadzio does not have consistently direct contact with Aschenbach and is not consciously trying to manipulate the writer to follow any plan of action. Tadzio could be interpreted as the "pale and lovely Summoner" (71) who gently and surreptitiously summons and guides Aschenbach to another world beyond everyday mortality. Tadzio even has the aura of a Hermes-like figure who, as the messenger of the gods, announces Aschenbach's death.

Although neither Solness in *The Master Builder* nor Aschenbach in "Death in Venice" approaches the end of his life aggressively, that is, with a passionate inclination to enter the realm of the dead, both characters are certainly aware, perhaps sometimes more subconsciously than consciously, that their final action involves the possibility of experiencing death. Solness knows that his proposed climb of the tower is extremely dangerous and Aschenbach is aware that the disease-ridden atmosphere in Venice could seriously threaten his health.

One might claim that Solness, despite the obvious anxiety of Mrs. Solness (an anxiety which shows that despite their outward conflicts she does care about him) that this physical endeavor is too dangerous and too precarious, climbs to the top of the structure to prove his vitality to himself or to Hilde. As Hilde knows that such a climb would be perilous for Solness, one could perhaps view her as a siren-like character who leads another individual or other individuals to their death as a compensation for or as a punishment for the suffering she has experienced in life.

In Clemens Brentano's poem about the Lorelei, "Die Lore Lay," she admits to the bishop that she is tired of life because everyone who sees her must perish. Lorelei is so distraught and upset because her lover once deserted her. It is noteworthy that in Brentano's version of this myth Lorelei is not a vicious and vindictive siren who enjoys destroying lives. Rather, she is critically self-aware of her own power and even asserts that she would prefer not to have such a destructive capability and would even rather perish herself. This inclination distinguishes her from Hilde who, as Hedda in Ibsen's *Hedda Gabler*, definitely enjoys possessing a controlling, potentially destructive power over others.

At the end of Brentano's poem this enchanting individual is led by three knights towards a cloister where she seemingly intends to spend the rest of her mortal days as a nun. However, as they climb into the rocky hills above the Rhine River she claims suddenly that she sees a ship cruising along the river which might contain her love—then she leans over the precipice and plunges into the river. Her three knightly companions also perish for once they have climbed into the rocky labyrinths above the majestic river there is no viable path for them to use for a descent.

Unlike Lorelei, Hilde as a siren does survive, though perhaps in a diminished capacity. For she is described as being bewildered at the end, though she also feels triumphant. It does not seem as if Hilde feels any remorse for having encouraged and exhorted the master builder to ascend to his demise. However, perhaps she is disappointed that the vitality of which she felt herself to be an important part ten years ago when Solness climbed to the tower in her home town no longer exists as the master builder plunges to his death. Hilde is bewildered because her dream of seeing Solness at the top of the building conversing with God and laying the foundation of her "castle in the air" has been undermined and vanquished.

Hilde is perhaps even more similar to the characterization or presentation of the Lorelei figure in Heinrich Heine's poem "Ich weiss nicht, was soll es bedeuten." Heine's Lorelei is described from a distance; she does not speak in the poem and we are not informed about her thoughts and feelings as we are in Brentano's lyrical version of the myth. Heine's Lorelei is portrayed as a most beautiful woman who sits on the rocks high above the Rhine River, combing her golden hair and singing a powerfully poignant melody which lures sailors to their deaths and ships to their inevitable destruction. The source of the negative and destructive power of Heine's Lorelei is her song—and she seems indifferent to the baleful, harmful consequences of her haunting melodies. In contrast, Brentano's Lorelei exerts her special powers through the beauty of her lovely face and gorgeous eyes.

Inga-Stina Ewbank affirms the power of Hilde over Solness: "The Lysanger episode comes alive in the play, not so much by gradual reconstruction as by Hilde imposing her construction of it on the Master Builder who, whether or not it is a fiction, is ever more willing to make it his own truth" (McFarlane 142). Solness initially attempts to deny that Hilde's recollections are true, but ultimately seems to accept her version of the past. This could be interpreted as a passive acceptance by Solness of Hilde's position. However, as Solness feels gradually encouraged to become a more active participant in the dialogue with Hilde, this might also suggest a temporary enhancement of the master builder's own sense of vitality.

It is possible that Solness makes the climb to the top of the new structure to converse with God as he claimed he did on a previous occasion. The ascent of the tower also gives Solness a sense of spiritual freedom and emotional liberation from the cares and tribulations of everyday mortality and reality. That Solness does seem tired of and exhausted by his professional career does provide a plausible reason for his suicide, if one would interpret the fall in such a way. Moreover, his final conversation with Hilde offers several hints about this possibility as well. Solness tells Hilde that when he reaches the top of the structure he will tell God that he will only build "one thing . . . the loveliest thing in the whole world" (351). One might wonder whether Solness means one type of structure, castles in the air, or whether he implies just one building, one final architectural creation, one ultimate castle in the air.

Solness seems mesmerized by Hilde at the end, for in his final conversation with her he even revives parts of the narrative of the past encounter which they had (that is, according to Hilde's version of the event) in Hilde's home town ten years ago. Perhaps the final act does represent Solness fulfilling his dream of creating "a castle in the air." As this phrase refers to the realm of the ideal one might interpret Solness and Ibsen as suggesting that castles in the air have no tangible place in the world of everyday mortality among the hardships and struggles of reality. The castle in the air of Solness, as the exceptional space of Atlantis which Anselmus and Serpentina inhabit in their blissful love, is only truly viable and vital in the world of the ideal and in the realm of the imagination.

Errol Durbach asserts that the castles in the air, as well as the Kingdom of Orangia, are "symbols of reality but not reality itself" (135). The inherent problem in the quest for such romantic structures, says Durbach, is that it signifies "an ascent into the no man's land of stasis, from which all human vitality has been purged and drained away" (135). Or perhaps one could say that the vitality has already been achieved and demonstrated by Solness in his career as a preparation for this final romantic quest of creating a "castle in the air."

Durbach proceeds to argue that "in *The Master Builder*, with its empty nurseries and uninhabitable houses and illusory castles, the impossibility of constructing such an innovative architecture underscores the tragedy of Solness's and Hilde's romanticism" (136). The empty nurseries and the houses which are uninhabitable or appear to be so certainly reinforce the aura of tragedy in the drama. However, I would say that the "castle in the air" represents a more positive, a more emotionally and spiritually vital entity. The castle in the air signifies for Solness the creation of the ideal and of an ideal image and structure which transcends the limitations and sufferings inherent in and perceptible in everyday mortality. As Solness declares in Act 3 that up to that point of his career he has not really accomplished anything, the opportunity to create a castle in the air could also represent the possibility of a strategy of self-revitalization. Solness might view the challenge to create such an extraordinary structure as an occasion to revitalize his creative energies and capacities.

The final statement of Nathaniel Hawthorne's "The Artist of the Beautiful" offers an interesting parallel to the situation of Solness in Act 3 of

The Master Builder: "When the artist rose high enough to achieve the beautiful, the symbol by which he made it perceptible to mortal senses became of little value in his eyes while his spirit possessed itself in the enjoyment of the reality" (Hawthorne 95). The grandson and spiritual heir of the arch-realist Peter Hovenden has just destroyed the beautiful and magical butterfly which the romantic Owen Warland created. Hawthorne, in the final sentence of the story, suggests that what really matters to this artist of the beautiful is the achievement of the ideal. Even though the real manifestation of his art work has been ruined, the ideal, once achieved, is eternal.

One could argue that Solness has risen to achieve the beautiful, his "castle in the air," and now the "real" construction of his structure to the top of which he has climbed is irrelevant. In speaking to the divine being or realm, the spirit of Solness is possessing "itself in the enjoyment of the reality" as Owen Warland does in the Hawthorne story. Unlike Solness, of course, Owen Warland does physically survive his immediate contact with the deleterious realism symbolized by Peter Hovenden and the blacksmith Robert Danforth. However, just as Solness has died to life so presumably will Owen. Solness has removed himself literally from the tribulations and vicissitudes of the world of everyday mortality. Owen Warland in "The Artist of the Beautiful" will presumably separate himself literally and symbolically from everyday mortality by isolating himself further after this painful contact with the doubting and unsupportive world around him.

In the quest for a sense of transcendent space, for a "castle in the air," for a sanctuary away from the world of everyday mortality, there is another related issue: namely, the quest of Solness to achieve something extraordinary, something exceptional in his life. This striving of Solness is comparable to that of J.S. Mill's "energetic individual" who aspires to achieve innovation as well as an exemplary creativity. The word "troll" in *The Master Builder* encompasses the manifold dimensions of the striving of Solness for exceptional achievement. The troll for Ibsen involves positive and creative features as well as negative and destructive aspects. The troll symbolizes the heroic attempt to achieve something extraordinary, unusual, and distinctive and to exert a controlling influence on others.

In Act 2 of *The Master Builder* Solness reveals his instinctive belief that he possesses extraordinary capacities. As a precursor to this assertion Solness suggested already in Act 1 that he had the ability to wish for certain things which would eventually happen. For example, when Kaja comes to the office for the first time, Solness wishes inwardly that she will stay and work for him; although he never said anything to her directly about this issue, she returns the next day assuming that she is part of his architectural firm. In Act 2 Solness speaks to Hilde of having the power to wish for various things and goals which are eventually and inevitably achieved.

Solness adds that such an exceptional individual with such a profound capacity often needs "helpers" who assist him in the completion of his work and in the attainment of his desires. It is noteworthy that these "helpers" must, according to Solness, be summoned not only imperiously but also inwardly. Perhaps Hilde functions as such a "helper" whom Solness summoned to aid him in achieving his ethereal sanctuary, his "castle in the air," and an honorable death. Perhaps Solness, having reached or having felt inwardly that he had reached a painful and unbearable sense of finality in his career and in his creative life "summons" Hilde to compel him to climb to the top of a structure, despite his considerable anxiety about heights, as he did ten years ago. Solness does not want to be excessively challenged or vanquished by youth, by the innovative designs of younger architects like Ragnar, so perhaps he decides to end his life before he can be officially eclipsed in his work. Solness, the master builder, exemplifies the inner conflict of creative and destructive inclinations which the figure of the troll symbolizes. The master builder has attained a pinnacle of creative achievement and public acclaim and does not wish to see the world of everyday reality encroach upon and diminish his considerable and vital past accomplishments.

Solness as an accomplished architect does not wish to confront for the rest of his life the prospect of a diminishing creative vitality and a decline in public appreciation and acclaim. However, perhaps there is even something of the spirit of Friedrich Hölderlin's poem "An die Parzen" ("To the Fates") in the experience and strategy of the master builder at the end of the Ibsen drama. In Hölderlin's "An die Parzen" the persona addresses "ihr Gewaltigen" (the powerful ones, presumably the gods), saying that once he has achieved the holy creation, the poem (perhaps even the perfect poem or a literary work of extraordinary artistic vitality), then he will be ready to leave this world and to die. This persona suggests that he will feel no regret because once in his life he can claim that he lived as the gods—and he does not require or expect more happiness and bliss than that. This sentiment could be viewed as similar to the willingness of Solness at the end of The Master Builder to pass on to another realm beyond mortality. In the attainment of his vision of the castle in the air Solness could feel that he has achieved his ultimate success and has no longer a desire to live in the realm of mortality.

In Ibsen's The Wild Duck the room with the duck offers the atmosphere of a sanctuary, of a timeless space. In Act 3 of The Wild Duck this special room is described in considerable detail in the conversation between Hedvig and Gregers. It is represented as a world of its own, with big cupboards containing various books with pictures as well as an old cabinet with compartments. This is a room where time no longer exists, symbolized by the presence of a huge clock which no longer functions properly. This room, although not as spatially extensive as Nansen's living-room in Siegfried Lenz's *The German Lesson*, contains a similarly vital aura of timelessness.

Hedvig stresses the mysterious nature of the wild duck, that no one really knows her or where she comes from. The aura of authority which the wild duck is given is due to her sense of isolation and to her representation of individualism and freedom; it is also noteworthy that the wild duck is described as having been in "the depths of the sea" (438)—this implies a capacity to explore beyond the confines and restraints of everyday mortality. Yet, the idealistic motivations and aspirations of Hjalmar and Gregers who strive to create a better world are undermined and shattered by the revelations about Gina and by Hedvig's death. The "enchantment" of the attic loft has been encroached upon by the misery and suffering of everyday reality—the sense of a potential sanctuary cannot be viably sustained.

Miss Julie in August Strindberg's *Miss Julie* yearns, as does Solness in Ibsen's *The Master Builder*, for a sense of sanctuary and for a better, more congenial, and more humane existential condition. The characters of Miss Julie and Solness reveal several interesting parallels. Both Solness and Miss Julie are discontented and dissatisfied with their present lives and long for a more beautiful and a more vital existence. The "kingdom of Orangia" which Solness has imagined for Hilde, and, by implication, for himself, is similar to Miss Julie's dream or vision of a paradise along a southern European lake. It is noteworthy that the visions of Solness and Miss Julie are both characterized in part by the image and idea of orange, a vibrant, dynamic color and aura.

Both Solness and Miss Julie have a dream or a vision relating to heights or an experience of climbing. Solness climbed to the top of the church tower in Hilde's home town to lay the wreath at the conclusion of the architectural work. Solness mentions the danger which he felt during this endeavor especially because a "little devil in white" (291), who was Hilde, was shouting at him so vociferously. Solness says that he almost grew dizzy at the sight of her waving her flag. The peril which Solness senses in this instance culminates in the final act of the drama when he falls to his death. The experience of Solness at the end of *The Master Builder* is strikingly similar to the dream which Miss Julie has of climbing up a pillar. As Solness, Miss Julie speaks of the fear of climbing down, of getting dizzy when she looks down, of longing to fall, of longing to reach the ground. One might claim that Miss Julie's dream foreshadows death, for she talks of desiring to "get down to the ground" (413) so she can be under the earth. Both Miss Julie and Solness could be said to have suicidal motivations.

One might also argue that both Solness and Miss Julie are the victims of the pressure and exhortation by others to strive for a goal which they do not truly desire. Miss Julie's servant encourages her to develop suicidal thoughts, just as Hilde exhorts Solness to risk his life by climbing to the top of the tower. Neither Jean nor Hilde, who are both conspicuously self-centered characters, seem to have genuinely caring and thoughtful feelings for the individuals they exhort or guide towards death.

The dream which Jean describes to Miss Julie is comparable to the desire of Hilde. Jean dreams of climbing up to the top of a high tree in a dark forest so that he can survey the surrounding landscape and take the golden eggs from the bird's nest at the top. Hilde's expectation of a kingdom from Solness is similar—she wants a kingdom with a tower and with an expansiveness of space. Such is Hilde's initial declaration, although by the end of Act 1 she seems to want most especially a personal and a professional connection to an important person such as the master builder, who can make her life more interesting and more worthwhile.

Another similarity between Jean and Hilde is that both want to escape or liberate themselves from the environment of their childhood and youth and the painful memories of that environment. Hilde feels emotionally and intellectually confined by her home town—her dream and expectation that Solness will provide her with a kingdom is in part a means to free herself from the unpleasant ambience and confining circumstances of her youth. Jean, whose socioeconomic condition in childhood was seemingly considerably more deprived than that of Hilde, describes his awareness of Miss Julie's house and garden as a Garden of Eden which he is prevented from entering but which he desires nevertheless.

As Miss Julie and Jean are contemplating the possibility of leaving together for a distant destination, Jean suggests that they travel to the Italian lakes where there is an eternal summer characterized by "oranges growing everywhere, laurel trees, always green" (416). This image of an earthly paradise, of a sanctuary beyond the exigencies and tribulations of everyday reality, is comparable in scope to Hilde's sense of the kingdom of Orangia, which she anticipates receiving from Solness. The dream of a happy future which Jean began to inspire Miss Julie to create is short-lived, for he soon criticizes her severely.

One might argue that Miss Julie, for various reasons, is more instinctively suicidal than Solness. Julie's dream implies a subtle longing for death, an inclination to welcome death. In contrast, when Solness climbed the tower in Hilde's home town he was presumably frightened of falling and feared death. Solness at the end of *The Master Builder* appears to have become more similar to Miss Julie with her implicit suicidal inclinations.

While Miss Julie and Solness both show a discontentment, disdain, and dissatisfaction with the life around them and with the world of everyday mortality, the source of their discontentment is different. Solness, as has been discussed, feels dismayed because he believes (and because he senses that other people believe this as well) that he has attained the pinnacle of his success as a master builder and that his professional position is threatened by the presence of youth. Miss Julie feels a sense of isolation and loneliness from the beginning of the Strindberg drama which seems to drive her into the arms of the superficially sympathetic and not profoundly sensitive Jean. As the drama progresses Julie becomes increasingly despondent, especially after she realizes that she has hastily yielded to someone who is certainly unworthy of her. In the "Ballet" scenario Julie even prays to God to end her wretched life and to save her from mortal anguish.

Julie and Solness are also similar in that they appear to wish to have someone guide their lives or one might say that they are powerless to prevent another person from exhorting them to do what they might otherwise not have done. When Julie senses that she is caught in an impossible, unresolvable position, she asks Jean to order her to do something. Solness, although not as abject or desolate as Julie, does allow Hilde to compel him to climb to the top of the tower at the end of *The Master Builder,* though he knows it might very likely mean his death. Jean gives Miss Julie the razor at the end of *Miss Julie* to enable her to commit suicide.

One of the most important and profound similarities between Miss Julie and Solness is that they are both instinctively romantic and idealistic characters. For example, Julie wishes to take her greenfinch with her on the proposed trip with Jean which she momentarily contemplates. In claiming that the greenfinch is the only living being that loves her, Julie pleads with Jean to allow her to take the bird along with them. In response, Jean, the cold-hearted realist, kills the bird because of the problem of carrying a birdcage with them on their planned journey. Julie is thoroughly horrified by Jean's brutal action and curses the moment when she first saw him.

Another example of Miss Julie's romanticism is revealed in her ensuing conversation with Kristine. Julie informs Kristine of the plan to travel to

Switzerland with Jean so the three of them can open a hotel. It is noteworthy that Julie mentions that along the way to Switzerland and the Alps they can visit the castles of King Ludwig, another quintessentially romantic character who was consistently misunderstood and undervalued by his contemporary society. Julie's statement to Kristine that Ludwig's castles are "like castles in fairy tales" (424) is as much an attempt to persuade Kristine of the value and vitality of the journey as it is to affirm to herself that the ideal beauty of which these castles are an exquisite earthly embodiment truly does exist.

Julie is trying desperately to create a beautiful and a viable vision and to nurture the dream of a lovely sanctuary of light and harmony to elevate her life above the sordidness and anguish of her everyday reality. Sadly, Kristine's question, after Julie's description of this picturesque vision, whether she really believes what she has just said challenges and undermines Julie's fragile dream. Julie's interest in visiting the beautiful castles of King Ludwig as symbols of an earthly paradise and sanctuary is analogous to the commitment of Solness to build castles in the air. A castle in the air signifies a vision of extraordinary beauty and symbolizes the triumph of the ideal over the real—such an image of an etherial sanctuary represents a tribute to the power of creativity and the imagination.

There are interesting and evocative depictions of other sanctuaries of light and of quests to achieve a sanctuary of light in various literary works of the first several decades of the twentieth century. In F. Scott Fitzgerald's *The Great Gatsby*, for example, Gatsby tries to create a sanctuary of extraordinary luminescence, his esoteric mansion, to attract the interest of Daisy Buchanan. It is noteworthy that Gatsby creates this "sanctuary" not as a place of beauty to be admired and valued in its own right—rather this "sanctuary" with its lavish parties and cosmopolitan architecture is only important to Gatsby as a means to attract and to impress Daisy. Even though Gatsby is described as an Apollonian figure, as a "patron of light," his Romantic presence and vision cannot withstand the encroachment of Tom Buchanan's world of crass materialism and harsh reality. The sanctuary of radiance which Gatsby created to attract and to celebrate Daisy, his former love, fades and vanishes with his death.

Hermann Hesse's *Steppenwolf* and *Siddhartha* represent other twentieth-century sanctuaries of light and seclusion beyond the world of everyday mortality. In *Steppenwolf* the experience of the Magic Theater is an opportunity to enrich, expand, and stimulate the self beyond the limits and constraints of everyday reality. The Magic Theater signifies a sense of sanctuary in a vibrant interior. One might even say that Harry Haller's experience in the Magic

Theater is analogous to the experience of Anselmus in the "magic theater" of Lindhorst's house. Both spaces are mind-expanding and spirit-entrancing sanctuaries of light and color. The sense of sanctuary in *Siddhartha* is exemplified most vitally and most nobly by the protagonist of the work. Siddhartha, a Buddha-like figure, embodies in his own heart and soul a sanctuary of luminescence and profound serenity. The sanctuary of tranquility and wisdom which Siddhartha instinctively represents is reaffirmed by the lovely and relatively peaceful natural environment around him.

The most exceptional refuge of light and serenity in early to mid-twentieth-century European literature is perhaps the sanctuary of Shangri-La in James Hilton's *Lost Horizon*. The first sight of the lamasery of Shangri-La is a dazzling, yet tranquil, vision of a timeless world, a cultural and intellectual oasis physically isolated from the world of everyday mortality. For Conway the initial perception of the lamasery might have been a vision deriving from his sense of physical tranquility and harmony which he feels during the climb to this mountainous retreat. The description of the first view of Shangri-La is memorable not only for the emphasis on the ethereal nature of the ambience but also because it initiates Conway into the seemingly timeless world:

> It was, indeed, a strange and half-incredible sight. A group of colored pavilions clung to the mountain-side with none of the grim deliberation of a Rhineland castle, but rather with the chance delicacy of flowerpetals impaled upon a crag. It was superb and exquisite. An austere emotion carried the eye upward from milk-blue roofs to the gray rock bastion above, tremendous as the Wetterhorn above Grindelwald. Beyond that, in a dazzling pyramid, soared the snow slopes of Karakal. (81)

The otherworldliness of the Tibetan ambience of Shangri-La is reinforced by the sense that the air, "clean as from another planet, was more precious with every intake" (74). The conscious and deliberate breathing which resulted inevitably in such an atmosphere produced ultimately "an almost tranquility of mind" (74) and "a single rhythm of breathing, walking and thinking" (74).

As Anselmus in Hoffmann's "Der goldene Topf" has the appropriate character to appreciate and to understand Serpentina and the imaginative world of the Archivist Lindhorst, so Conway in *Lost Horizon* is portrayed as having the appropriate character and life-philosophy to appreciate the profound serenity and timeless ambience of Shangri-La. Conway had been initially chosen to be among those destined for Shangri-La, for this extraordinary sanctuary beyond the ravages of mortality, because he was perceived as a compassionate, sensitive, thoughtful, and wise individual who maintained a resilient balance of inner energy and dynamic spectatorship.

The dream-like aura of Shangri-La gives Conway an exceptional sense of tranquility. This sense of peacefulness is complemented by Conway's initial impression of the lamasery as being spacious, warm, and clean. He feels that he has entered a new world of elegant serenity and ethereal beauty. The aura of Shangri-La represents in the intellectual and aesthetic tradition of Andre Malraux's *The Voices of Silence* a purification of the world and a serenely Promethean revolt against the temporal flux and vicissitudes of mortality.

At the beginning of chapter four there is a description of the life-philosophy which pervades Shangri-La and which Conway has cultivated instinctively in his own life: "He was enjoying that pleasant mingling of physical ease and mental alertness which seemed to him, of all sensations, the most truly civilized" (85). Shangri-La, despite its geographical isolation in the Himalayas, does possess the material accoutrements of civilized society such as central heating. Perhaps most importantly for its self-defined mission of cultural-intellectual preservation Shangri-La fuses features of Western and Eastern civilization (for example, containing in its library significant literary texts of both traditions).

Conway's quest for timelessness, for a timeless sanctuary, is simultaneously a quest for aesthetic enrichment. Conway's experience of the sanctuary of Shangri-La will not only develop his sense of time and potential timelessness—it will also enhance his aesthetic awareness and sensibility. Perhaps these two features of personal development are inextricably linked. The aesthetic education of Conway is strengthened in his perception of treasures that museums and millionaires alike would be interested in. These treasures include pearl blue Sung ceramics, paintings in tinted inks, and beautiful lacquers.

The exquisitely fragile beauty of the artistic objects is reinforced in the following description of the Shangri-La aura: "A world of incomparable refinements still lingered tremulously in porcelain and varnish, yielding an instant of emotion before its dissolution into purest thought" (114). The dissolution of the instant of emotion into purest thought transforms the vitality of the aesthetic image (in Pound's sense of the image as an emotional and intellectual complex in an instant of time) into an aura of artistically vital and profoundly ethereal contemplation. By appreciating the delicate beauty of such lovely art objects, Conway participates aesthetically and emotionally in the world of Shangri-La.

The timeless ambience of Shangri-La is enhanced by the presence of "the gleaming pyramid of Karakal" (97), which has a seemingly mesmerizing effect on Conway, infusing his spirit with a profound sense of repose. Conway envisions Karakal, meaning Blue Moon, as a lighthouse brooding serenely over the valley beyond the world of mortality. Conway's adventure in Shangri-La might be described as a series of enchanted moments which transcend any possible transitoriness, culminating in the supreme enchanted moment of his congenially ethereal encounter with the High Lama. Like the perfected mind in Shelley's *Prometheus Unbound* that achieves a sense of illimitable time, so Conway, through his acquaintance with Shangri-La, experiences a sanctuary of relative timelessness and of the emotional and spiritual expansiveness of the inner self.

The description of the library at Shangri-La reinforces the serenely wise tone of the lamasery. The library is a sanctuary characterized by and infused with an ambience of lofty spaciousness as well as of good manners, intellectual and aesthetic vitality, and profound wisdom. As the material, physical aspects of the lamasery, the library at Shangri-La represents a harmonious balance of Western and Eastern aspects and texts. Conway feels very much at home in this atmosphere of quiet elegance and profound harmony.

Shangri-La, as most of the other successful and viable sanctuaries of light and serenity in twentieth-century European literature, exists at a distance from the world of everyday mortality. In the depiction of other literary sanctuaries, this sense of distance may be literal or symbolic, but it is always present if the sanctuary is to attain and preserve its integrity and vitality. Despite this sense of physical and geographical distance from the idiosyncrasies and exigencies of the world of everyday mortality, Shangri-La, as the High Lama, Father Perrault, explains to Conway, can only diminish the tempo of life and postpone mortality. For Shangri-La offers a relative timelessness, an exemplary aura of timelessness, which has nevertheless not made a conquest of death.

The High Lama asserts that Shangri-La has a definite and an important private and public function. For Shangri-La exists to preserve the cultural and intellectual legacy of humanity and to preserve a vision of hope, moderation, and wisdom in a world which has often seemingly the penchant to revel in excessive violence, suffering, and war and has the tragically undeniable potential to destroy itself. The High Lama cherishes the hope and the vision, as strong as it is fragile, that Shangri-La will overcome any doomsday cataclysm which may destroy the world as humankind currently knows it. The High Lama embraces the instinctively vibrant hope that Shangri-La, as a sanctuary with an important cultural heritage to bequeath, will be ignored by the tempestuousness and the violence of the world.

The conversations between the High Lama, the embodiment of Plato's philosopher-king, and Conway, his spiritual heir, end as they begin—in an atmosphere of ethereal serenity, intellectual elegance, and profound harmony. Hilton describes the supremely congenial meetings between these two kindred spirits, the High Lama and Conway, as aesthetically, intellectually, and spiritually close to one another as Thomas Cole and William Cullen Bryant in Asher Durand's painting *Kindred Spirits* (1849), as distinguished by a sumptuous tranquility. This is a tranquility which by its very nature reaffirms the aura of timeless calm and benevolent wisdom of Shangri-La.

Conway is enraptured by Karakal and Shangri-La, from the vision of the gleaming, pure, and elusive mountains to the perception of the silvery tones of the harpsichord floating across the lotus-pool. In the aura of enchantment Conway, like the protagonist in H. G. Wells' *The Time Machine*, feels that he has time for everything. Conway feels that the aura of Shangri-La has given him an exuberance of time. Conway has time for everything that he wished to happen, so much time that desire itself was satisfied in the certainty of fulfillment. Conway exemplifies the individual who, having developed a Shangri-La life-philosophy, no longer considers time as an inimical antagonist. There exists a complementary relation between such an individual and time. Such an individual suspends mortality in his own self-determined, self-generated conception of time and fulfills the challenge and the promise of Walt Whitman's persona in "Song of Myself," who laughs at dissolution (the dissolution of the self through mortality) and asserts that he knows the amplitude of time.

The various and profound sanctuaries of light, harmony, and serenity in Wordsworth, Hoffmann, Eichendorff, and C. Brontë may exist perpetually, consistently, occasionally, or periodically. They may establish a vital integrity which makes them impregnable and unassailable by mortality; or they may represent places which are instinctively sanctuaries of light and tranquility, but which are sometimes so encroached upon or impacted by everyday reality that the sense of sanctuary is temporarily diminished or undermined before being ultimately revitalized after the imminence and influence of everyday mortality is vanquished. Such sanctuaries of luminescence and peacefulness may even exist as enchanted moments which are as transitory as they are dynamic. Yet what all of these sanctuaries, regardless of their temporal duration share, is a sense of permanence, eternity, and consecration to an extraordinary space.

Whether or not Conway is able to find his way back to the geographically remote Shangri-La at the end of the novel, he has achieved his quest for a sanctuary with a timeless aura. By participating devotedly and wholeheartedly in the world of Shangri-La during his sojourn there Conway becomes forever an integral part of its serene timelessness. Conway's experience in Shangri-La is comparable to that of Hugo in Heinrich Böll's *Billiards at Half-Past Nine* who, having been given a sense of eternity by participating in Robert Faehmel's enchanted moment of timelessness in the billiard-room, feels that he has always had it, that it has always signified a vital aspect of his inner being.

A truly vital sanctuary of light and serenity, once it exists, is always present and eternal and perpetually possesses a temporal versatility, whether or not it appears to be outwardly dynamic and vibrant. Such a sanctuary, as the "Attic shape" (41) in the "Ode on a Grecian Urn" by John Keats, will remain "a friend to man" (48) as one generation succeeds the next in the flux of mortality. In affirming to humanity its permanence and its capacity to inspire, the Grecian urn proclaims: "Beauty is truth, truth beauty,–that is all / Ye know on earth, and all ye need to know" (49–50).

Hugo Walter's "The Morning Dew Is a Dance of Divine Whispers" similarly creates a sanctuary of light which celebrates the reciprocal vitality of beauty and truth and affirms the capacity of nature to develop, nurture, and strengthen the ambience of a lovely refuge:

> The morning dew is a dance of divine whispers
>
> Shaping the first azalea-refulgent incantations
>
> Of Artemisian-lavender, gladiolus-soaring light
>
> In heliotrope-mimosa, cypress-floating reveries
>
> Of swan-gloaming, marigold-seraphic butterflies;
>
> The morning dew is an Eden-crystalline oasis
>
> Of jasmine-diaphanous, astral-winged silences
>
> Conceiving sapphire-lambent, asphodel-pure synergies
>
> Of Aurora-sophic, silken-altared omens and lilac-
>
> Sparkling, Orangerie-sunset ballerinas. (1–5, 12–16)

In "Marigold-Germinating Chalices" Walter depicts a beautiful natural environment which creates and sustains its own sense of sanctuary beyond mortality:

> Marigold-germinating chalices of light rise from the hydrangea-sacred
>
> Pond as amaryllis-madrigal winds seal camellia-vaned dusks
>
> Of Aeolian-dewed timelessness in hyacinth-embering silences
>
> Of chrysalis-jade, orchid-weaving dreams,
>
> Amber-soft angels ripple across clover-mullioned pools
>
> Of edelweiss-sibylline radiance in cypress-opulent rhythms

As the ancestral-pinioned call of the golden-necked swan
Converges saffron-diaphanous voices in amaryllis-streaming,
Wisteria-pealing rainbows of magenta-translucent,
Lily-diapason, sunflower-lambent light.

The conclusion of Percy Shelley's "The Sensitive Plant" argues similarly that the beautiful garden, the sanctuary of light and color, and the Eve who wanders through the garden "In truth have never passed away: / 'Tis we, 'tis ours, are changed; not they" (132–33). The lovely sanctuary of luminescence and peacefulness, and the lady who is an integral dimension of this beauty, signify a permanent aspect of this vision. Shelley affirms the permanence of the ideal in the last quatrain of the poem: "For love, and beauty, and delight, / There is no death nor change" (134–35). This gorgeous sanctuary, this delightful Garden of Eden, will be eternal. The capacity of humankind to observe and to appreciate the beauty and the vitality of this natural sanctuary may change or be transfigured, but the beauty of this special natural place is eternal.

The sanctuaries in the works of Wordsworth, Hoffmann, Eichendorff, and Brontë are all permeated, nurtured, and sustained by a glorious effulgence as vital as the light of Shelley's "Hymn to Intellectual Beauty" which gives "grace and truth to life's unquiet dream" (36), by a sense of the spatial expansiveness of the soul as profound as the experience of Anselmus and Serpentina in Hoffmann's "The Golden Pot" and in Eichendorff's "Sehnsucht," by the spirit of hope and faith as vibrant as that of Jane in Brontë's *Jane Eyre*, by a sense of serenity as pure and as strong as that of Eichendorff's Taugenichts in the natural ambience of the palace in Vienna or Jane in the splendid seclusion of Ferndean, and by a devotion to and belief in the power of the light as profound as that of Wordsworth's persona in stanza nine of the Immortality Ode when he speaks of the "first affections" (148) which are "the fountain-light of all our day" (151) and the "master-light of all our seeing" (152). Such sanctuaries of light signify, as Wordsworth says of nature in "Tintern Abbey," the guide and guardian of the heart and soul and a refuge of beautiful radiance, effulgent serenity, and sublime harmony.

✳ *Works Consulted*

Introduction

Allison, Alexander W., Arthur J. Carr, and Arthur Eastman, eds. *Masterpieces of the Drama*. New York: Macmillan, 1974. Print.

Arnold, Matthew. *Selected Poems and Prose*. Ed. Miriam Allott. London: J. M. Dent, 1978. Print.

Beja, Morris. *Epiphany in the Modern Novel*. Seattle: U of Washington P, 1979. Print.

Brontë, Charlotte. *Jane Eyre*. New York: Signet, 1982. Print.

Buckley, Jerome H. *The Triumph of Time*. Cambridge, Mass.: Harvard UP, 1966. Print.

Burke, Edmund. *Philosophical Enquiry into the Origin of Our Ideas of the Sublime and the Beautiful*. London, 1757. Print.

Echtermeyer, Ernst T. und Benno von Wiese, eds. *Deutsche Gedichte von den Anfängen bis zur Gegenwart*. Düsseldorf: A. Bagel, 1962. Print.

Fitzgerald, F. Scott. *The Great Gatsby*. New York: Scribner, 1995. Print.

Gray, Thomas. *The Poems and Letters of Thomas Gray*. Ed. William Mason. London, 1820. Print.

Hazlitt, William. *The Spirit of the Age*. London, 1825. Print.

Hilton, James. *Lost Horizon*. New York: William Morrow, 1934. Print.

Hoffmann, E. T. A. *The Nutcracker and The Golden Pot*. New York: Dover, 1993. Print.

——. *Tales of Hoffmann*. Trans. R. J. Hollingdale. New York: Penguin, 2004. Print.

Houghton, Walter E., and G. Robert Stange. *Victorian Poetry and Poetics*. 2nd ed. Boston: Houghton Mifflin, 1968. Print.

Hungerford, Edward B. *Shores of Darkness*. Cleveland: World Publishing, 1963. Print.

Knight, Richard Payne. *Analytical Inquiry into the Principles of Taste*. London, 1805. Print.

Kroeber, Karl. *Romantic Landscape Vision: Constable and Wordsworth*. Madison: U of Wisconsin P, 1975. Print.

Liu, Alan, ed. Home page. *Voice of the Shuttle*. Dept. of English, U of California, Santa Barbara. Web. 3 June 2009.

Mill, John Stuart. *The Spirit of the Age*. Ed. Frederick A. von Hayek. Chicago: U of Chicago P, 1942. Print.

Perkins, David, ed. *English Romantic Writers*. New York: Harcourt Brace, 1967. Print.

Tatar, Maria, ed. *The Classic Fairy Tales*. New York: Norton, 1999. Print.

Untermeyer, Louis. *Modern American and Modern British Poetry*. New York: Harcourt Brace, 1955. Print.

Williams, Oscar, ed. *Immortal Poems of the English Language*. New York: Simon and Schuster, 1952. Print.

Williams, Raymond. *Culture and Society: 1780–1950*. New York: Columbia UP, 1960. Print.

Wordsworth, William. *The Prelude (1799, 1805, 1850)*. Ed. Jonathan Wordsworth, M. H. Abrams, and Stephen Gill. New York: W. W. Norton, 1979. Print.

Chapter 1—William Wordsworth

Abrams, M. H. *The Mirror and the Lamp: Romantic Theory and the Critical Tradition*. New York: The Norton Library, 1958. Print.

——. "Revolutionary Romanticism 1790–1990." *Wordsworth in Context*. Ed. Pauline Fletcher and John Murphy. Lewisburg: Bucknell UP, 1992. 19–34. Print.

——, ed. *Wordsworth–A Collection of Critical Essays*. Englewood Cliffs: Prentice-Hall, 1972. Print.

Averill, James H. *Wordsworth and Human Suffering*. Ithaca: Cornell UP, 1980. Print.

Baetjer, Katharine, ed. *Glorious Nature: British Landscape Painting 1750–1850*. Denver Art Museum; New York: Hudson Hills Press, 1993. Print.

Baillie, John. *An Essay on the Sublime*. 1747. Los Angeles: The Augustan Society, 1953. Print.

Baker, Carlos, ed. *The Prelude; With a Selection from the Shorter Poems and the Sonnets*. New York: Rinehart, 1954. Print.

Baker, Jeffrey. *Time and Mind in Wordsworth's Poetry*. Detroit: Wayne State UP, 1980. Print.

Bate, Jonathan. *Romantic Ecology: Wordsworth and the Environmental Tradition*. London: Routledge, 1991. Print.

Beer, John. *Wordsworth in Time*. London: Faber, 1979. Print.

Bewell, Alan. *Wordsworth and the Enlightenment: Nature, Man, and Society in the Experimental Poetry*. New Haven: Yale UP, 1989. Print.

Bloom, Harold. *The Visionary Company: A Reading of English Romantic Poetry*. Garden City, N.Y.: Doubleday, 1961. Print.

——, ed. and intro. *William Wordsworth's 'The Prelude.'* New York: Chelsea House, 1986. Print.

Brooks, Cleanth. *The Well-Wrought Urn*. London: Denis Dobson, 1968. Print.

Butler, Marilyn. *Romantics, Rebels, and Reactionaries*. Oxford: Oxford UP, 1981. Print.

Curran, Stuart. *Poetic Form and British Romanticism*. New York: Oxford UP, 1986. Print.

Durrant, Geoffrey. *Wordsworth and the Great System*. Cambridge: Cambridge UP, 1986. Print.

Fletcher, Pauline, and John Murphy, eds. *Wordsworth in Context*. Lewisburg: Bucknell UP, 1992. Print.

Friedman, Michael H. *The Making of a Tory Humanist: William Wordsworth and the Idea of Community*. New York: Columbia UP, 1979. Print.

Fry, Paul H. *Wordsworth and the Poetry of What We Are*. New Haven: Yale UP, 2008. Print.

Gerard, Alexander. *An Essay on Taste*. 3rd ed. Edinburg, 1780. Print.

Gill, Stephen. *Cambridge Companion to Wordsworth*. Cambridge, U.K.; New York: Cambridge UP, 2003. Print.

——. *William Wordsworth: A Life*. Oxford: Clarendon P, 1989. Print.

——, ed. *William Wordsworth's The Prelude: A Casebook*. Oxford: Oxford UP, 2006. Print.

Gilpin, George H., ed. *Critical Essays on William Wordsworth*. Boston: G. K. Hall, 1990. Print.

Hanley, Keith. "'A Poet's History': Wordsworth and Revolutionary Discourse." *Wordsworth in Context*. Ed. Pauline Fletcher and John Murphy. Lewisburg: Bucknell UP, 1992. 35–65. Print.

Hartman, Geoffrey. "The Romance of Nature and the Negative Way." *William Wordsworth's The Prelude*. Ed. Harold Bloom. New York: Chelsea House, 1986. 57–75. Print.

——. *The Unremarkable Wordsworth*. Minneapolis: UP of Minnesota, 1987. Print.

——. *Wordsworth's Poetry, 1787–1814*. New Haven: Yale UP, 1964. Print.

Hazlitt, William. *The Spirit of the Age*. London, 1825. Print.

Heffernan, James A. W. *The ReCreation of Landscape: A Study of Wordsworth, Coleridge, Constable, and Turner*. Hanover, N.H.: UP of New England, 1984. Print.

Jacobus, Mary. "Apostrophe and Lyric Voice in 'The Prelude.'" *William Wordsworth's The Prelude*. Ed. Harold Bloom. New York: Chelsea House, 1986. 145–59. Print.

Jarvis, Simon. *Wordsworth's Philosophic Song*. New York: Cambridge UP, 2007. Print.

Johnson, Karl R. *The Written Spirit: Thematic and Rhetorical Structure in Wordsworth's "The Prelude."* Salzburg: Salzburg Studies in English, 1978. Print.

Johnston, Kenneth R., and Gene W. Ruoff, eds. *The Age of William Wordsworth: Critical Essays on the Romantic Tradition*. New Brunswick, N.J.: Rutgers UP, 1987. Print.

Johnston, Kenneth R. *The Hidden Wordsworth*. New York: W. W. Norton, 1998. Print.

Knight, Richard Payne. *Analytical Inquiry into the Principles of Taste*. London: 1805. Print.

Kroeber, Karl. *Romantic Landscape Vision: Constable and Wordsworth*. Madison: U of Wisconsin P, 1975. Print.

Langbaum, Robert. *The Mysteries of Identity*. Oxford: Oxford UP, 1979. Print.

Lindenberger, Herbert. *On Wordsworth's Prelude*. Princeton: Princeton UP, 1963. Print.

——. "The Structural Unit: 'Spots of Time.'" *William Wordsworth's "The Prelude."* Ed. Harold Bloom. New York: Chelsea House, 1986. 77–88. Print.

Liu, Alan, ed. Home page. *Voice of the Shuttle*. Dept. of English, U of California, Santa Barbara. Web. 3 June 2009.

Liu, Alan. *Wordsworth: The Sense of History*. Stanford: Stanford UP, 1989. Print.

Manning, Peter. *Reading Romantics: Texts and Contexts*. New York: Oxford UP, 1990. Print.

Mill, John Stuart. *The Spirit of the Age*. Ed. Frederick A. von Hayek. Chicago: U of Chicago P, 1942. Print.

Miller, Christopher R. *The Invention of Evening: Perception and Time in Romantic Poetry.* Cambridge, U.K.; New York: Cambridge UP, 2006. Print.

Nichols, Ashton. "The Revolutionary 'I': Wordsworth and the Politics of Self-Presentation." *Wordsworth in Context.* Ed. Pauline Fletcher and John Murphy. Lewisburg: Bucknell UP, 1992. 66-84. Print.

Owen, W. J. B. *The Fourteen-Book Prelude by William Wordsworth.* Ithaca: Cornell UP, 1985. Print.

Perkins, David, ed. *English Romantic Writers.* San Diego: Harcourt Brace, 1967. Print.

Pirie, David. *William Wordsworth: The Poetry of Grandeur and of Tenderness.* London: Methuen, 1982. Print.

Prickett, Stephen. *Coleridge and Wordsworth: The Poetry of Growth.* Cambridge: Cambridge UP, 1970. Print.

Priestly, Joseph. *A Course of Lectures on Oratory and Criticism.* London, 1777. Print.

Rosen, David. *Power, Plain English, and the Rise of Modern Poetry.* New Haven: Yale UP, 2006. Print.

Schiller, Friedrich. *Essays.* Ed. Walter Hinderer and Daniel O. Dahlstrom. New York: Continuum. Print.

Simpson, David E. "The Spots of Time: Spaces for Refiguring." *William Wordsworth's "The Prelude."* Ed. Harold Bloom. New York: Chelsea House, 1986. 137-44. Print.

——. *Wordsworth, Commodification, and Social Concern: the Poetics of Modernity.* Cambridge, U.K.; New York: Cambridge UP, 2009.

Stillinger, Jack. *Romantic Complexity: Keats, Coleridge, and Wordsworth.* Urbana: U of Illinois P, 2006.

Vendler, Helen. "'Tintern Abbey': Two Assaults." *Wordsworth in Context.* Ed. Pauline Fletcher and John Murphy. Lewisburg: Bucknell UP, 1992. 173-90. Print.

Venning, Barry. *Constable.* London: Studio Editons, 1993. Print.

Walter, Hugo. *Space and Time on the Magic Mountain: Studies in Nineteenth- and Early-Twentieth-Century European Literature.* New York: Peter Lang, 1999. Print.

Ward, J. P. *Wordsworth's Language of Man.* Sussex: The Harvester P, 1984. Print.

Welsford, Enid. *Salisbury Plain: A Study in the Development of Wordsworth's Mind and Art.* Oxford: Oxford UP, 1966. Print.

Wesling, Donald. *Wordsworth and the Adequacy of Landscape.* London: Routledge and Kegan Paul, 1970. Print.

Williams, Raymond. *Culture and Society: 1780-1950.* New York: Columbia UP, 1960. Print.

Wlecke, Albert O. *Wordsworth and the Sublime.* Berkeley: U of California P, 1973. Print.

Woof, Robert, ed. *William Wordsworth: The Critical Heritage.* London; New York: Routledge, 2001. Print.

Wordsworth, Jonathan. *The Borders of Vision.* Oxford: Clarendon P, 1982. Print.

———, ed. *The Prelude: the Four Texts (1798, 1799, 1805, 1850)*. London; New York: Penguin Books, 1995. Print.

Wordsworth, William. *The Complete Poetical Works of William Wordsworth*. *Bartleby Library Online*, n.d. Web. 15 August 2009.

———. *The Complete Poetical Works of Wordsworth*. Boston: Houghton Mifflin, 1932. Print.

———. *The Poems: Volume Two*. Ed. John O. Hayden. New Haven: Yale UP, 1981. Print.

———. *The Prelude (1799, 1805, 1850)*. Ed. Jonathan Wordsworth, M. H. Abrams, and Stephen Gill. New York: W. W. Norton, 1979. Print.

———. *The Prelude*. Cambridge: Chadwyck-Healey, 1992. Web. 7 August 2009.

———. *The Prelude: 1850*. Oxford; New York: Woodstock Books, 1993. Print.

———. *William Wordsworth's The Prelude*. *Bartleby Library* Online, n.d. Web. 15 August 2009.

Zimmerman, Sarah M. *Romanticism, Lyricism, and Writing*. Albany: State University of New York P, 1999. Print.

Chapter 2–E. T. A. Hoffmann

Barkhoff, Jürgen. *Magnetische Fiktionen: Literarisierungen des Mesmerismus in der Romantik*. Stuttgart: Metzler, 1995. Print.

Bleiler, E. F., ed. *The Best Tales of Hoffmann*. New York: Dover, 1967. Print.

Bomhoff, Katrin. *Bildende Kunst und Dichtung: Die Selbstinterpretation E. T. A. Hoffmanns in der Kunst Jacques Callots und Salvator Rosas*. Freiburg: Rombach, 1999. Print.

Braun, Peter. *E. T. A. Hoffmann: Dichter, Zeichner, Musiker: Biographie*. Düsseldorf: Artemis & Winkler, 2004. Print.

Chantler, Abigail. *E. T. A. Hoffmann's Musical Aesthetics*. Burlington, VT: Ashgate, 2006. Print.

Daemmrich, Horst S. *The Shattered Self: E. T. A. Hoffmann's Tragic Vision*. Detroit: Wayne State UP, 1973. Print.

Deterding, Klaus. *Hoffmanns Erzählungen: Eine Einführung in das Werk E. T. A. Hoffmanns*. Würzburg: Königshausen und Neumann, 2007. Print.

———. *Allerwunderbarste Märchen*. Würzburg: Königshausen und Neumann, 2003. Print.

———. *Magie des poetischen Raums: E.T.A. Hoffmanns Dichtung und Weltbild*. Heidelberg: C. Winter, 1999. Print.

Dobat, Klaus-Dieter. *Musik als romantische Illusion: Eine Untersuchung zur Bedeutung der Musikvorstellung E.T.A. Hoffmanns für sein literarisches Werk*. Tübingen: Niemeyer, 1984. Print.

Ellis, John. "Hoffmann's 'Das Fräulein von Scuderi.'" *Modern Language Review* 64 (1969): 340-50. Print.

Fühmann, Franz. *Fräulein Veronika Paulmann aus der Pirnaer Vorstadt: oder, Etwas über das Schauerliche bei E. T. A. Hoffmann*. Hamburg: Hoffmann und Campe, 1980. Print.

Gray, William. *Fantasy, Myth, and the Measure of Truth: Tales of Pullmann, Lewis, Tolkien, MacDonald, and Hoffmann.* Basingstoke, England; New York: Palgrave Macmillan, 2009. Print.

Harnischfeger, Johannes. *Die Hieroglyphen der inneren Welt: Romantikkritik bei E.T.A. Hoffmann.* Opladen: Westdeutscher Verlag, 1988. Print.

Hewett-Thayer, Harvey W. *Hoffmann: Author of the Tales.* Princeton: Princeton UP, 1948. Print.

Hoffmann, E. T. A. *The Nutcracker and The Golden Pot.* New York: Dover, 1993. Print.

———. *Tales of Hoffmann.* Trans. R. J. Hollingdale. New York: Penguin, 2004. Print.

Jennings, Lee B. "The Downward Transcendence: Hoffmanns 'Bergwerke zu Falun.'" *Deutsche Vierteljahrsschrift für Literaturwissenschaft und Geistesgeschichte* 59 (1985): 278–89. Print.

Keil, Werner. *E. T. A. Hoffmann als Komponist: Studien zur Kompositionstechnik an ausgewählten Werken.* Wiesbaden: Breitkopf & Härtel, 1986. Print.

Klessman, Eckart. *E. T. A. Hoffmann: oder die Tiefe zwischen Stern und Erde: eine Biographie.* Stuttgart: Deutsche Verlags-Anstalt, 1988. Print.

Kremer, Detlef. *E. T. A. Hoffmann: Erzählungen und Romane.* Berlin: E. Schmidt, 1999. Print.

———. *Romantische Metamorphosen: E. T. A. Hoffmanns Erzählungen.* Stuttgart, Weimar: Metzler, 1993. Print.

Kropf, David G. *Authorship as alchemy: subversive writing in Pushkin, Scott, and Hoffmann.* Stanford: Stanford UP, 1994. Print.

Liebrand, Claudia. *Aporie des Kunstmythos: Die Texte E. T. A. Hoffmanns.* Freiburg: Rombach, 1996. Print.

Liu, Alan, ed. Home page. *Voice of the Shuttle.* Dept. of English, U of California, Santa Barbara. Web. 6 June 2009.

Loecker, Armand de. *Zwischen Atlantis und Frankfurt: Märchendichtung und goldenes Zeitalter bei E. T. A. Hoffmann.* Frankfurt am Main: Peter Lang, 1983. Print.

McGlathery, James. *E. T. A. Hoffmann.* New York: Twayne, 1997. Print.

Negus, Kenneth. *E. T. A. Hoffmann's Other World: The Romantic Author and His 'New Mythology.'* Philadelphia: U of Pennsylvania P, 1965. Print.

Nehring, Wolfgang. *Spätromantiker: Eichendorff und E. T. A. Hoffmann.* Göttingen: Vandenhoeck & Ruprecht, 1997. Print.

Orosz, Magdolna. *Identität, Differenz, Ambivalenz: Erzählstrukturen und Erzählstrategien bei E. T. A. Hoffmann.* Frankfurt: Peter Lang, 2001. Print.

Reher, Stephan. *Leuchtende Finsternis: Erzählen in Callots Manier.* Köln: Böhlau Verlag, 1997.

Robertson, Ritchie. *The Golden Pot and Other Tales: A New Translation.* New York: Oxford UP, 2009. Print.

Röder, Birgit. *A Study of the Major Novellas of E. T. A. Hoffmann*. Rochester, N.Y.: Camden House, 2003. Print.

Safranski, Rüdiger. *E. T. A. Hoffmann: das Leben eines skeptischen Phantasten*. München: C. Hanser, 1984. Print.

Schmidt, Ricarda. *Wenn mehrere Künste im Spiel sind: Intermedialität bei E. T. A. Hoffmann*. Göttingen: Vandenhoeck & Ruprecht, 2006. Print.

Steinecke, Hartmut. *E. T. A. Hoffmann*. Stuttgart: P. Reclam, 1997. Print.

——. *Kunst der Fantasie: E. T. A. Hoffmanns Leben und Werk*. Frankfurt: Insel, 2004. Print.

Tatar, Maria. "E. T. A. Hoffmann's 'Der Sandmann': Reflection and Romantic Irony." *Modern Language Notes* 95 (1980): 585-608. Print.

Triebel, Odila. *Staatsgespenster: Fiktionen des Politischen bei E. T. A. Hoffmann*. Köln: Böhlau Verlag, 2003. Print.

Winter, Ilse. *Untersuchungen zum serapiontischen Prinzip E. T. A. Hoffmanns*. The Hague: Mouton, 1976. Print

Wührl, Paul-Wolfgang. *E. T. A. Hoffmann: Der goldene Topf*. Paderborn: F. Schöningh, 1988. Print.

Chapter 3—Joseph von Eichendorff

Alewyn, Richard. "Ein Wort über Eichendorff." *Eichendorff Heute*. Ed. Paul Stöcklein. München: Bayerischer Schulbuch-Verlag, 1960. 7-18. Print.

Dennerle, Dieter. *Kunst als Kommunikationsprozess—Zur Kunsttheorie Clemens Brentanos*. Bern: H. Lang, 1976. Print.

Echtermeyer, Ernst T., und Benno von Wiese, eds. *Deutsche Gedichte von den Anfängen bis zur Gegenwart*. Düsseldorf: A. Bagel, 1962. Print.

Engelen, Bernhard. *Die Synästhesien in der Dichtung Eichendorffs*. Köln: 1966. Print.

Fetzer, John F. *Romantic Orpheus—Profiles of Clemens Brentano*. Berkeley: U of California P, 1974. Print.

Goebel, Robert O. *Eichendorff's Scholarly Reception: A Survey*. Columbia, SC: Camden House, 1993. Print.

Gössmann, Wilhelm, und Christoph Hollender. *Joseph von Eichendorff: seine literarische und kulturelle Bedeutung*. Paderborn: Schöningh, 1995. Print.

Hachmeister, Gretchen. *Italy in the German Literary Imagination: Goethe's "Italian Journey" and its Reception by Eichendorff, Platen, and Heine*. Rochester, N.Y.: Camden House, 2002. Print.

Kach, Rudolf. *Eichendorffs Taugenichts und Taugenichtsfiguren bei Gottfried Keller und Hermann Hesse*. Bern: P. Haupt, 1988. Print.

Krabiel, Klaus-Dieter. *Tradition und Bewegung. Zum sprachlichen Verfahren Eichendorffs*. Stuttgart: W. Kohlhammer, 1973. Print.

Kunisch, Hermann. "Freiheit und Bann—Heimat und Fremde." *Eichendorff Heute*. Ed. Paul Stöcklein. München: Bayerischer Schulbuch-Verlag, 1960. 131-64. Print.

Kunz, Josef. *Eichendorff–Höhepunkt und Krise der Spätromäntik.* Darmstadt: Wissenschaftliche Buchgesellschaft, 1967. Print.

Löhr, Katja. *Sehnsucht als poetologisches Prinzip bei Joseph von Eichendorff.* Würzburg: Königshausen & Neumann GmbH, 2003. Print.

Lüthi, Hans Jürg. *Dichtung und Dichter bei Joseph von Eichendorff.* Bern: Francke Verlag, 1966. Print.

Möbus, Gerhard. "Eichendorff und Novalis." *Eichendorff Heute.* Ed. Paul Stöcklein. München: Bayerischer Schulbuchverlag, 1960. 165-79. Print.

Ohff, Heinz. *Joseph Freiherr von Eichendorff.* Berlin: Stapp, 1983. Print.

Paulsen, Wolfgang. *Eichendorff und sein Taugenichts: die innere Problematik des Dichters in seinem Werk.* Bern: Francke Verlag, 1976. Print.

Radner, Lawrence. *Eichendorff: The Spiritual Geometer.* Lafayette, Indiana: Purdue University Studies, 1970. Print.

Regener, Ursula. *Formelsuche: Studien zu Eichendorffs lyrischem Frühwerk.* Tübingen: Niemeyer, 2001. Print.

Ryder, Frank G., ed. *German Romantic Stories.* New York: Continuum, 1988. Print.

Schaum, Konrad. *Poesie und Wirklichkeit in Joseph von Eichendorffs 'Ahnung und Gegenwart.'* Heidelberg: Winter, 2008. Print.

Schultz, Hartwig. *Joseph von Eichendorff: Aus dem Leben eines Taugenichts.* Stuttgart: P. Reclam, 1994. Print.

Schwartz, Egon. *Joseph von Eichendorff.* New York: Twayne, 1972. Print.

Schwarz, Peter. *Die Bedeutung der Tageszeiten in der Dichtung Eichendorffs.* Bamberg: 1964. Print.

Schwarz, Peter Paul. *Aurora–Zur romantischen Zeitstruktur bei Eichendorff.* Bad Homburg v.d.h.: Verlag Gehlen, 1970. Print.

Seidlin, Oskar. *Versuche über Eichendorff.* Göttingen: Vandenhoeck & Ruprecht, 1965. Print.

Stöcklein, Paul, ed. *Eichendorff Heute.* München: Bayerischer Schulbuch Verlag, 1960. Print.

Walter, Hugo. *The Apostrophic Moment in Nineteenth- and Twentieth- Century German Lyric Poetry.* New York: Peter Lang, 1988. Print.

Weisrock, Katharina. *Götterblick und Zaubermacht: Auge, Blick und Wahrnehmung in Aufklärung und Romantik.* Opladen: Westdeutscher Verlag, 1990. Print.

Chapter 4—Charlotte Brontë

Berg, Maggie. *Jane Eyre-Portrait of a Life.* Boston: Twayne, 1987. Print.

Blom, Margaret. *Charlotte Brontë.* Boston: Twayne, 1977. Print.

Bloom, Harold, ed. and intro. *Modern Critical Interpretations–Charlotte Brontë's Jane Eyre.* New York: Chelsea House, 1987. Print.

——, ed. and intro. *Modern Critical Interpretations–Charlotte Brontë's Jane Eyre*. New York: Chelsea House, 2007. Print.

Bodenheimer, Rosemarie. "Jane Eyre in Search of Her Story." *Modern Critical Interpretations–Charlotte Brontë's Jane Eyre*. New York: Chelsea House, 1987. 97–112. Print.

Brontë, Charlotte. *Jane Eyre*. New York: Signet, 1982. Print.

——. *Selected Letters*. Ed. Margaret Smith. Oxford; New York: Oxford UP, 2007. Print.

Christ, Carol T. "Imaginative Constraint, Feminine Duty, and the Form of Charlotte Brontë's Fiction." *Critical Essays on Charlotte Brontë*. Ed. Barbara Timm Gates. Boston: G. K. Hall, 1990. 60–67. Print.

Colby, Robert. "*Villette* and the Life of the Mind." *Critics on Charlotte and Emily Brontë*. Ed. Judith O'Neill. Coral Gables, FL: U of Miami P, 1968. Print.

Corbett, Mary Jean. *Family Likeness: Sex, Marriage, and Incest from Jane Austen to Virginia Woolf*. Ithaca: Cornell UP, 2008. Print.

Craik, W. A. *The Brontë Novels*. London: Methuen, 1968. Print.

——. "The Shape of the Novel." *Modern Critical Interpretations–Charlotte Brontë's Jane Eyre*. New York: Chelsea House, 1987. 7–20. Print.

DeLamotte, Eugenia C. *Perils of the Night: A Feminist Study of Nineteenth Century Gothic*. New York: Oxford UP, 1990. Print.

Duthie, Enid L. *Brontës and Nature*. New York: St. Martin's P, 1986. Print.

Eagleton, Terry. "Class, Power, and Charlotte Brontë." *Critical Essays on Charlotte Brontë*. Ed. Barbara Timm Gates. Boston: G. K. Hall, 1990. 50–60. Print.

——. "*Jane Eyre*: A Marxist Study." *Modern Critical Interpretations–Charlotte Brontë's Jane Eyre*. New York: Chelsea House, 1987. 29–46. Print.

——. *Myths of Power: A Marxist Study of the Brontës*. New York: Barnes and Noble, 1975. Print.

Fraser, Rebecca. *The Brontës*. New York: Crown, 1988. Print.

Gaskell, Elizabeth. *The Life of Charlotte Brontë*. Harmondsworth: Penguin, 1975. Print.

Gates, Barbara T., ed. *Critical Essays on Charlotte Brontë*. Boston: G. K. Hall, 1990. Print.

Gerin, Winifred. *Charlotte Brontë: The Evolution of Genius*. Oxford: Clarendon P, 1967. Print.

Gilbert, Sandra, and Susan Gubar. "A Dialogue of Self and Soul: Plain Jane's Progress." *Modern Critical Interpretations–Charlotte Brontë's Jane Eyre*. New York: Chelsea House, 1987. 63–96. Print.

Gilbert, Sandra, and Susan Gubar. *The Madwoman in the Attic: The Woman Writer and the Nineteenth-Century Literary Imagination*. New Haven: Yale UP, 1979. Print.

Glen, Heather, ed. *Cambridge Companion to the Brontës*. Cambridge, U.K.; New York: Cambridge UP, 2002.

Gordon, Lyndall. *Charlotte Brontë: A Passionate Life*. New York: W. W. Norton, 1995. Print.

Hardy, Barbara. *The Appropriate Form: An Essay on the Novel.* Evanston: Northwestern UP, 1970. Print.

——. "Providence Invoked: Dogmatic Form in *Jane Eyre* and *Robinson Crusoe.*" *Modern Critical Interpretations–Charlotte Brontë's Jane Eyre.* New York: Chelsea House, 1987. 21–28. Print.

Heilman, Robert B. "Charlotte Brontë, Reason, and the Moon." *Critical Essays on Charlotte Brontë.* Ed. Barbara Timm Gates. Boston: G.K. Hall, 1990. 34–49. Print.

Hook, Andrew D. "Charlotte Brontë, the Imagination, and *Villette.*" *The Brontës: A Collection of Critical Essays.* Ed. Ian Gregor. Englewood Cliffs, N.J.: Prentice- Hall, 1970. 137–156. Print.

Imlay, Elizabeth. *Charlotte Brontë and the Mysteries of Love: Myth and Allegory in Jane Eyre.* New York: St. Martin's P, 1989. Print.

Ingham, Patricia. *Brontës.* New York: Oxford UP, 2006. Print.

Knies, Earl. *The Art of Charlotte Brontë.* Athens: Ohio University P, 1969. Print.

Lenz, Siegfried. *The German Lesson.* Trans. Ernst Kaiser and Eithne Wilkins. New York: Hill and Wang, 1972. Print.

Linder, Cynthia. *Romantic Imagery in the Novels of Charlotte Brontë.* London: MacMillan, 1978. Print.

Liu, Alan, ed. Home page. *Voice of the Shuttle.* Dept. of English, U of California, Santa Barbara. Web. 3 July 2009.

Lodge, David. "Fire and Eyre: Charlotte Brontë's War of Earthly Elements." *The Brontës: A Collection of Critical Essays.* Ed. Ian Gregor. Englewood Cliffs, N.J.: Prentice-Hall, 1970. 110–136. Print.

Moglen, Helene. *Charlotte Brontë–The Self-Conceived.* New York: W. W. Norton, 1976. Print.

——. "The End of *Jane Eyre* and the Creation of a Feminist Myth." *Modern Critical Interpretations–Charlotte Brontë's Jane Eyre.* New York: Chelsea House, 1987. 47–62. Print.

Nestor, Pauline. *Charlotte Brontë.* Totowa, N.J.: Barnes and Noble, 1987. Print.

O'Neill, Judith, ed. *Critics on Charlotte and Emily Brontë.* Coral Gables, FL: U of Miami P, 1968. Print.

Parkin-Gounelas, Ruth. *Fictions of the Female Self: Charlotte Brontë, Olive Schreiner, Katherine Mansfield.* London: Macmillan, 1991. Print.

Passel, Anne. *Charlotte and Emily Brontë–An Annotated Bibliography.* New York; London: Garland Publishing, 1979. Print.

Perkins, David. *English Romantic Writers.* New York: Harcourt, Brace, 1967. Print.

Peters, Margot. *Unquiet Soul: A Biography of Charlotte Brontë.* Garden City, N.Y.: Doubleday, 1975. Print.

Praz, Mario. *The Hero in Eclipse in Victorian Fiction.* London: 1956. Print.

Thormahlen, Marianne. *Brontës and Education.* Cambridge: Cambridge UP, 2007. Print.

Tillotson, Kathleen. *Novels of the Eighteen Forties*. Oxford: Clarendon P, 1954. Print.

Torgerson, Beth E. *Reading the Brontë Body: Disease, Desire, and the Constraints of Culture*. New York: Palgrave Macmillan, 2005. Print.

Van Ghent, Dorothy. *The English Novel: Form and Function*. New York: 1953. Print.

Wheat, Patricia H. *Adytum of the Heart*. Rutherford: Fairleigh Dickinson UP, 1992. Print.

Williams, Judith. *Perception and Expression in the Novels of Charlotte Brontë*. Ann Arbor: UMI Press, 1988.

Winnifrith, Tom. *New Life of Charlotte Brontë*. Basingstoke, Hampshire: MacMillan, 1988. Print.

Conclusion

Allison, Alexander W., Arthur J. Carr, and Arthur Eastman, eds. *Masterpieces of the Drama*. New York: Macmillan, 1974. Print.

Bloom, Harold. *Shelley's Mythmaking*. New Haven: Yale UP, 1959. Print.

——. *The Visionary Company: A Reading of English Romantic Poetry*. Garden City, N.Y.: Doubleday, 1961. Print.

Böll, Heinrich. *Billiards at Half-Past Nine*. New York: McGraw-Hill, 1962. Print.

Brontë, Charlotte. *Jane Eyre*. New York: Signet, 1982. Print.

Durbach, Errol. *Ibsen the Romantic*. Athens: U of Georgia P, 1982. Print.

Echtermeyer, Ernst T. und Benno von Wiese, eds. *Deutsche Gedichte von den Anfängen bis zur Gegenwart*. Düsseldorf: A. Bagel, 1962. Print.

Fitzgerald, F. Scott. *The Great Gatsby*. New York: Scribner, 1995. Print.

Fjelde, Rolf, ed. *Twentieth Century Views on Ibsen*. New York: 1965. Print.

Hawthorne, Nathaniel. *Young Goodman Brown and Other Short Stories*. New York: Dover, 1992. Print.

Heck, Francis S. "The Domain as a Symbol of a Paradise Lost: *Lost Horizon* and *Brideshead Revisited*." *Nassau Review* 4 (3): 24-29. Print.

Hesse, Hermann. *Siddhartha*. Trans. Hilde Rosner. New York: New Directions, 1957. Print.

——. *Steppenwolf*. New York: Holt, Rinehart and Winston. 1970. Print.

Hilton, James. *Lost Horizon*. New York: William Morrow, 1934. Print.

Hoffmann, E. T. A. *The Nutcracker and The Golden Pot*. New York: Dover, 1993. Print.

——. *Tales of Hoffmann*. Trans. R. J. Hollingdale. New York: Penguin, 2004. Print.

Honour, Hugh. *Romanticism*. New York: Harper and Row, 1979. Print.

Ibsen, Henrik. *Four Major Plays*. Trans. James McFarlane. New York: Oxford UP, 1998. Print.

Lyons, Charles R. *Henrik Ibsen: The Divided Consciousness*. Carbondale, IL: U of Southern Illinois P, 1972. Print.

Mann, Thomas. *Death in Venice and Seven Other Stories*. Trans. H. T. Lowe-Porter. New York: Vintage, 1989. Print.

McFarlane, James, ed. *The Cambridge Companion to Ibsen*. Cambridge: Cambridge UP, 1994. Print.

——, ed. *Henrik Ibsen*. London: Penguin, 1970. Print.

——. *Ibsen and Meaning*. Norwich, England: Norwich P, 1989. Print.

Northam, John. *Ibsen: A Critical Study*. Cambridge: Cambridge UP, 1973. Print.

Paulson, Ronald. *Emblem and Expression: Meaning in English Art of the Eighteenth Century*. Cambridge, Mass.: Harvard UP, 1975. Print.

Perkins, David. *English Romantic Writers*. New York: Harcourt Brace, 1967. Print.

Pyle, Forest. *The Ideology of Imagination*. Stanford: Stanford UP, 1995. Print.

Ryder, Frank G., ed. *German Romantic Stories*. New York: Continuum, 1988. Print.

Walter, Hugo. *A Purple-Golden Renascence of Eden-Exalting Rainbows*. Santa Barbara, California: Fithian P, 2001. Print.

——. *Space and Time on the Magic Mountain: Studies in Nineteenth- and Early-Twentieth-Century European Literature*. New York: Peter Lang, 1999. Print.

Wordsworth, Jonathan, et al. *Wordsworth and the Age of English Romanticism*. New Brunswick, N.J.: Rutgers UP, 1987. Print.

Wordsworth, William. *The Prelude (1799, 1805, 1850)*. Ed. Jonathan Wordsworth, M. H. Abrams, and Stephen Gill. New York: W. W. Norton, 1979. Print.

❋ Index

Studies on Themes and Motifs in Literature

The series is designed to advance the publication of research pertaining to themes and motifs in literature. The studies cover cross-cultural patterns as well as the entire range of national literatures. They trace the development and use of themes and motifs over extended periods, elucidate the significance of specific themes or motifs for the formation of period styles, and analyze the unique structural function of themes and motifs. By examining themes or motifs in the work of an author or period, the studies point to the impulses authors received from literary tradition, the choices made, and the creative transformation of the cultural heritage. The series will include publications of colloquia and theoretical studies that contribute to a greater understanding of literature.

For additional information about this series or for the submission of manuscripts, please contact:

Dr. Heidi Burns
Peter Lang Publishing
P.O. Box 1246
Bel Air, MD 21014-1246

To order other books in this series, please contact our Customer Service Department:

800-770-LANG (within the U.S.)
212-647-7706 (outside the U.S.)
212-647-7707 FAX

Or browse online by series at:

www.peterlang.com